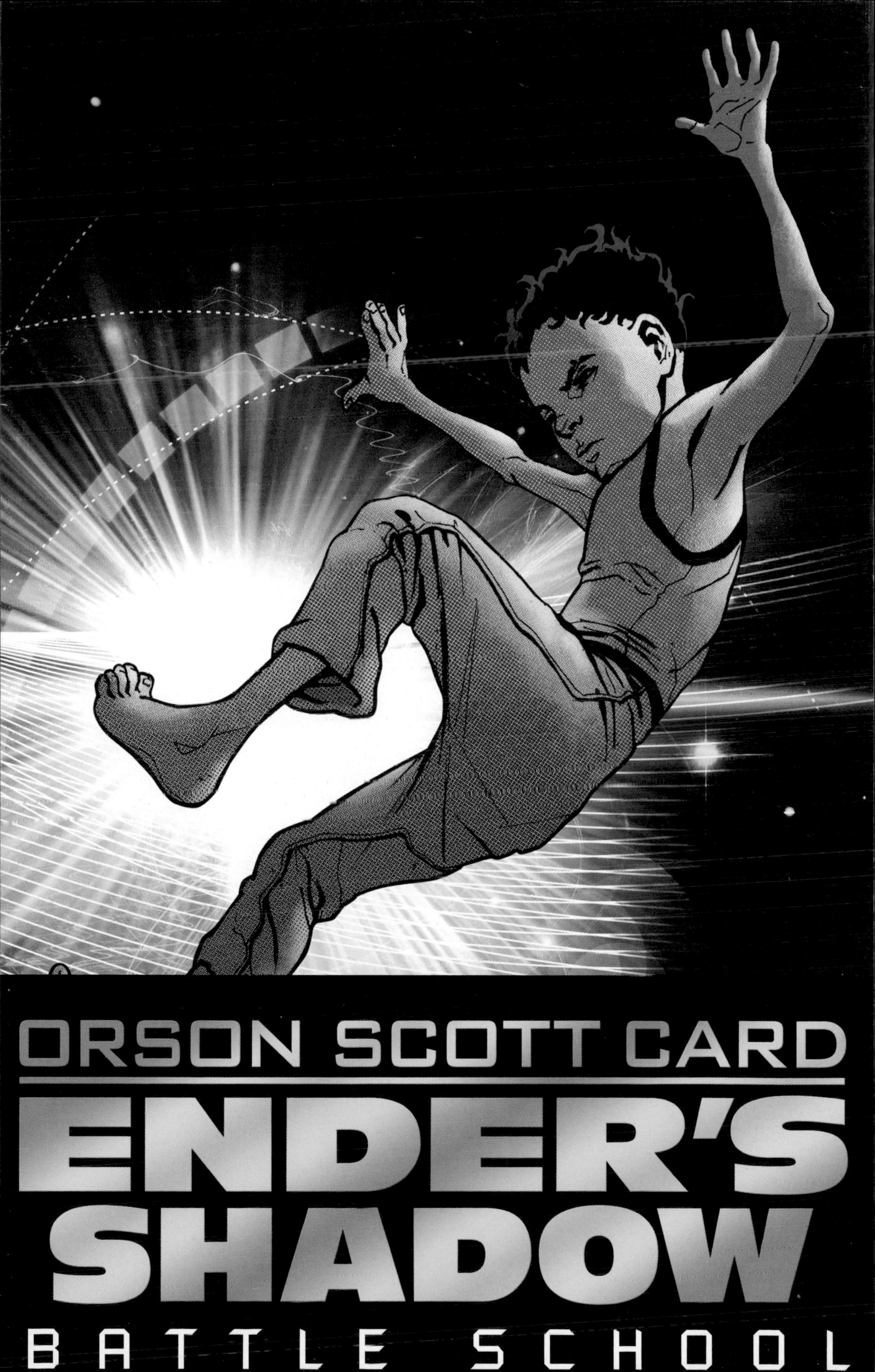

ORSON SCOTT CARD

ENDER'S SHADOW

BATTLE SCHOOL

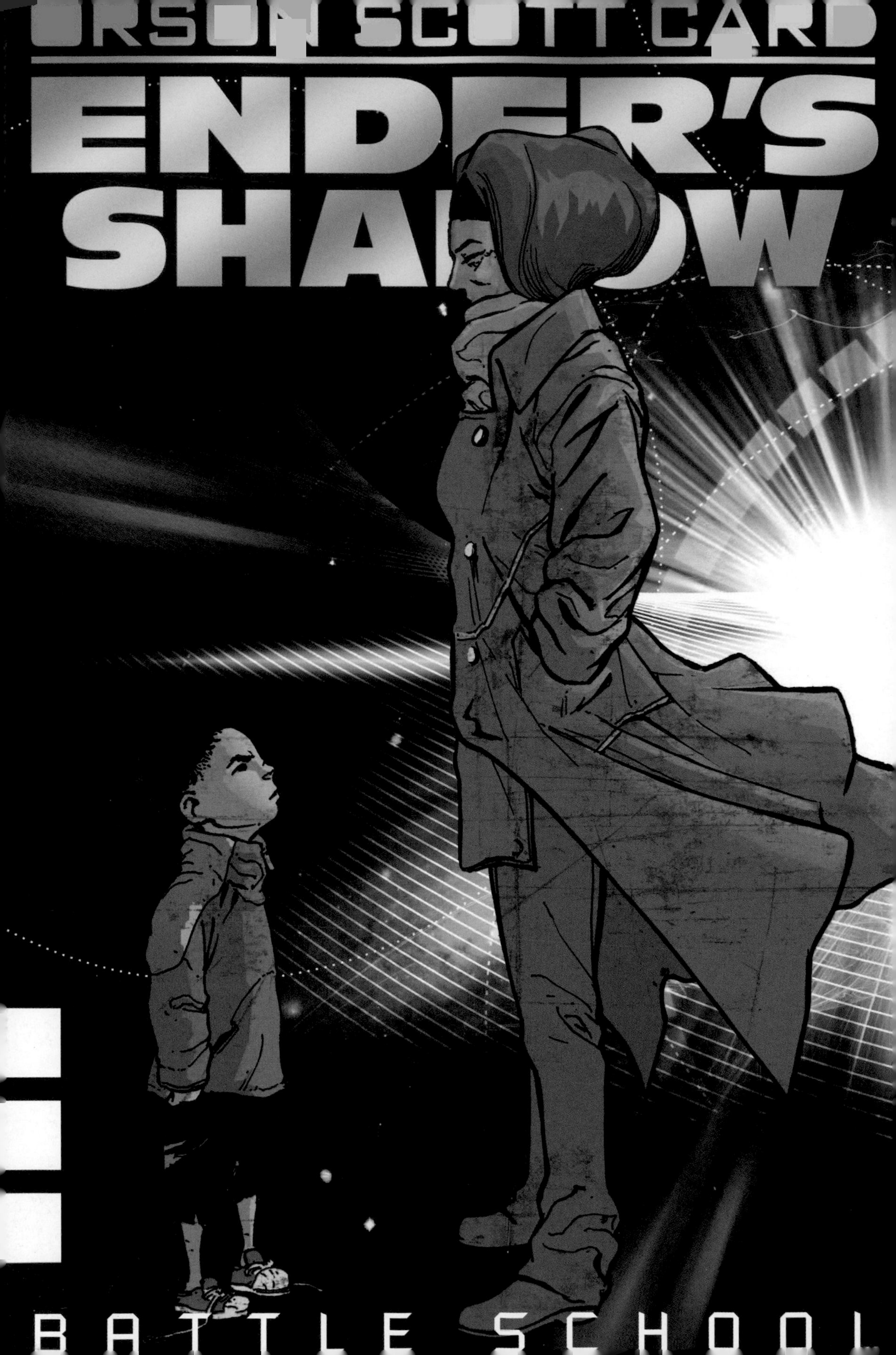
ORSON SCOTT CARD
ENDER'S SHADOW
BATTLE SCHOOL

Creative Director & Executive Director:
ORSON SCOTT CARD
Script: **MIKE CAREY**
Art: **SEBASTIAN FIUMARA**
Color Art: **GIULIA BRUSCO**
Lettering: **VC'S CORY PETIT**
Story Consultant: **JAKE BLACK**
Cover Art: **JIM CHEUNG &
MORRY HOLLOWELL** (Issue #1)
and **TIMOTHY GREEN II**
Editor: **JORDAN D. WHITE**
Consulting Editor: **NICK LOWE**
Senior Editor: **MARK PANICCIA**

Special thanks to **KRISTINE CARD,
KATHLEEN BELLAMY,
DARIEN ROBBINS,
ANDREW BAUGHAN,
RALPH MACCHIO,
LAUREN SANKOVITCH,
JIM NAUSEDAS,
JIM MCCANN,
ARUNE SINGH,
CHRIS ALLO
& JEFF SUTER**

Collection Editor: **JENNIFER GRÜNWALD**
Editorial Assistant: **ALEX STARBUCK**
Assistant Editors: **CORY LEVINE
& JOHN DENNING**
Editor, Special Projects:
MARK D. BEAZLEY
Senior Editor, Special Projects:
JEFF YOUNGQUIST
Senior Vice President of Sales:
DAVID GABRIEL
Senior Vice President of Strategic
Development: **RUWAN JAYATILLEKE**
Book designer: **RODOLFO MURAGUCHI**

Editor in Chief: **JOE QUESADA**
Publisher: **DAN BUCKLEY**
Executive Producer: **ALAN FINE**

ENDER'S SHADOW: BATTLE SCHOOL. Contains material originally published in magazine form as ENDER'S SHADOW: BATTLE SCHOOL #1-5. First printing 2009. ISBN# 978-0-7851-3596-8. Published by MARVEL PUBLISHING, INC., a subsidiary of MARVEL ENTERTAINMENT, INC. OFFICE OF PUBLICATION: 417 5th Avenue, New York, NY 10016. Copyright © 2009 Orson Scott Card. All rights reserved. $24.99 per copy in the U.S. (GST #R127032852); Canadian Agreement #40668537. All characters featured in this issue and the distinctive names and likenesses thereof, and all related indicia are trademarks of Orson Scott Card. No similarity between any of the names, characters, persons, and/or institutions in this magazine with those of any living or dead person or institution is intended, and any such similarity which may exist is purely coincidental. **Printed in the U.S.A.** ALAN FINE, CEO Marvel Publishing Division and EVP & CMO Marvel Characters B.V.; DAN BUCKLEY, President of Publishing - Print & Digital Media; JIM SOKOLOWSKI, Chief Operating Officer; DAVID GABRIEL, SVP of Publishing Sales & Circulation; DAVID BOGART, SVP of Business Affairs & Talent Management; MICHAEL PASCIULLO, VP Merchandising & Communications; JIM O'KEEFE, VP of Operations & Logistics; DAN CARR, Executive Director of Publishing Technology; JUSTIN F. GABRIE, Director of Publishing & Editorial Operations; SUSAN CRESPI, Editorial Operations Manager; ALEX MORALES, Publishing Operations Manager; STAN LEE, Chairman Emeritus. For information regarding advertising in Marvel Comics or on Marvel.com, please contact Mitch Dane, Advertising Director, at mdane@marvel.com. For Marvel subscription inquiries, please call 800-217-9158.

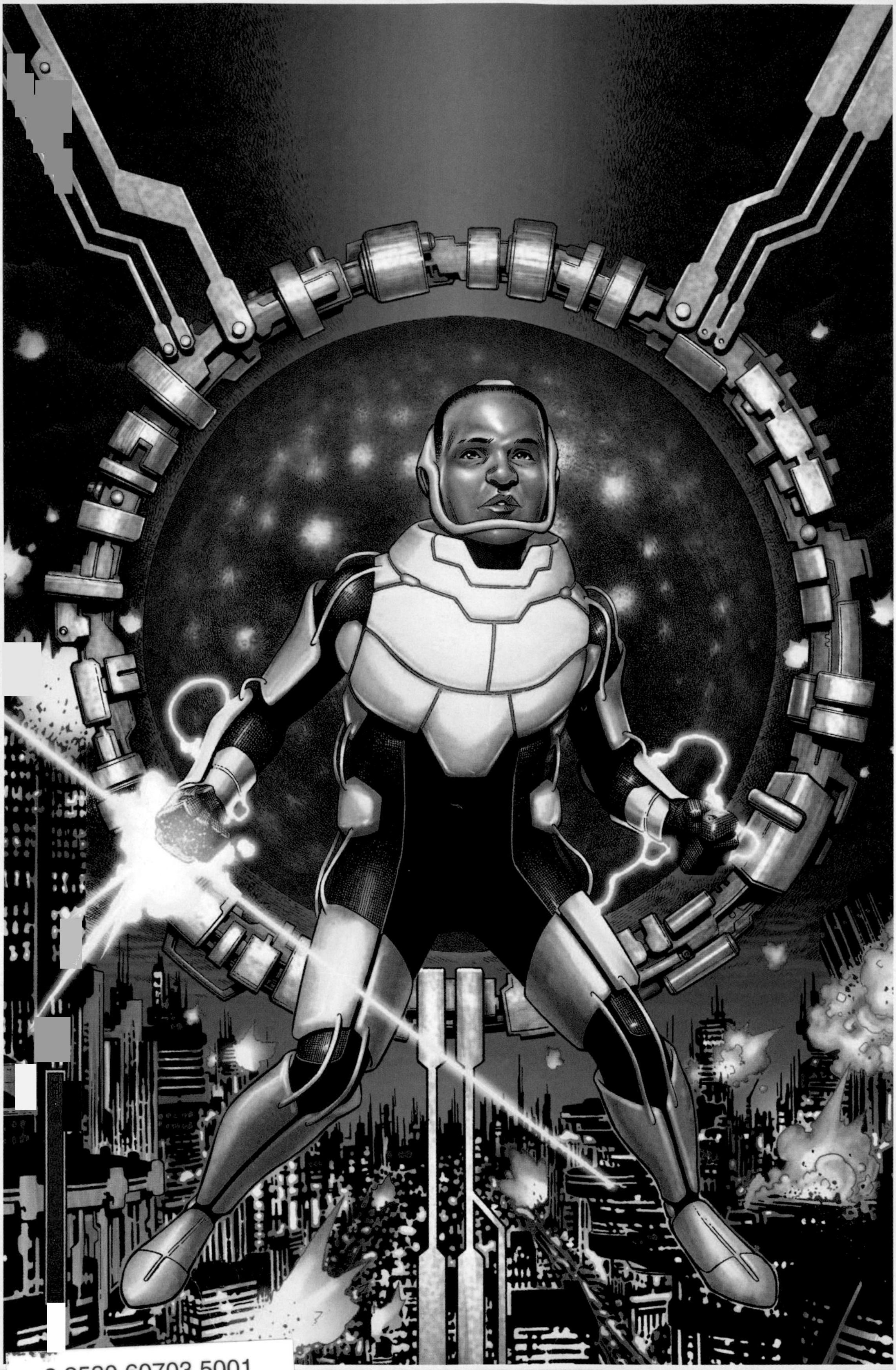

"You think you've found somebody, so suddenly my program gets the axe?"

"It's not about the kid that Graff found. It's about the low quality of what you've been finding."

"We knew it was long odds. But the kids I'm working with are actually fighting a war just to stay alive."

"Your kids are so malnourished that they suffer severe mental degradation before you even begin testing them. Most of them haven't formed any normal human bonds. They're so messed up, they can't get through a day without finding something they can steal, break, or disrupt."

"I think I have someone for you."

"You've thought that before."

"But I should warn you. He doesn't meet your physical specifications..."

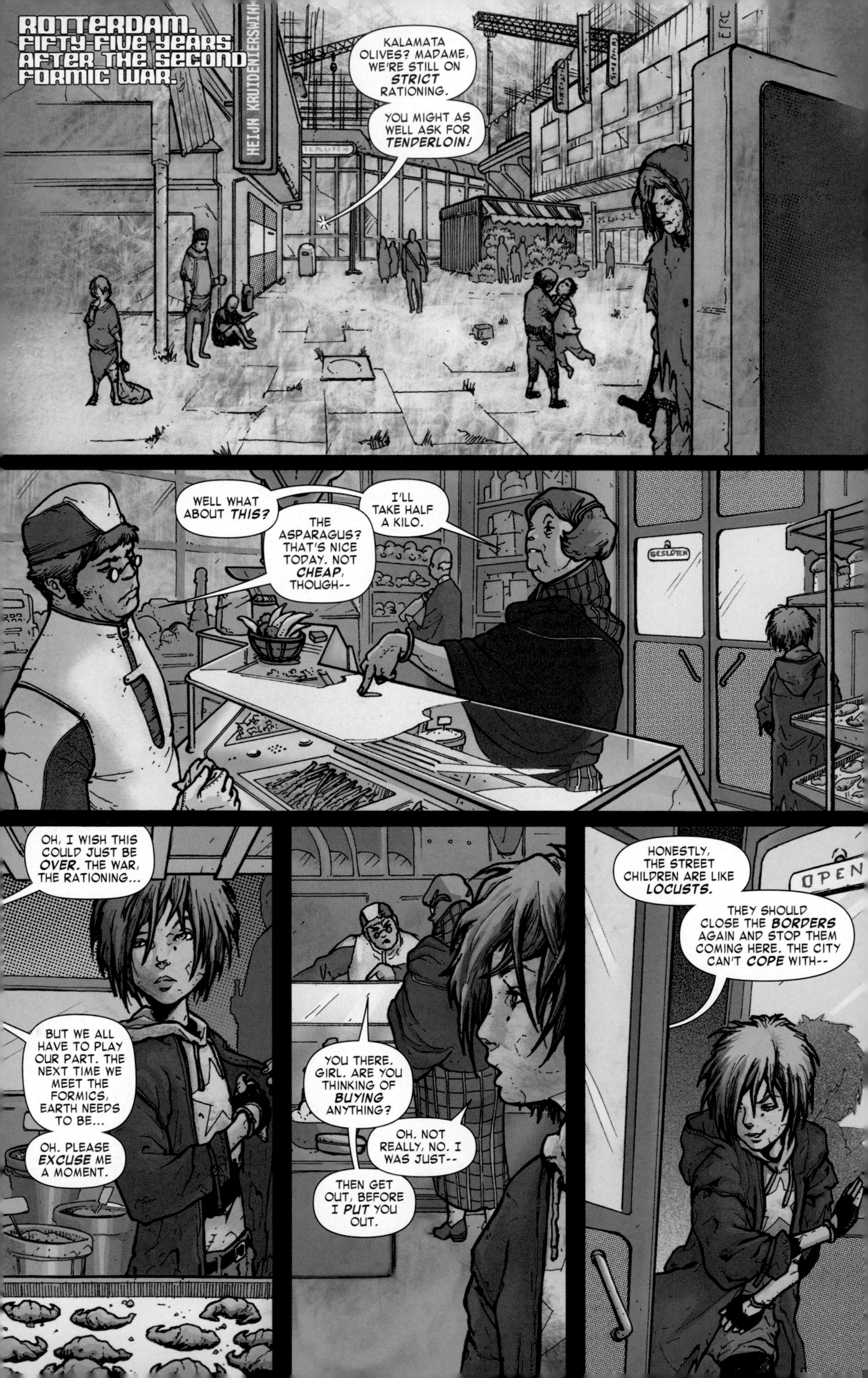
ROTTERDAM. FIFTY-FIVE YEARS AFTER THE SECOND FORMIC WAR.
HEIJN KRUIDENIERSWINK
KALAMATA OLIVES? MADAME, WE'RE STILL ON STRICT RATIONING.
YOU MIGHT AS WELL ASK FOR TENDERLOIN!
WELL WHAT ABOUT THIS?
I'LL TAKE HALF A KILO.
THE ASPARAGUS? THAT'S NICE TODAY. NOT CHEAP, THOUGH--
GESLOTEN
OH, I WISH THIS COULD JUST BE OVER. THE WAR, THE RATIONING...
BUT WE ALL HAVE TO PLAY OUR PART. THE NEXT TIME WE MEET THE FORMICS, EARTH NEEDS TO BE...
OH. PLEASE EXCUSE ME A MOMENT.
YOU THERE. GIRL. ARE YOU THINKING OF BUYING ANYTHING?
OH. NOT REALLY, NO. I WAS JUST--
THEN GET OUT, BEFORE I PUT YOU OUT.
OPEN
HONESTLY, THE STREET CHILDREN ARE LIKE LOCUSTS.
THEY SHOULD CLOSE THE BORDERS AGAIN AND STOP THEM COMING HERE. THE CITY CAN'T COPE WITH--

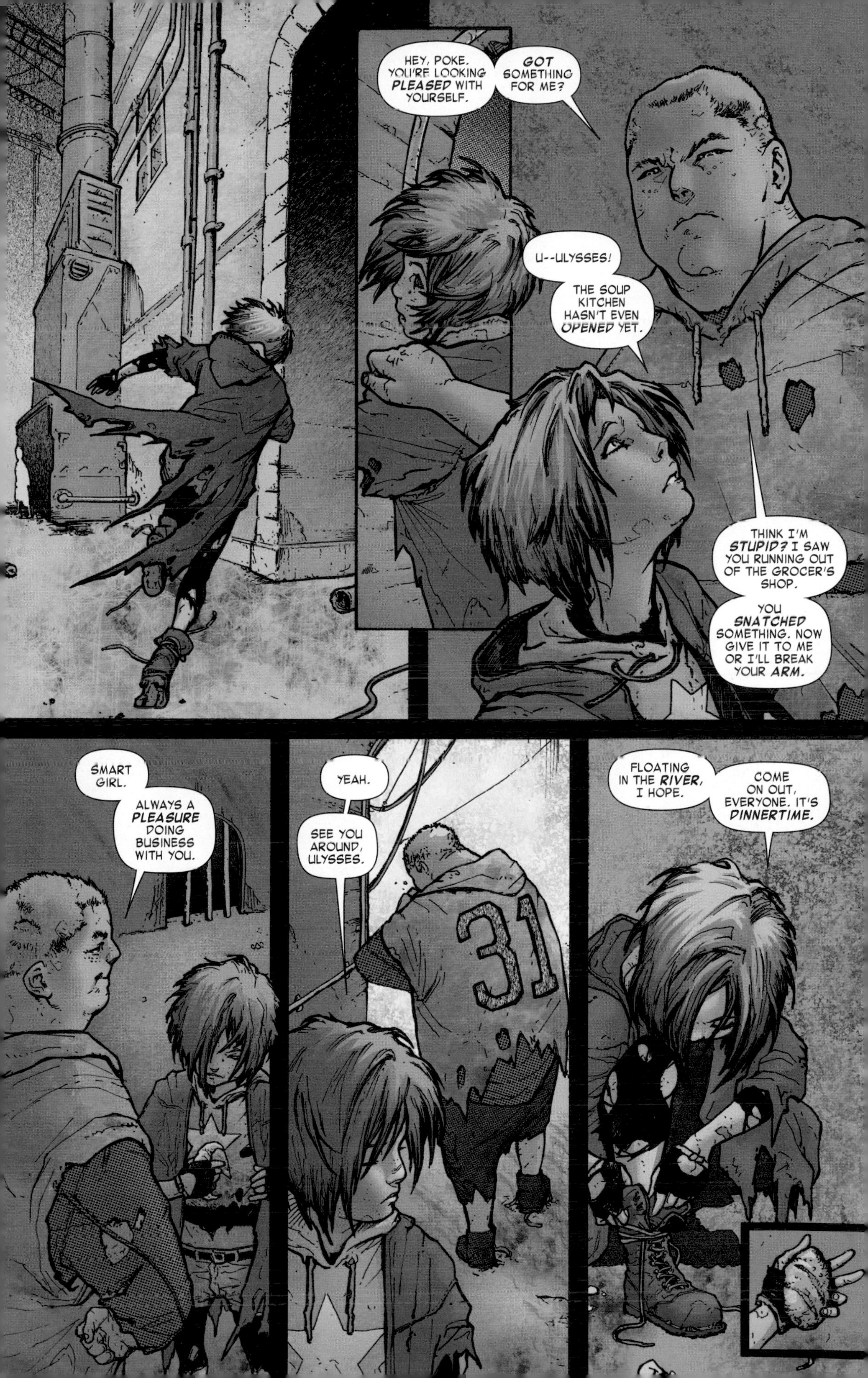
HEY, POKE. YOU'RE LOOKING PLEASED WITH YOURSELF.
GOT SOMETHING FOR ME?
U--ULYSSES!
THE SOUP KITCHEN HASN'T EVEN OPENED YET.
THINK I'M STUPID? I SAW YOU RUNNING OUT OF THE GROCER'S SHOP.
YOU SNATCHED SOMETHING. NOW GIVE IT TO ME OR I'LL BREAK YOUR ARM.
SMART GIRL.
ALWAYS A PLEASURE DOING BUSINESS WITH YOU.
YEAH.
SEE YOU AROUND, ULYSSES.
FLOATING IN THE RIVER, I HOPE.
COME ON OUT, EVERYONE. IT'S DINNERTIME.

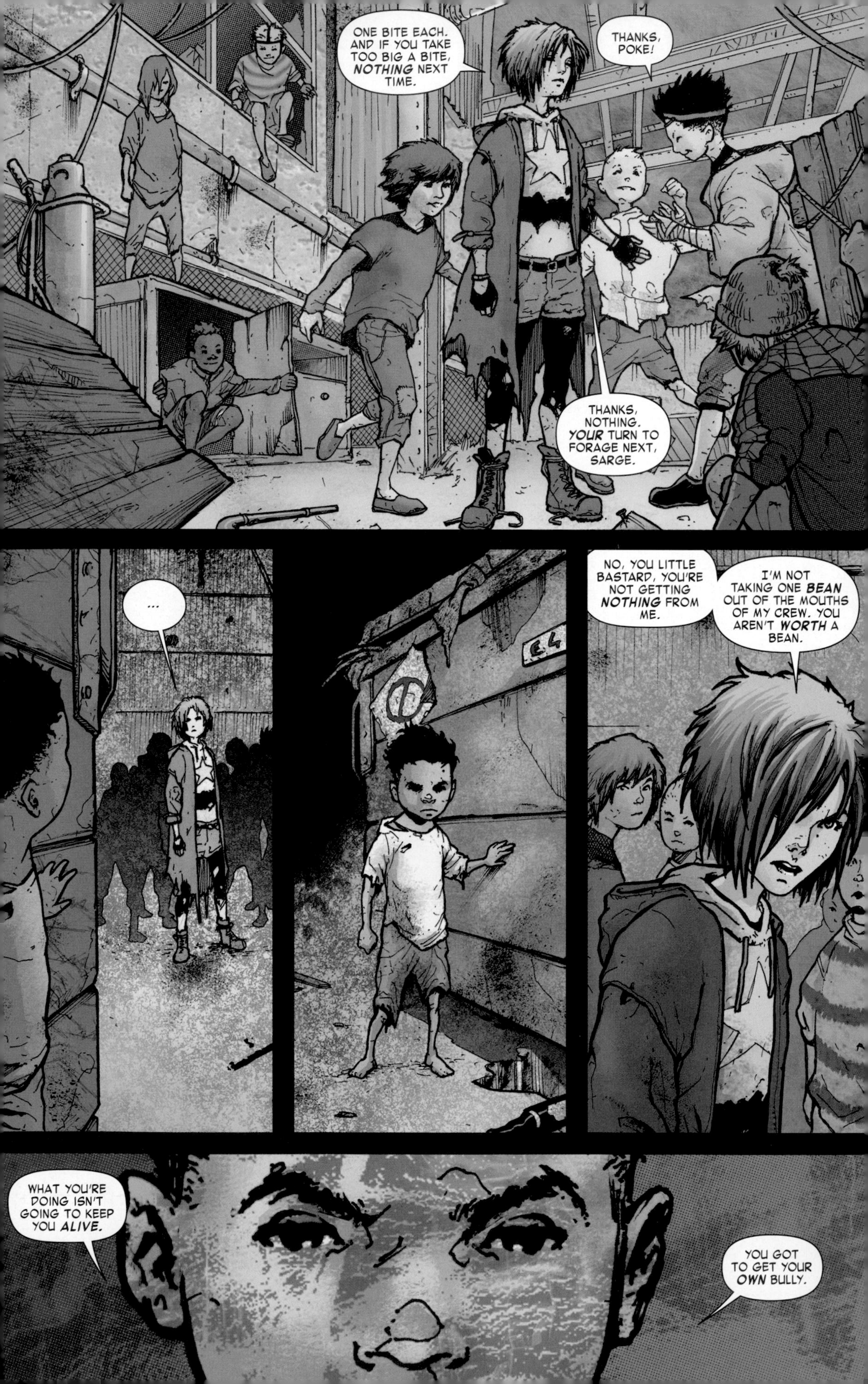
ONE BITE EACH. AND IF YOU TAKE TOO BIG A BITE, *NOTHING* NEXT TIME.
THANKS, POKE!
THANKS, NOTHING. *YOUR* TURN TO FORAGE NEXT, SARGE.
...
NO, YOU LITTLE BASTARD, YOU'RE NOT GETTING *NOTHING* FROM ME.
I'M NOT TAKING ONE *BEAN* OUT OF THE MOUTHS OF MY CREW. YOU AREN'T *WORTH* A BEAN.
WHAT YOU'RE DOING ISN'T GOING TO KEEP YOU *ALIVE.*
YOU GOT TO GET YOUR *OWN* BULLY.

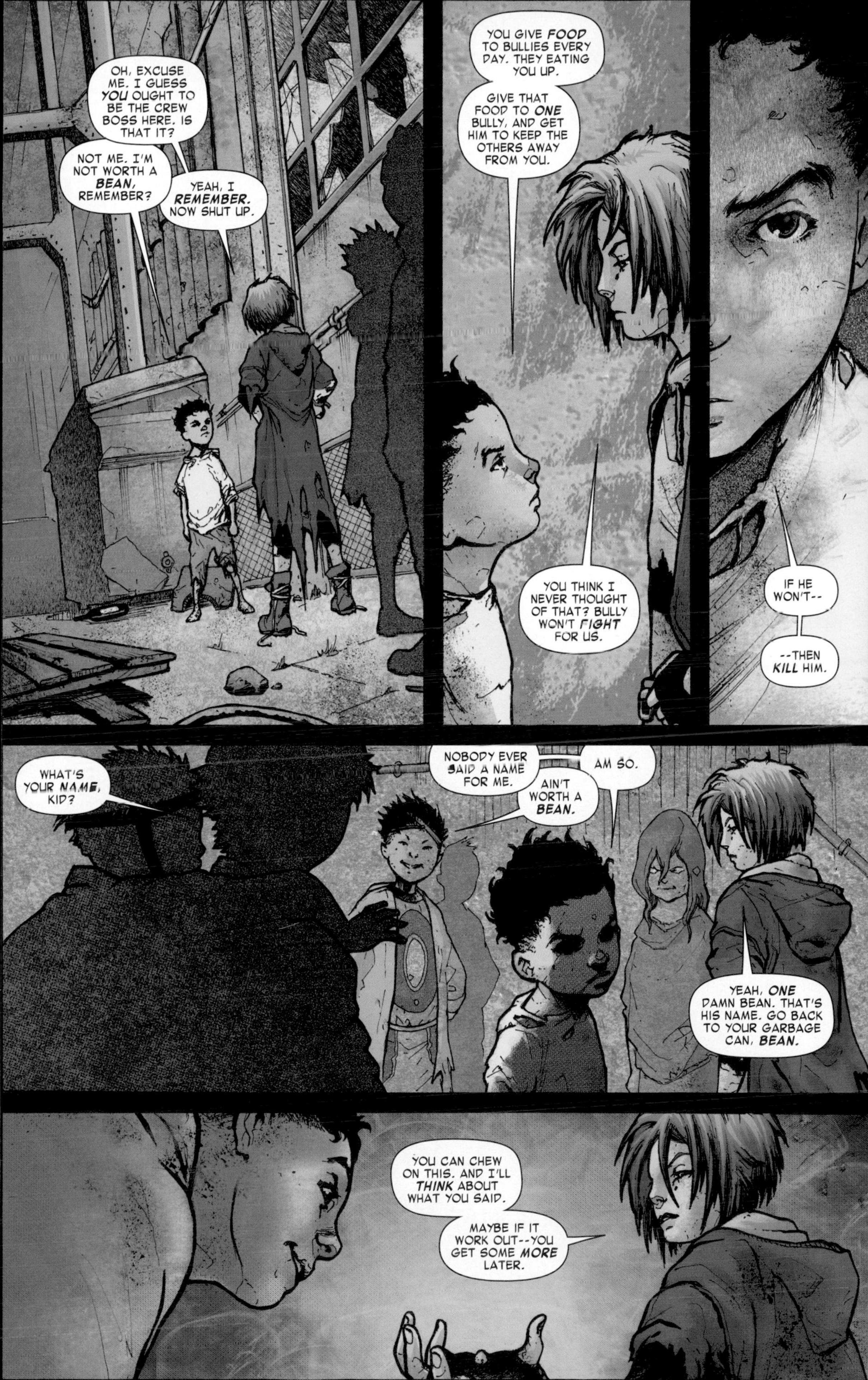

OH, EXCUSE ME. I GUESS *YOU* OUGHT TO BE THE CREW BOSS HERE. IS THAT IT?
NOT ME. I'M NOT WORTH A *BEAN*, REMEMBER?
YEAH, I *REMEMBER*. NOW SHUT UP.
YOU GIVE *FOOD* TO BULLIES EVERY DAY. THEY EATING YOU UP.
GIVE THAT FOOD TO *ONE* BULLY, AND GET HIM TO KEEP THE OTHERS AWAY FROM YOU.
YOU THINK I NEVER THOUGHT OF THAT? BULLY WON'T *FIGHT* FOR US.
IF HE WON'T--
--THEN *KILL* HIM.
WHAT'S YOUR *NAME*, KID?
NOBODY EVER SAID A NAME FOR ME.
AIN'T WORTH A *BEAN.*
AM SO.
YEAH, *ONE* DAMN BEAN. THAT'S HIS NAME. GO BACK TO YOUR GARBAGE CAN, *BEAN.*
YOU CAN CHEW ON THIS. AND I'LL *THINK* ABOUT WHAT YOU SAID.
MAYBE IF IT WORK OUT--YOU GET SOME *MORE* LATER.

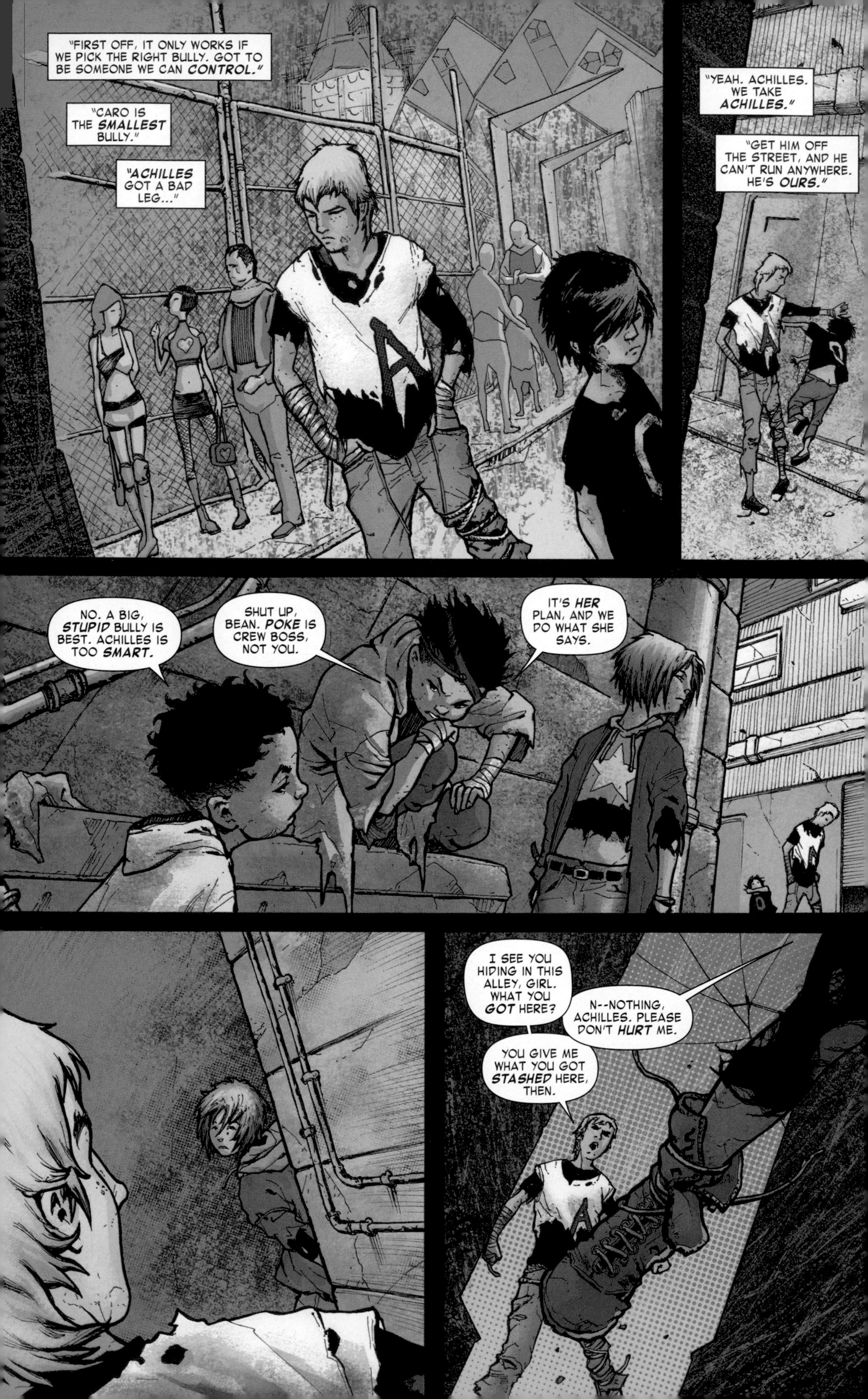
"FIRST OFF, IT ONLY WORKS IF WE PICK THE RIGHT BULLY. GOT TO BE SOMEONE WE CAN CONTROL."
"CARO IS THE SMALLEST BULLY."
"ACHILLES GOT A BAD LEG..."
"YEAH. ACHILLES. WE TAKE ACHILLES."
"GET HIM OFF THE STREET, AND HE CAN'T RUN ANYWHERE. HE'S OURS."
NO. A BIG, STUPID BULLY IS BEST. ACHILLES IS TOO SMART.
SHUT UP, BEAN. POKE IS CREW BOSS, NOT YOU.
IT'S HER PLAN, AND WE DO WHAT SHE SAYS.
I SEE YOU HIDING IN THIS ALLEY, GIRL. WHAT YOU GOT HERE?
N--NOTHING, ACHILLES. PLEASE DON'T HURT ME.
YOU GIVE ME WHAT YOU GOT STASHED HERE, THEN.

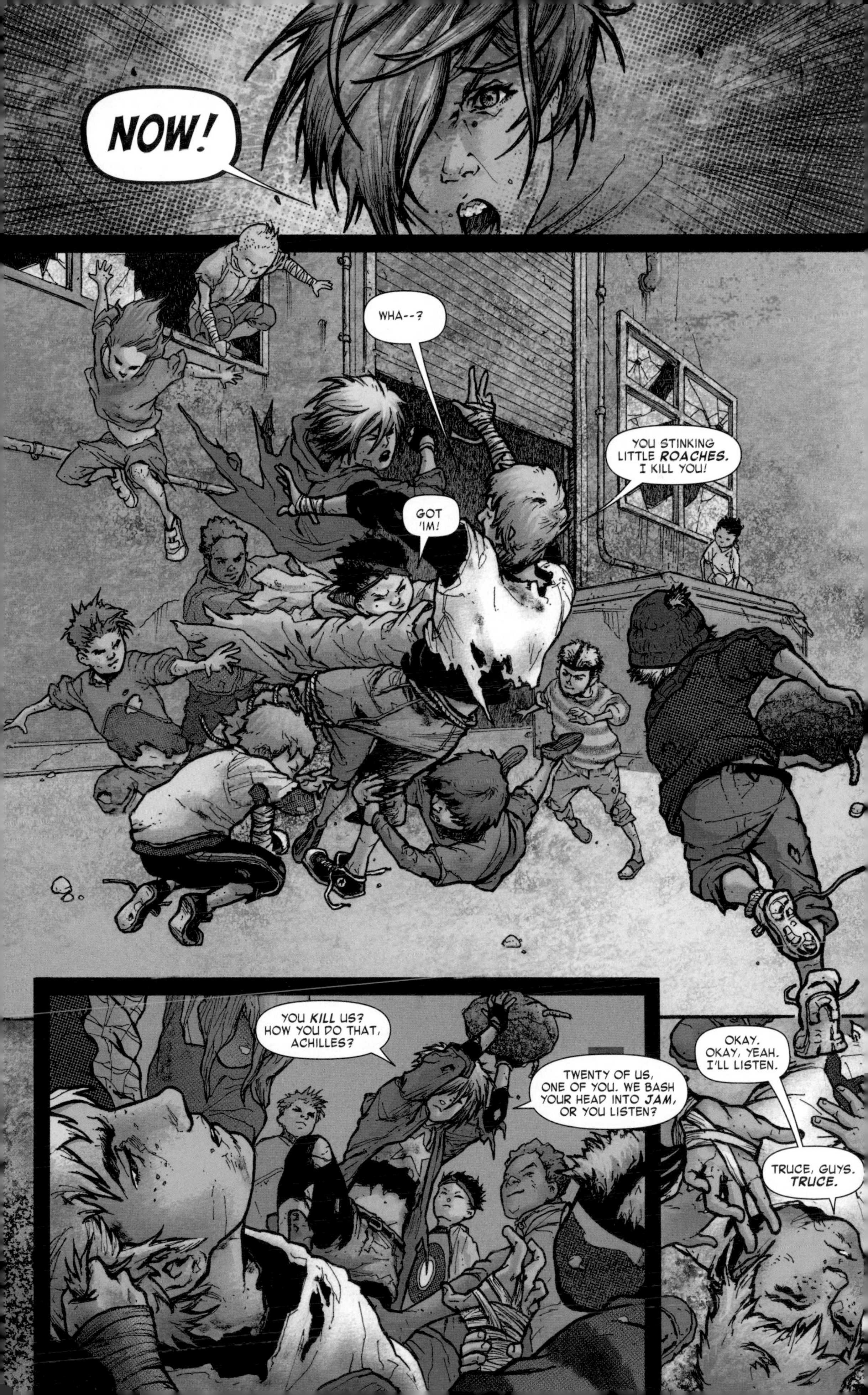
NOW!
WHA--?
YOU STINKING LITTLE ROACHES. I KILL YOU!
GOT 'IM!
YOU KILL US? HOW YOU DO THAT, ACHILLES?
TWENTY OF US, ONE OF YOU. WE BASH YOUR HEAD INTO JAM, OR YOU LISTEN?
OKAY. OKAY, YEAH. I'LL LISTEN.
TRUCE, GUYS. TRUCE.

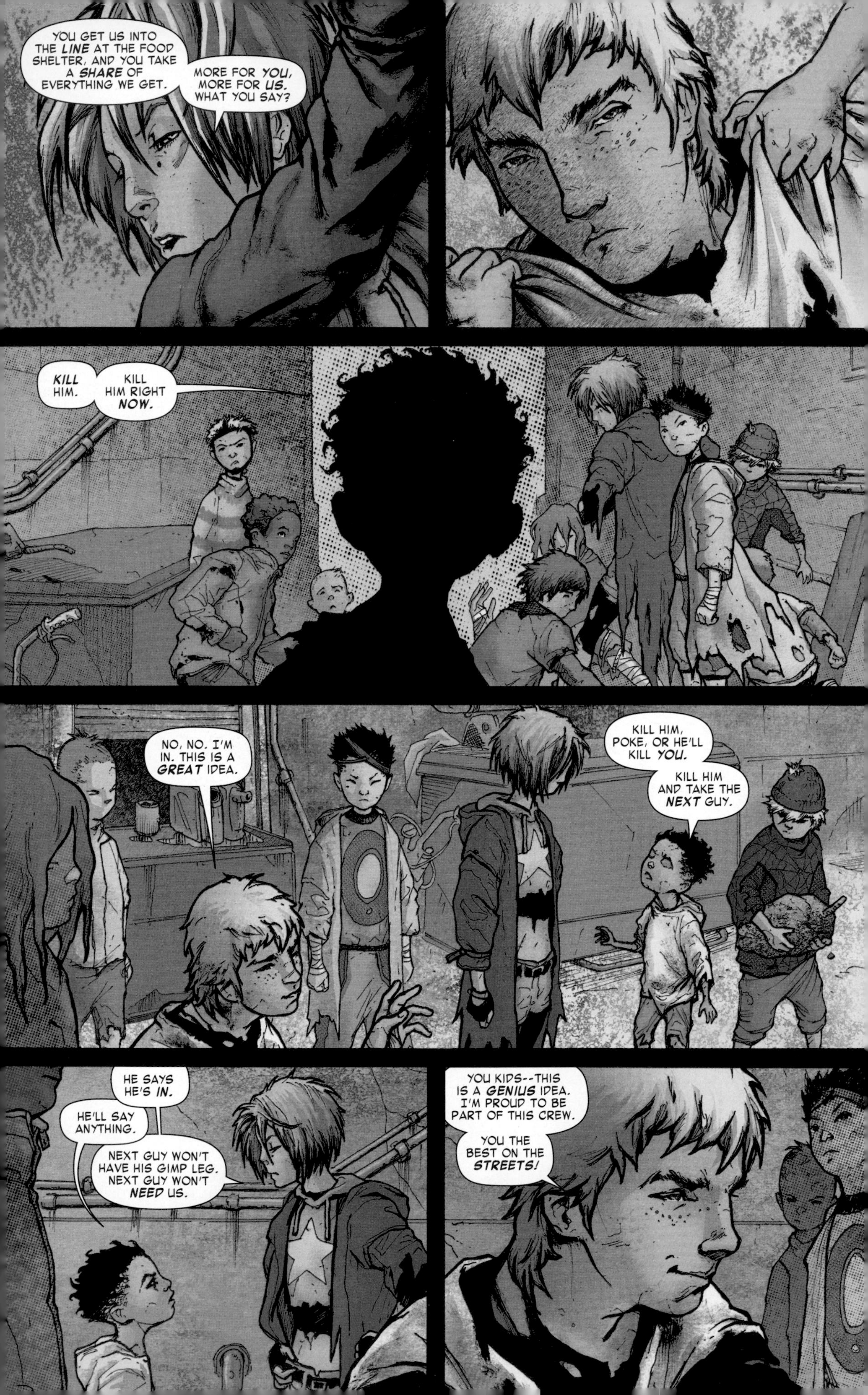
YOU GET US INTO THE LINE AT THE FOOD SHELTER, AND YOU TAKE A SHARE OF EVERYTHING WE GET.
MORE FOR YOU, MORE FOR US. WHAT YOU SAY?
KILL HIM.
KILL HIM RIGHT NOW.
NO, NO. I'M IN. THIS IS A GREAT IDEA.
KILL HIM, POKE, OR HE'LL KILL YOU.
KILL HIM AND TAKE THE NEXT GUY.
HE SAYS HE'S IN.
HE'LL SAY ANYTHING.
NEXT GUY WON'T HAVE HIS GIMP LEG. NEXT GUY WON'T NEED US.
YOU KIDS--THIS IS A GENIUS IDEA. I'M PROUD TO BE PART OF THIS CREW.
YOU THE BEST ON THE STREETS!

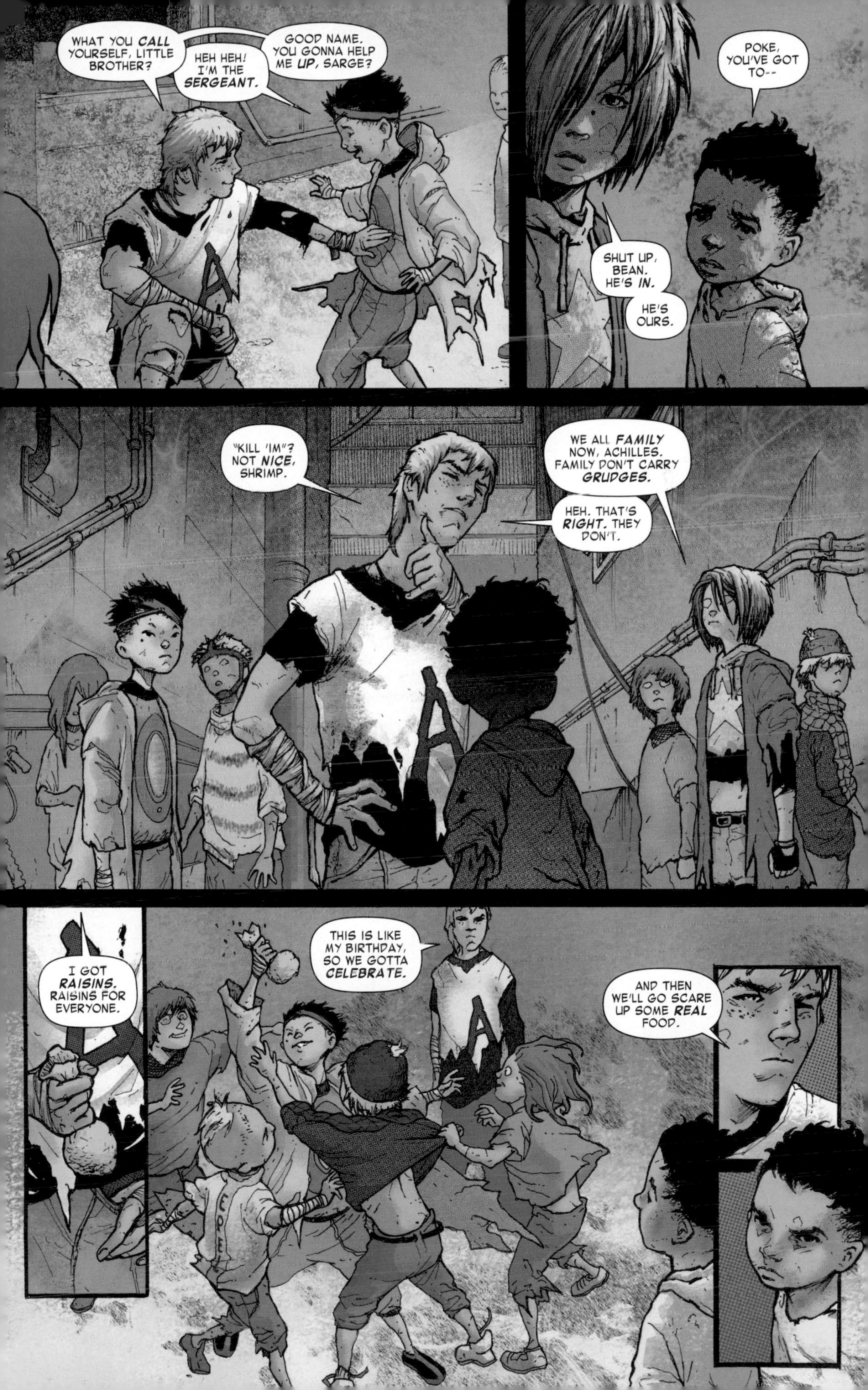
WHAT YOU CALL YOURSELF, LITTLE BROTHER?
HEH HEH! I'M THE SERGEANT.
GOOD NAME. YOU GONNA HELP ME UP, SARGE?
POKE, YOU'VE GOT TO--
SHUT UP, BEAN. HE'S IN.
HE'S OURS.
"KILL 'IM"? NOT NICE, SHRIMP.
WE ALL FAMILY NOW, ACHILLES. FAMILY DON'T CARRY GRUDGES.
HEH. THAT'S RIGHT. THEY DON'T.
I GOT RAISINS. RAISINS FOR EVERYONE.
THIS IS LIKE MY BIRTHDAY, SO WE GOTTA CELEBRATE.
AND THEN WE'LL GO SCARE UP SOME REAL FOOD.

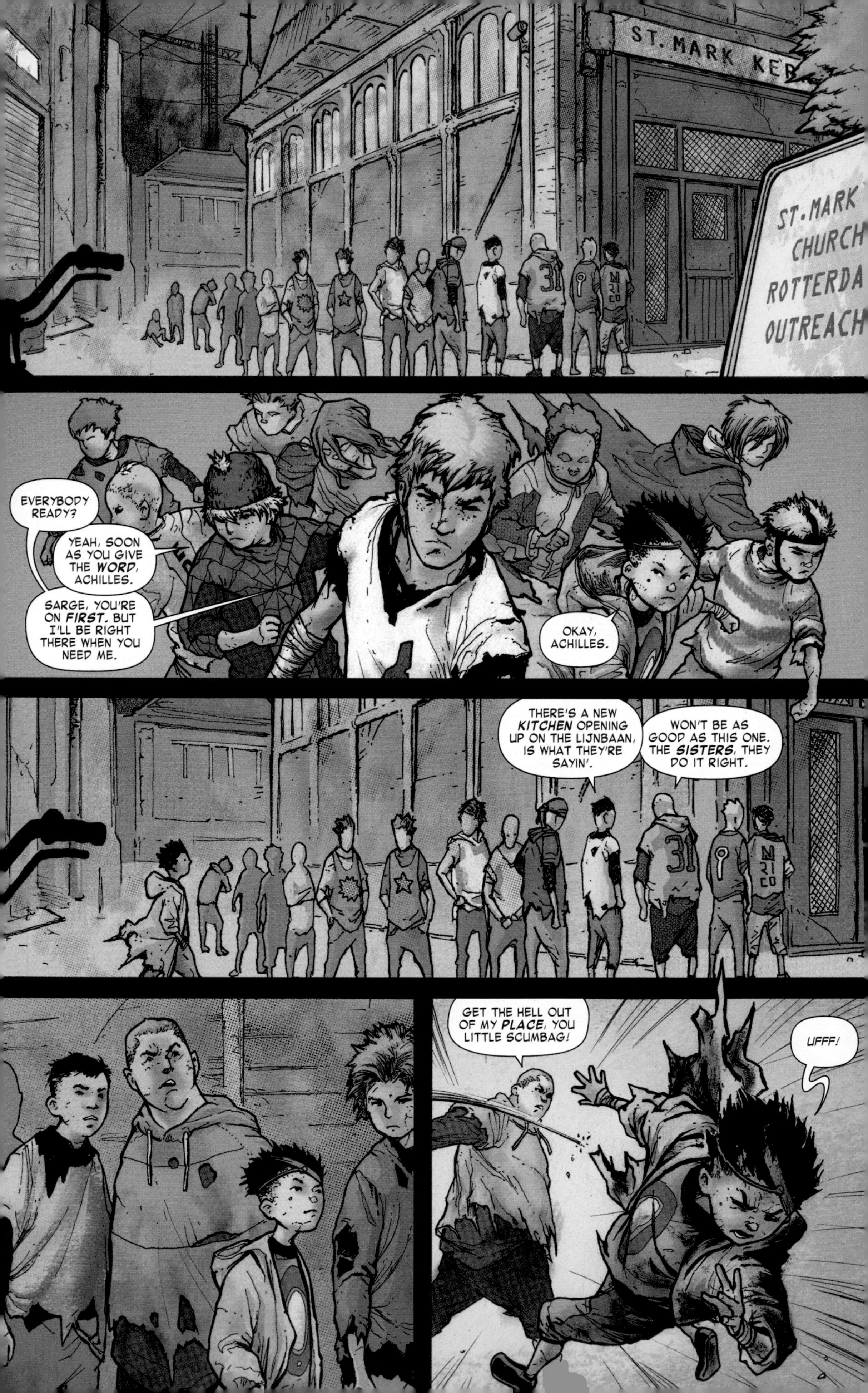
ST. MARK KER
ST. MARK CHURCH ROTTERDA OUTREACH
EVERYBODY READY?
YEAH, SOON AS YOU GIVE THE WORD, ACHILLES.
SARGE, YOU'RE ON FIRST. BUT I'LL BE RIGHT THERE WHEN YOU NEED ME.
OKAY, ACHILLES.
THERE'S A NEW KITCHEN OPENING UP ON THE LIJNBAAN, IS WHAT THEY'RE SAYIN'.
WON'T BE AS GOOD AS THIS ONE. THE SISTERS, THEY DO IT RIGHT.
GET THE HELL OUT OF MY PLACE, YOU LITTLE SCUMBAG!
UFFF!

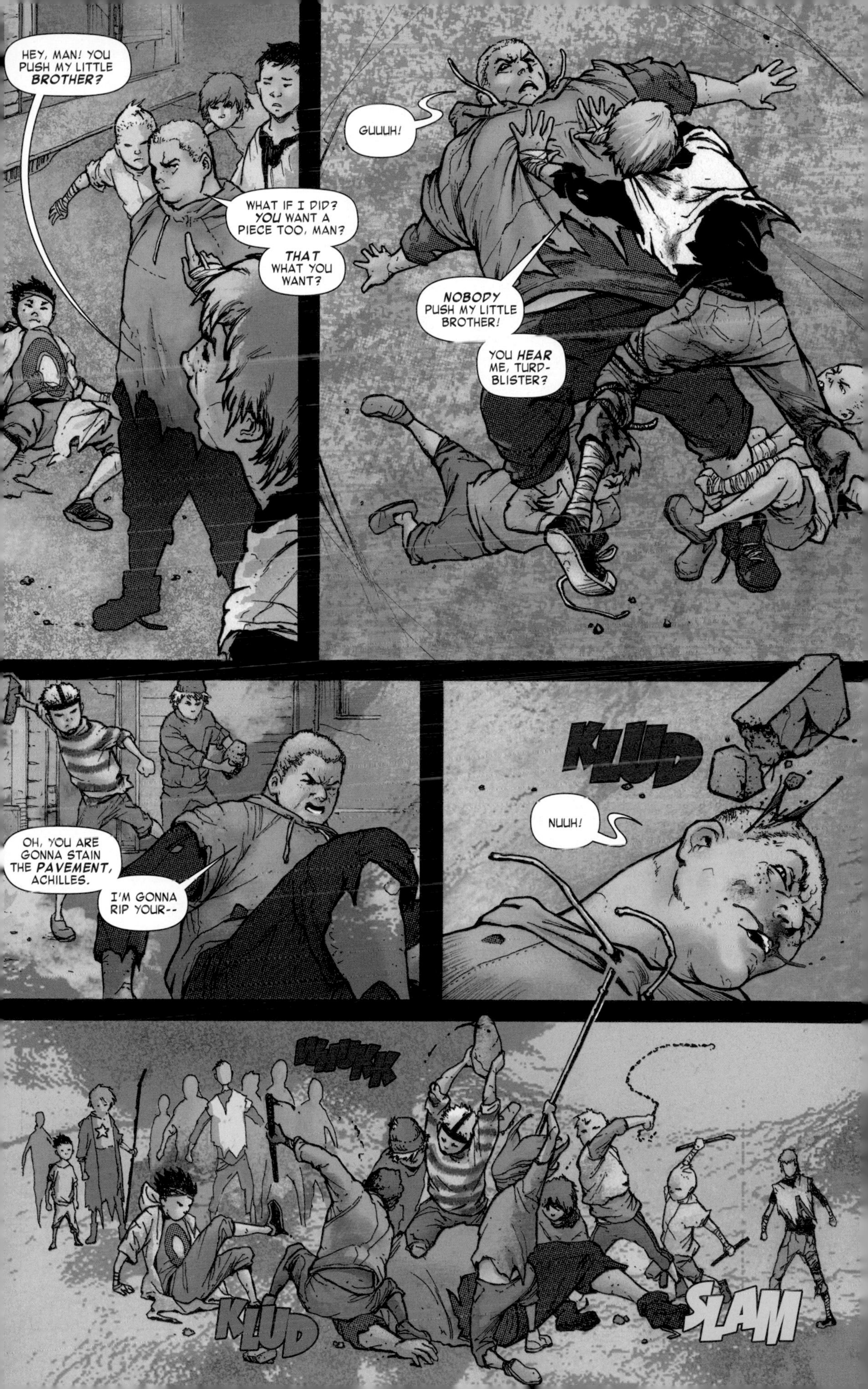
HEY, MAN! YOU PUSH MY LITTLE BROTHER?
WHAT IF I DID? YOU WANT A PIECE TOO, MAN?
THAT WHAT YOU WANT?
GUUUH!
NOBODY PUSH MY LITTLE BROTHER!
YOU HEAR ME, TURD-BLISTER?
OH, YOU ARE GONNA STAIN THE PAVEMENT, ACHILLES.
I'M GONNA RIP YOUR--
KLUD
NUUH!
KLUD
SLAM

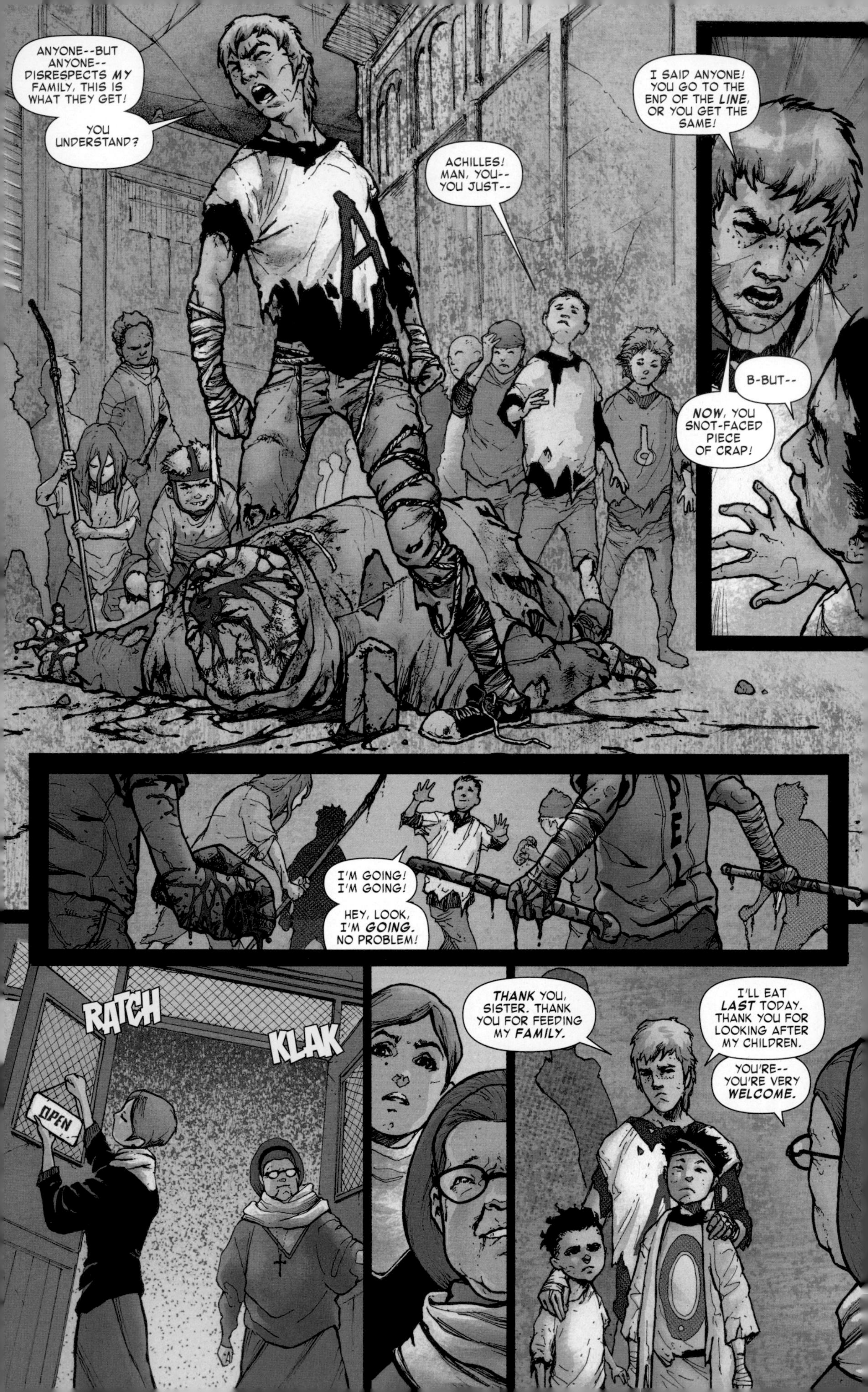
ANYONE--BUT ANYONE--DISRESPECTS *MY* FAMILY, THIS IS WHAT THEY GET!
YOU UNDERSTAND?
ACHILLES! MAN, YOU--YOU JUST--
I SAID ANYONE! YOU GO TO THE END OF THE *LINE*, OR YOU GET THE SAME!
B-BUT--
NOW, YOU SNOT-FACED PIECE OF CRAP!
I'M GOING! I'M GOING!
HEY, LOOK, I'M *GOING.* NO PROBLEM!
RATCH
KLAK
OPEN
THANK YOU, SISTER. THANK YOU FOR FEEDING MY *FAMILY.*
I'LL EAT *LAST* TODAY. THANK YOU FOR LOOKING AFTER MY CHILDREN.
YOU'RE--YOU'RE VERY *WELCOME.*

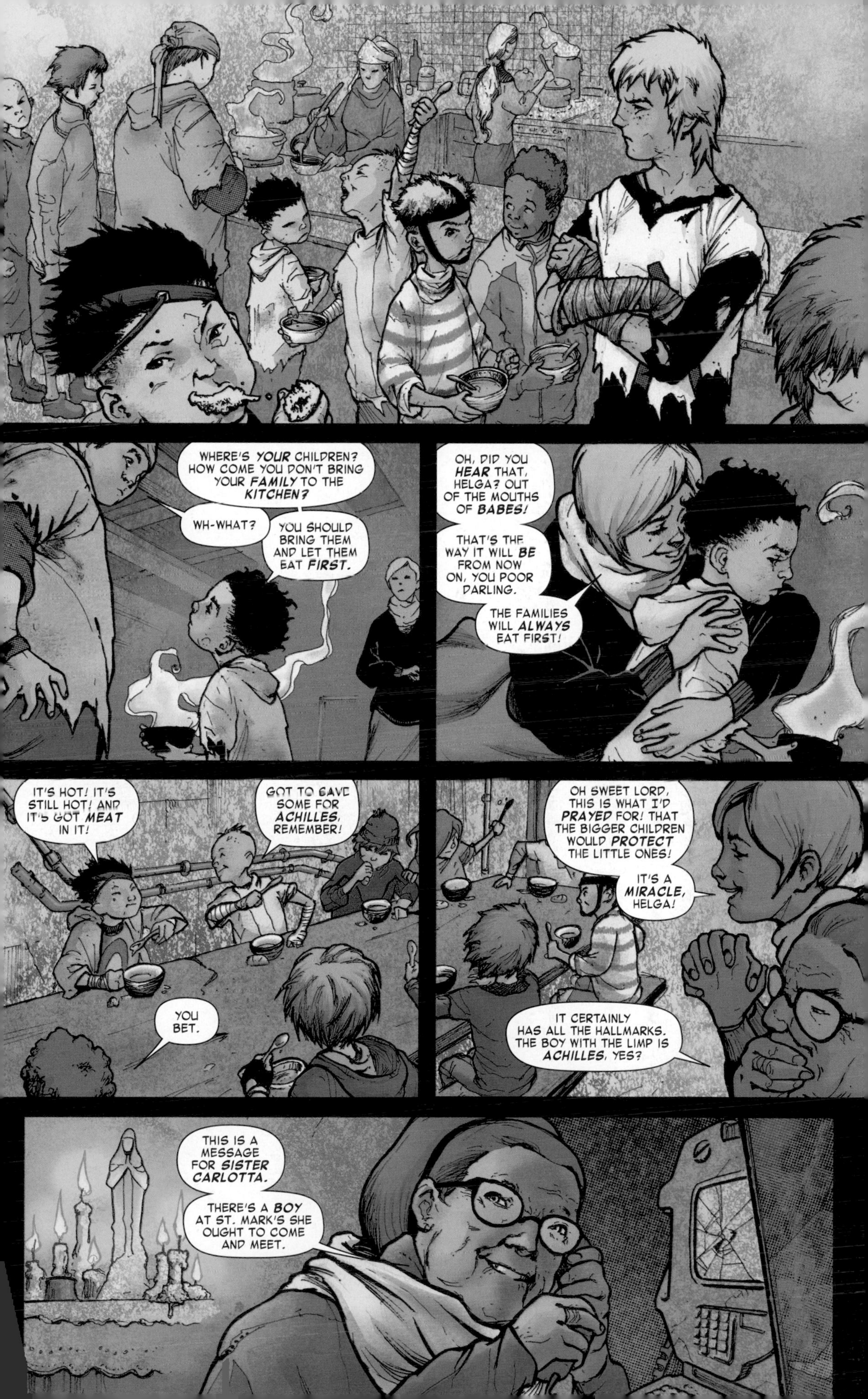
WHERE'S YOUR CHILDREN? HOW COME YOU DON'T BRING YOUR FAMILY TO THE KITCHEN?
WH-WHAT?
YOU SHOULD BRING THEM AND LET THEM EAT FIRST.
OH, DID YOU HEAR THAT, HELGA? OUT OF THE MOUTHS OF BABES!
THAT'S THE WAY IT WILL BE FROM NOW ON, YOU POOR DARLING.
THE FAMILIES WILL ALWAYS EAT FIRST!
IT'S HOT! IT'S STILL HOT! AND IT'S GOT MEAT IN IT!
GOT TO SAVE SOME FOR ACHILLES, REMEMBER!
YOU BET.
OH SWEET LORD, THIS IS WHAT I'D PRAYED FOR! THAT THE BIGGER CHILDREN WOULD PROTECT THE LITTLE ONES!
IT'S A MIRACLE, HELGA!
IT CERTAINLY HAS ALL THE HALLMARKS. THE BOY WITH THE LIMP IS ACHILLES, YES?
THIS IS A MESSAGE FOR SISTER CARLOTTA.
THERE'S A BOY AT ST. MARK'S SHE OUGHT TO COME AND MEET.

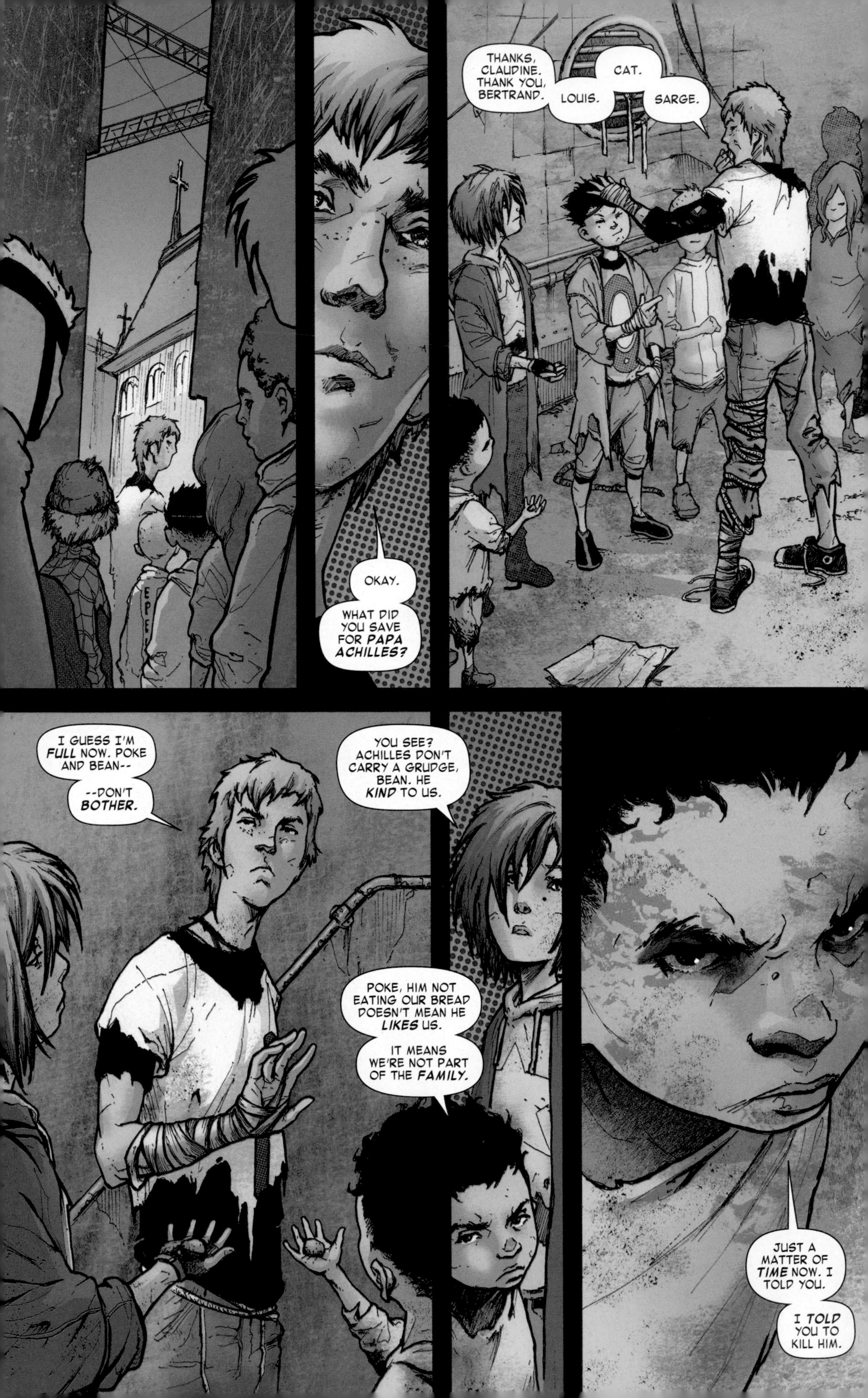
OKAY.
WHAT DID YOU SAVE FOR PAPA ACHILLES?
THANKS, CLAUDINE. THANK YOU, BERTRAND.
LOUIS.
CAT.
SARGE.
I GUESS I'M FULL NOW. POKE AND BEAN--
--DON'T BOTHER.
YOU SEE? ACHILLES DON'T CARRY A GRUDGE, BEAN. HE KIND TO US.
POKE, HIM NOT EATING OUR BREAD DOESN'T MEAN HE LIKES US.
IT MEANS WE'RE NOT PART OF THE FAMILY.
JUST A MATTER OF TIME NOW. I TOLD YOU.
I TOLD YOU TO KILL HIM.

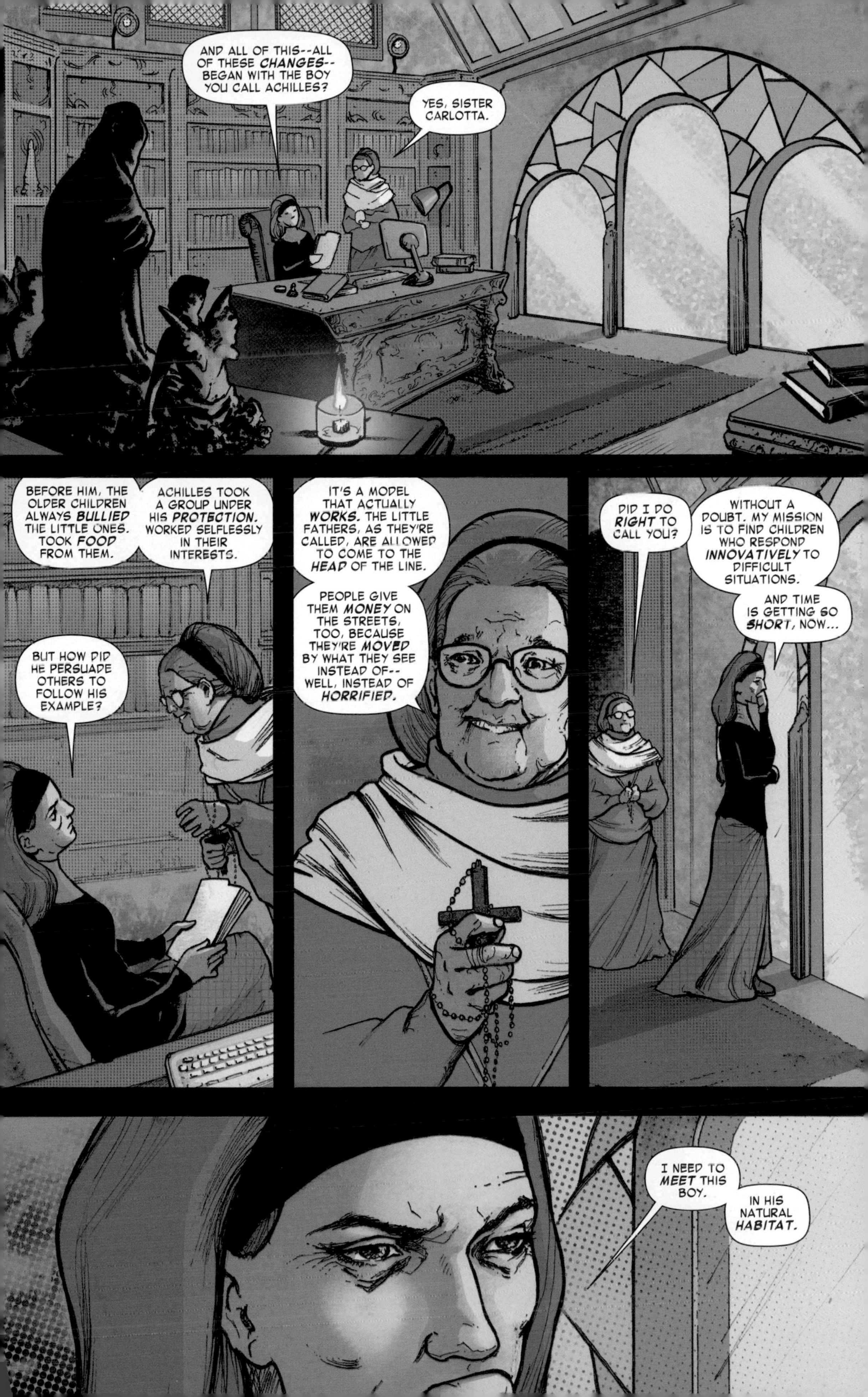
AND ALL OF THIS--ALL OF THESE CHANGES--BEGAN WITH THE BOY YOU CALL ACHILLES?
YES, SISTER CARLOTTA.
BEFORE HIM, THE OLDER CHILDREN ALWAYS BULLIED THE LITTLE ONES. TOOK FOOD FROM THEM.
ACHILLES TOOK A GROUP UNDER HIS PROTECTION. WORKED SELFLESSLY IN THEIR INTERESTS.
BUT HOW DID HE PERSUADE OTHERS TO FOLLOW HIS EXAMPLE?
IT'S A MODEL THAT ACTUALLY WORKS. THE LITTLE FATHERS, AS THEY'RE CALLED, ARE ALLOWED TO COME TO THE HEAD OF THE LINE.
PEOPLE GIVE THEM MONEY ON THE STREETS, TOO, BECAUSE THEY'RE MOVED BY WHAT THEY SEE INSTEAD OF--WELL, INSTEAD OF HORRIFIED.
DID I DO RIGHT TO CALL YOU?
WITHOUT A DOUBT. MY MISSION IS TO FIND CHILDREN WHO RESPOND INNOVATIVELY TO DIFFICULT SITUATIONS.
AND TIME IS GETTING SO SHORT, NOW...
I NEED TO MEET THIS BOY.
IN HIS NATURAL HABITAT.

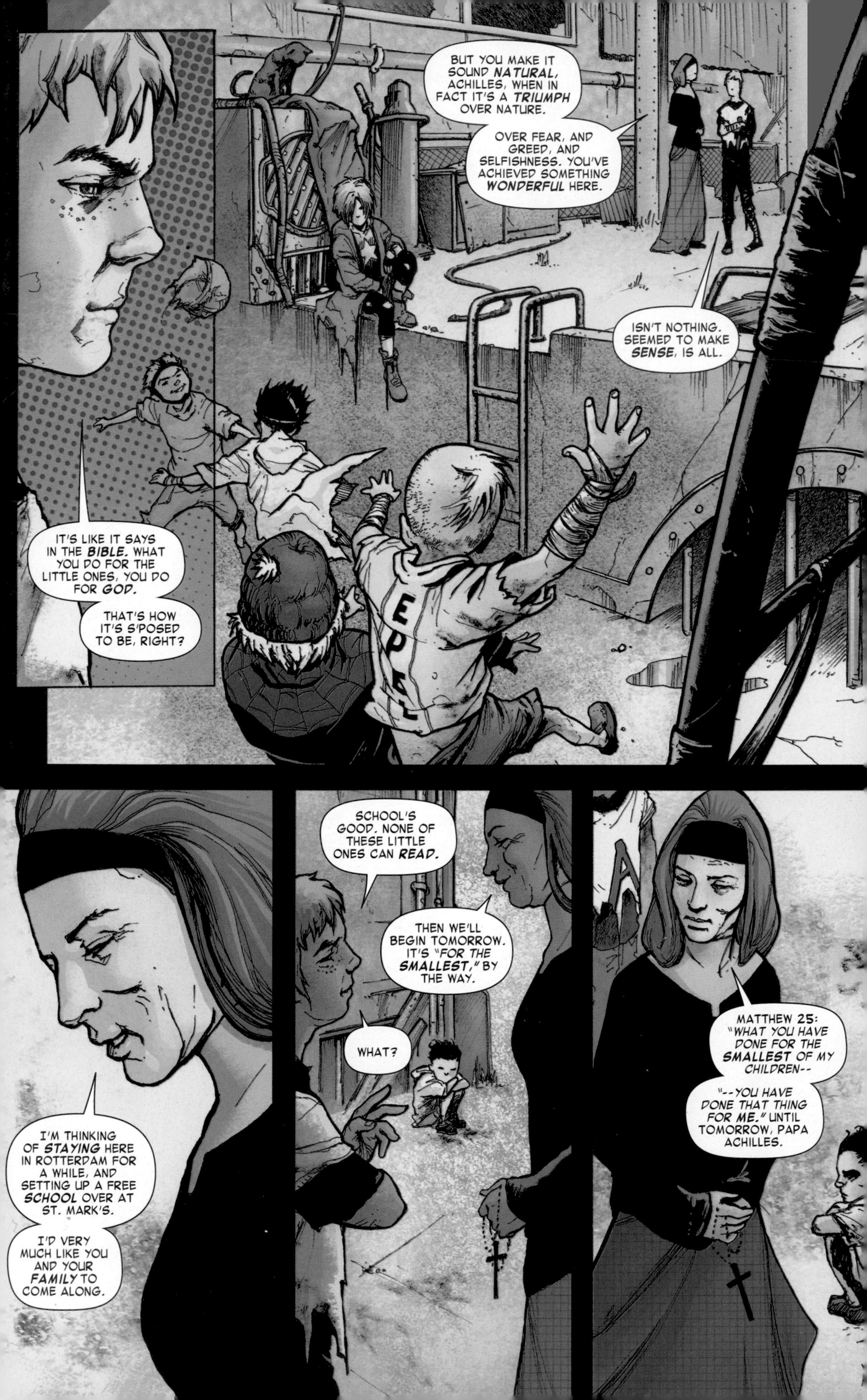
BUT YOU MAKE IT SOUND NATURAL, ACHILLES, WHEN IN FACT IT'S A TRIUMPH OVER NATURE.
OVER FEAR, AND GREED, AND SELFISHNESS. YOU'VE ACHIEVED SOMETHING WONDERFUL HERE.
ISN'T NOTHING. SEEMED TO MAKE SENSE, IS ALL.
IT'S LIKE IT SAYS IN THE BIBLE. WHAT YOU DO FOR THE LITTLE ONES, YOU DO FOR GOD.
THAT'S HOW IT'S S'POSED TO BE, RIGHT?
I'M THINKING OF STAYING HERE IN ROTTERDAM FOR A WHILE, AND SETTING UP A FREE SCHOOL OVER AT ST. MARK'S.
I'D VERY MUCH LIKE YOU AND YOUR FAMILY TO COME ALONG.
SCHOOL'S GOOD. NONE OF THESE LITTLE ONES CAN READ.
THEN WE'LL BEGIN TOMORROW. IT'S "FOR THE SMALLEST," BY THE WAY.
WHAT?
MATTHEW 25: "WHAT YOU HAVE DONE FOR THE SMALLEST OF MY CHILDREN--
"--YOU HAVE DONE THAT THING FOR ME." UNTIL TOMORROW, PAPA ACHILLES.

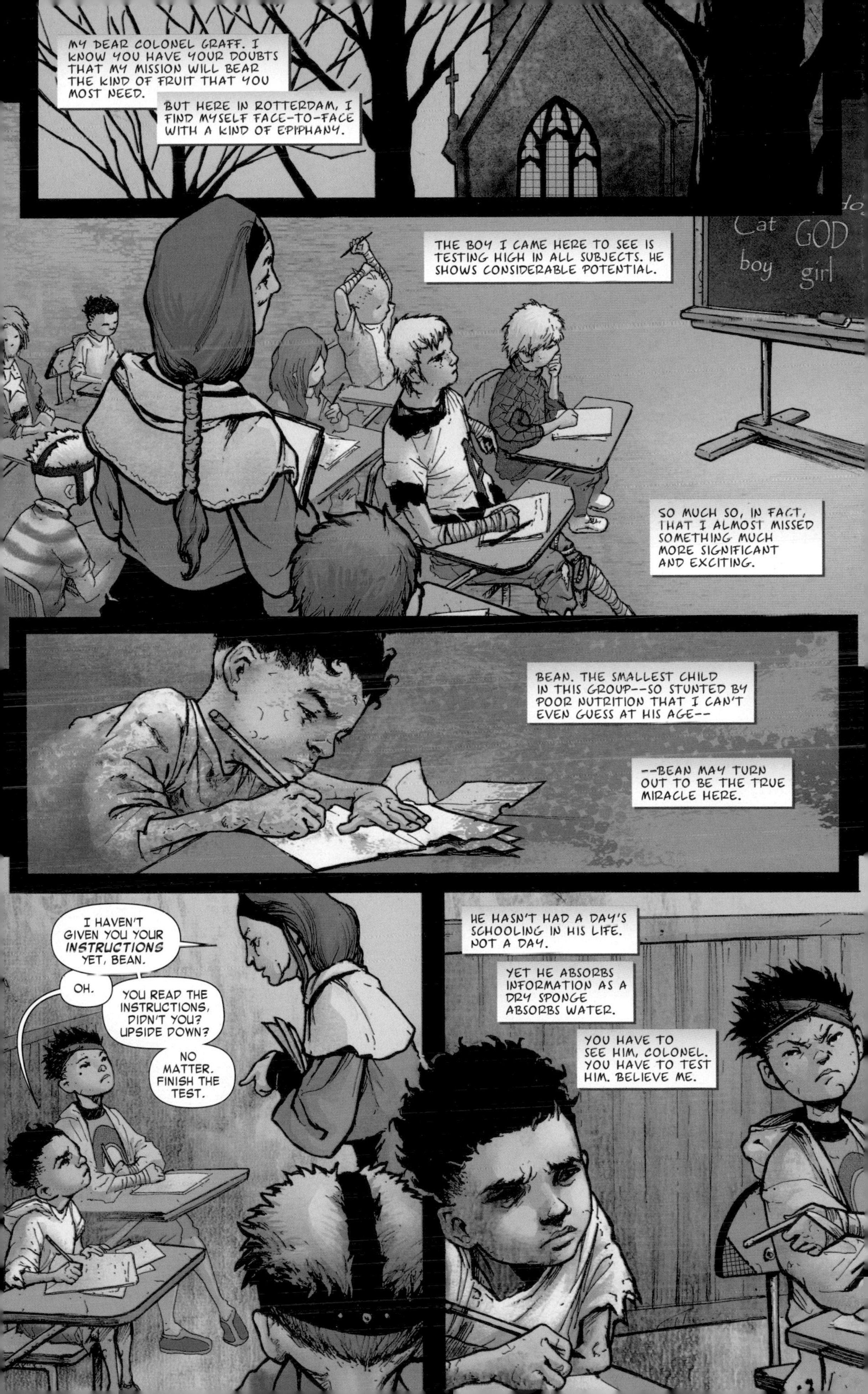
MY DEAR COLONEL GRAFF. I KNOW YOU HAVE YOUR DOUBTS THAT MY MISSION WILL BEAR THE KIND OF FRUIT THAT YOU MOST NEED.
BUT HERE IN ROTTERDAM, I FIND MYSELF FACE-TO-FACE WITH A KIND OF EPIPHANY.
THE BOY I CAME HERE TO SEE IS TESTING HIGH IN ALL SUBJECTS. HE SHOWS CONSIDERABLE POTENTIAL.
Cat GOD
boy girl
SO MUCH SO, IN FACT, THAT I ALMOST MISSED SOMETHING MUCH MORE SIGNIFICANT AND EXCITING.
BEAN. THE SMALLEST CHILD IN THIS GROUP--SO STUNTED BY POOR NUTRITION THAT I CAN'T EVEN GUESS AT HIS AGE--
--BEAN MAY TURN OUT TO BE THE TRUE MIRACLE HERE.
I HAVEN'T GIVEN YOU YOUR INSTRUCTIONS YET, BEAN.
OH.
YOU READ THE INSTRUCTIONS, DIDN'T YOU? UPSIDE DOWN?
NO MATTER. FINISH THE TEST.
HE HASN'T HAD A DAY'S SCHOOLING IN HIS LIFE. NOT A DAY.
YET HE ABSORBS INFORMATION AS A DRY SPONGE ABSORBS WATER.
YOU HAVE TO SEE HIM, COLONEL. YOU HAVE TO TEST HIM. BELIEVE ME.

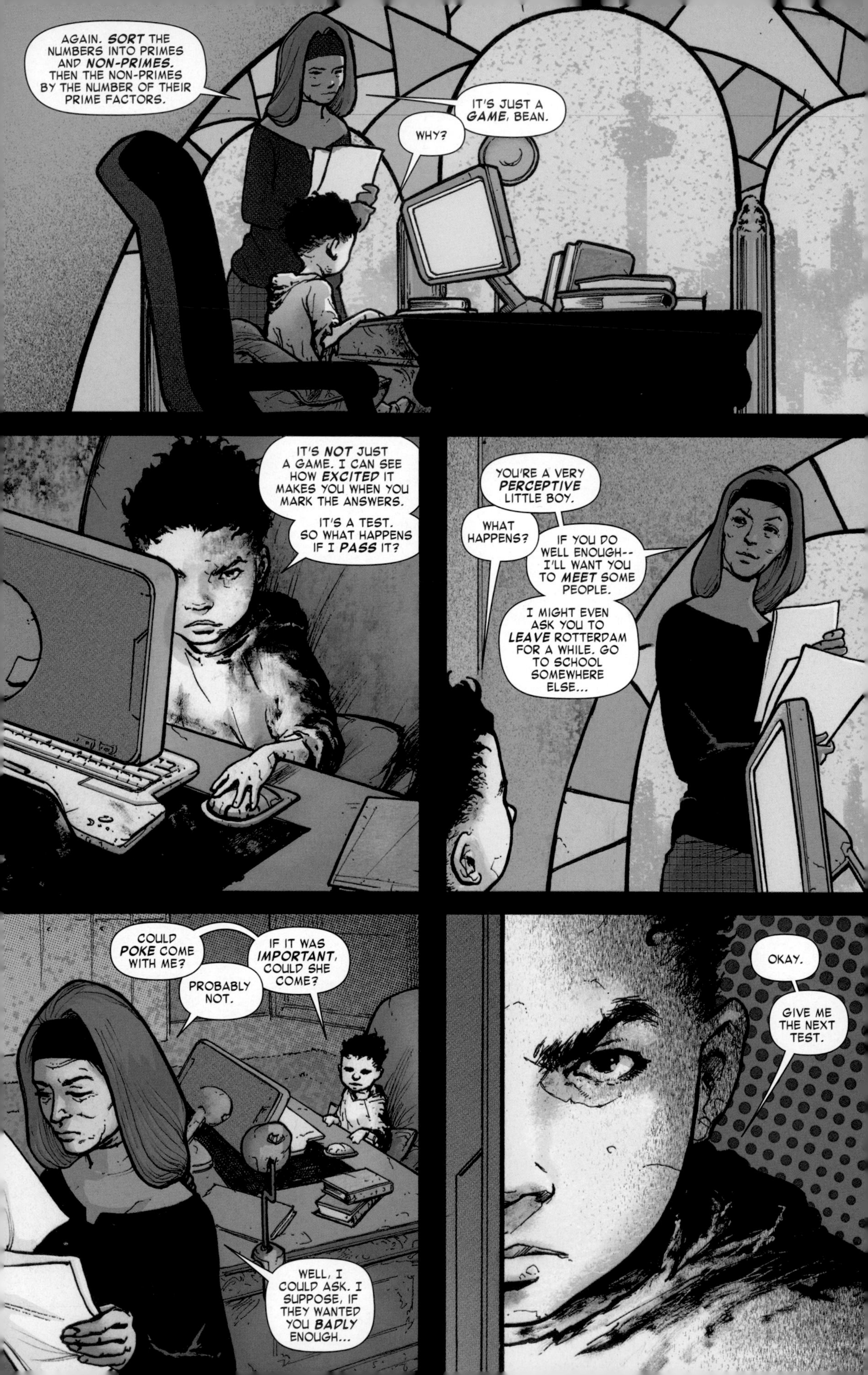
AGAIN. SORT THE NUMBERS INTO PRIMES AND NON-PRIMES. THEN THE NON-PRIMES BY THE NUMBER OF THEIR PRIME FACTORS.
WHY?
IT'S JUST A GAME, BEAN.
IT'S NOT JUST A GAME. I CAN SEE HOW EXCITED IT MAKES YOU WHEN YOU MARK THE ANSWERS.
IT'S A TEST. SO WHAT HAPPENS IF I PASS IT?
YOU'RE A VERY PERCEPTIVE LITTLE BOY.
WHAT HAPPENS?
IF YOU DO WELL ENOUGH-- I'LL WANT YOU TO MEET SOME PEOPLE.
I MIGHT EVEN ASK YOU TO LEAVE ROTTERDAM FOR A WHILE. GO TO SCHOOL SOMEWHERE ELSE...
COULD POKE COME WITH ME?
PROBABLY NOT.
IF IT WAS IMPORTANT, COULD SHE COME?
WELL, I COULD ASK. I SUPPOSE, IF THEY WANTED YOU BADLY ENOUGH...
OKAY.
GIVE ME THE NEXT TEST.

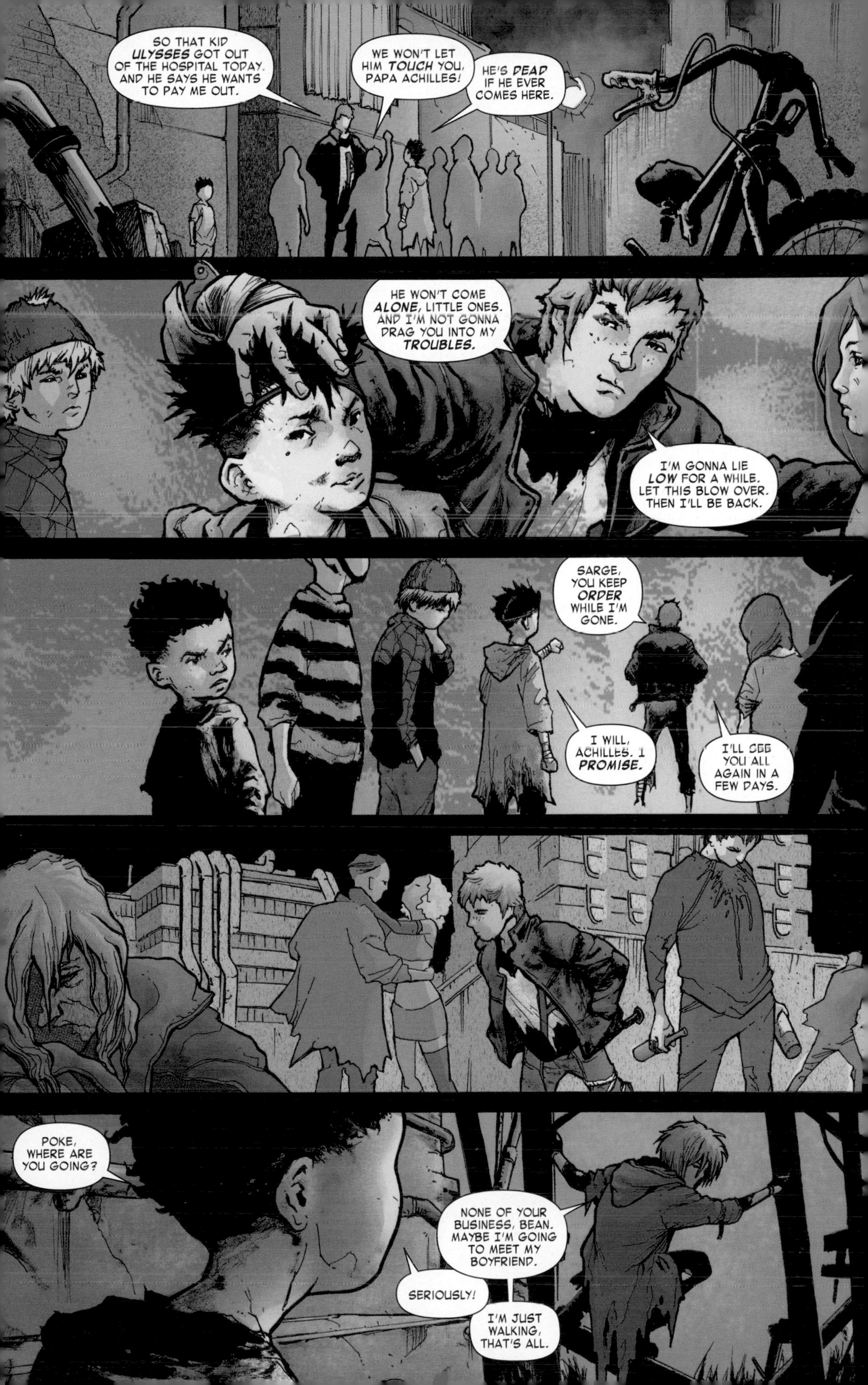
SO THAT KID ULYSSES GOT OUT OF THE HOSPITAL TODAY. AND HE SAYS HE WANTS TO PAY ME OUT.
WE WON'T LET HIM TOUCH YOU, PAPA ACHILLES!
HE'S DEAD IF HE EVER COMES HERE.
HE WON'T COME ALONE, LITTLE ONES. AND I'M NOT GONNA DRAG YOU INTO MY TROUBLES.
I'M GONNA LIE LOW FOR A WHILE. LET THIS BLOW OVER. THEN I'LL BE BACK.
SARGE, YOU KEEP ORDER WHILE I'M GONE.
I WILL, ACHILLES. I PROMISE.
I'LL SEE YOU ALL AGAIN IN A FEW DAYS.
POKE, WHERE ARE YOU GOING?
NONE OF YOUR BUSINESS, BEAN. MAYBE I'M GOING TO MEET MY BOYFRIEND.
SERIOUSLY!
I'M JUST WALKING, THAT'S ALL.

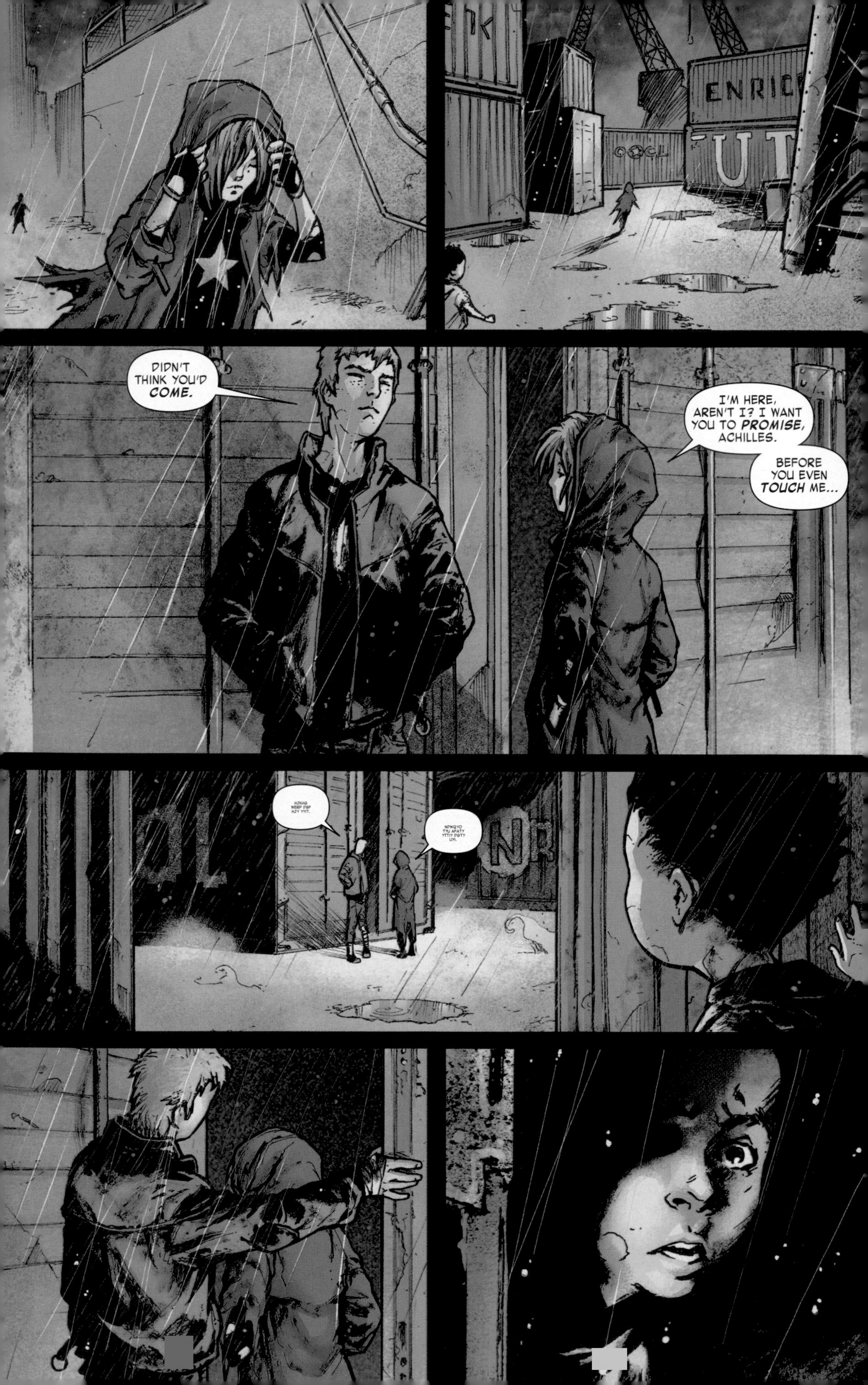
DIDN'T THINK YOU'D COME.
I'M HERE, AREN'T I? I WANT YOU TO PROMISE, ACHILLES.
BEFORE YOU EVEN TOUCH ME...

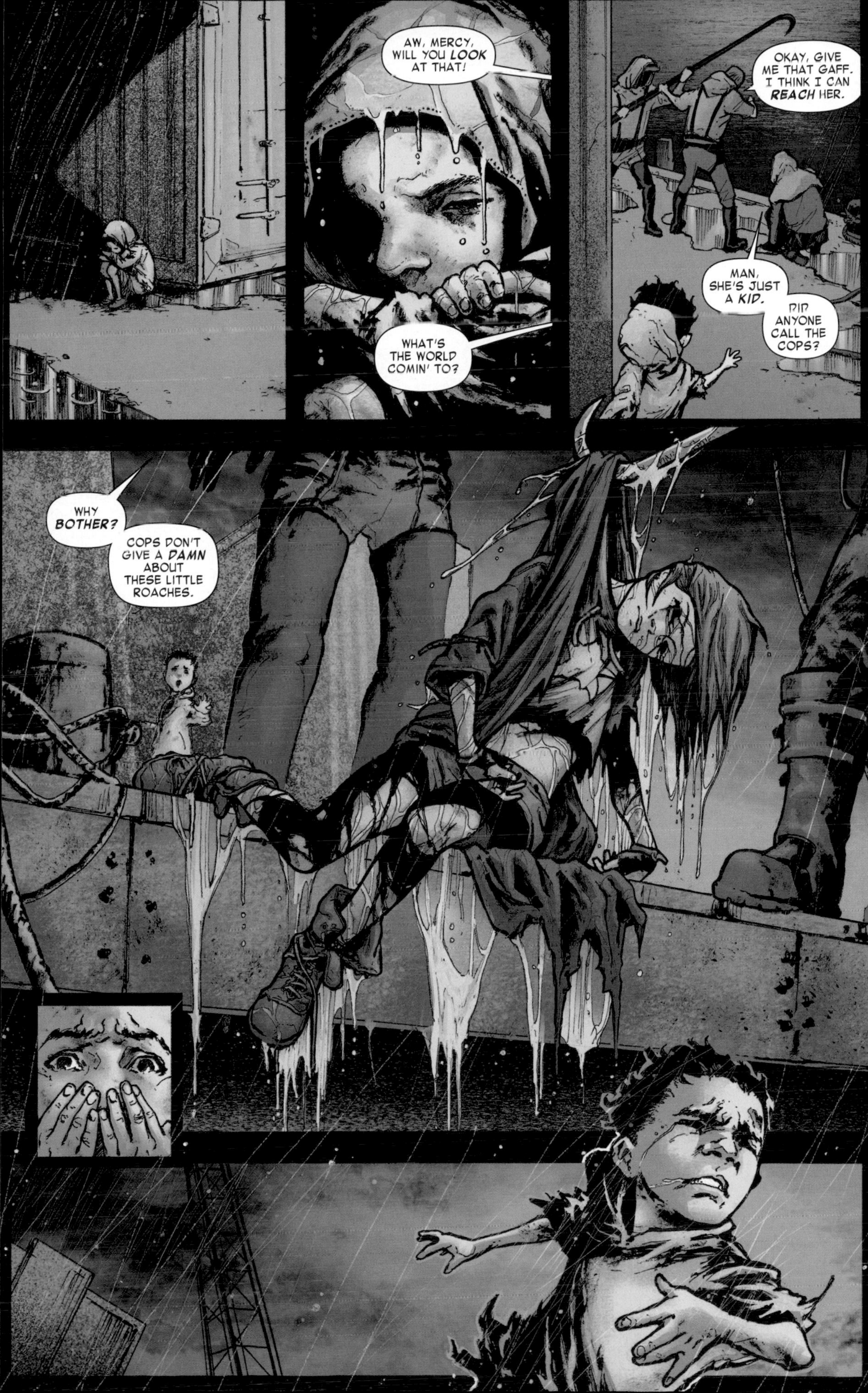
AW, MERCY, WILL YOU LOOK AT THAT!
WHAT'S THE WORLD COMIN' TO?
OKAY, GIVE ME THAT GAFF. I THINK I CAN REACH HER.
MAN, SHE'S JUST A KID.
DID ANYONE CALL THE COPS?
WHY BOTHER?
COPS DON'T GIVE A DAMN ABOUT THESE LITTLE ROACHES.

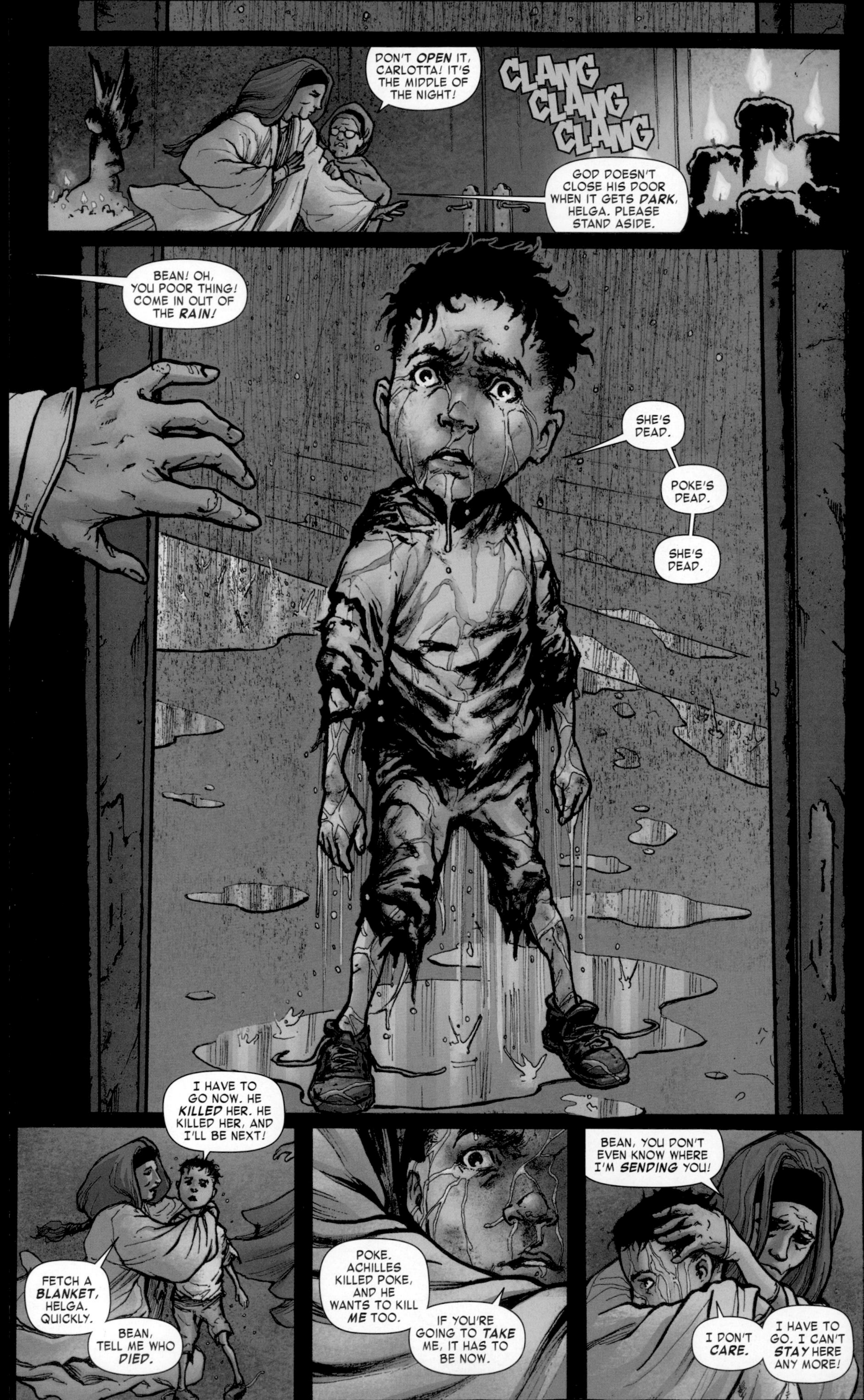
DON'T OPEN IT, CARLOTTA! IT'S THE MIDDLE OF THE NIGHT!
CLANG CLANG CLANG
GOD DOESN'T CLOSE HIS DOOR WHEN IT GETS DARK, HELGA. PLEASE STAND ASIDE.
BEAN! OH, YOU POOR THING! COME IN OUT OF THE RAIN!
SHE'S DEAD.
POKE'S DEAD.
SHE'S DEAD.
I HAVE TO GO NOW. HE KILLED HER. HE KILLED HER, AND I'LL BE NEXT!
FETCH A BLANKET, HELGA. QUICKLY.
BEAN, TELL ME WHO DIED.
POKE. ACHILLES KILLED POKE, AND HE WANTS TO KILL ME TOO.
IF YOU'RE GOING TO TAKE ME, IT HAS TO BE NOW.
BEAN, YOU DON'T EVEN KNOW WHERE I'M SENDING YOU!
I DON'T CARE.
I HAVE TO GO. I CAN'T STAY HERE ANY MORE!

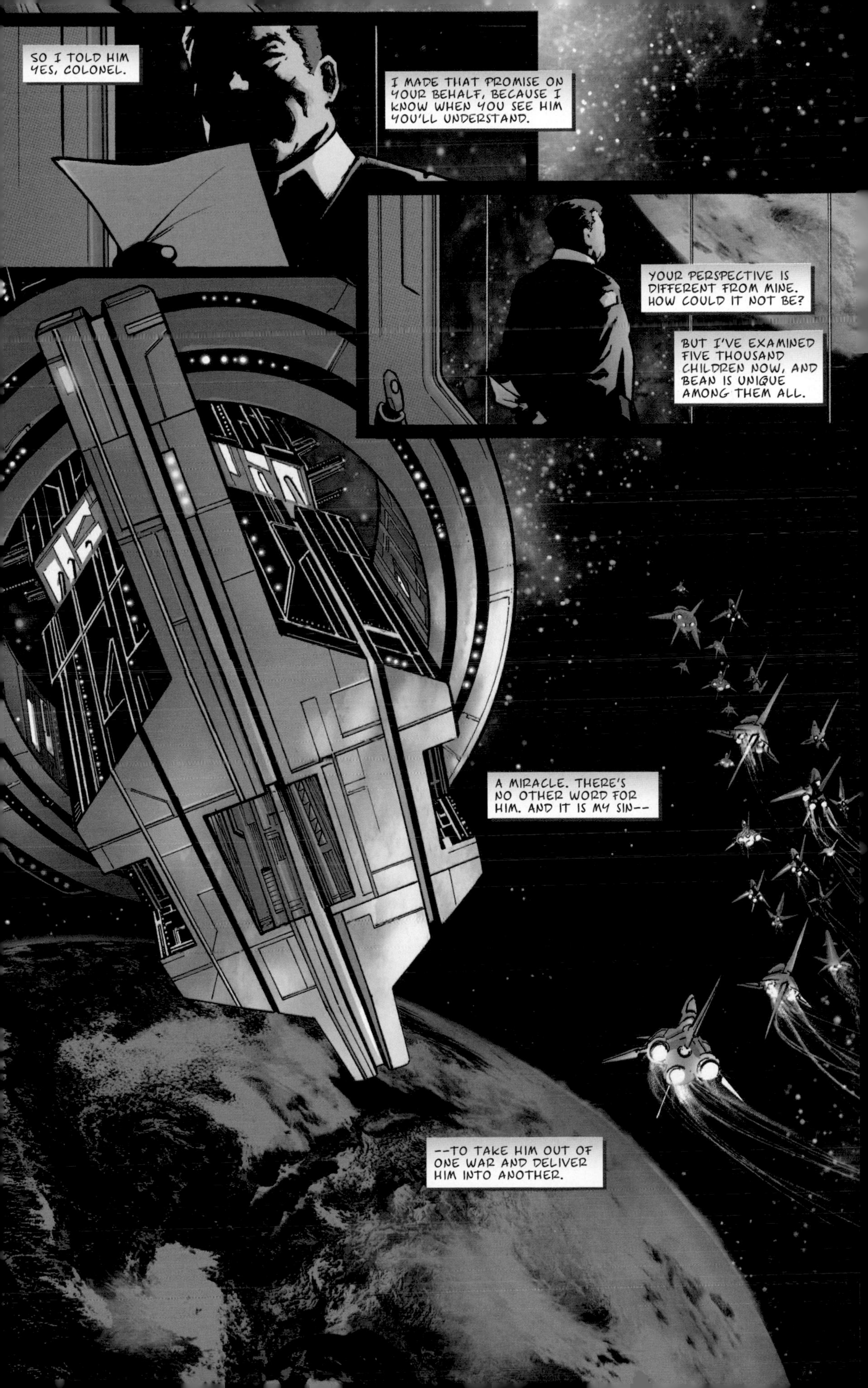
SO I TOLD HIM YES, COLONEL.
I MADE THAT PROMISE ON YOUR BEHALF, BECAUSE I KNOW WHEN YOU SEE HIM YOU'LL UNDERSTAND.
YOUR PERSPECTIVE IS DIFFERENT FROM MINE. HOW COULD IT NOT BE?
BUT I'VE EXAMINED FIVE THOUSAND CHILDREN NOW, AND BEAN IS UNIQUE AMONG THEM ALL.
A MIRACLE. THERE'S NO OTHER WORD FOR HIM. AND IT IS MY SIN--
--TO TAKE HIM OUT OF ONE WAR AND DELIVER HIM INTO ANOTHER.

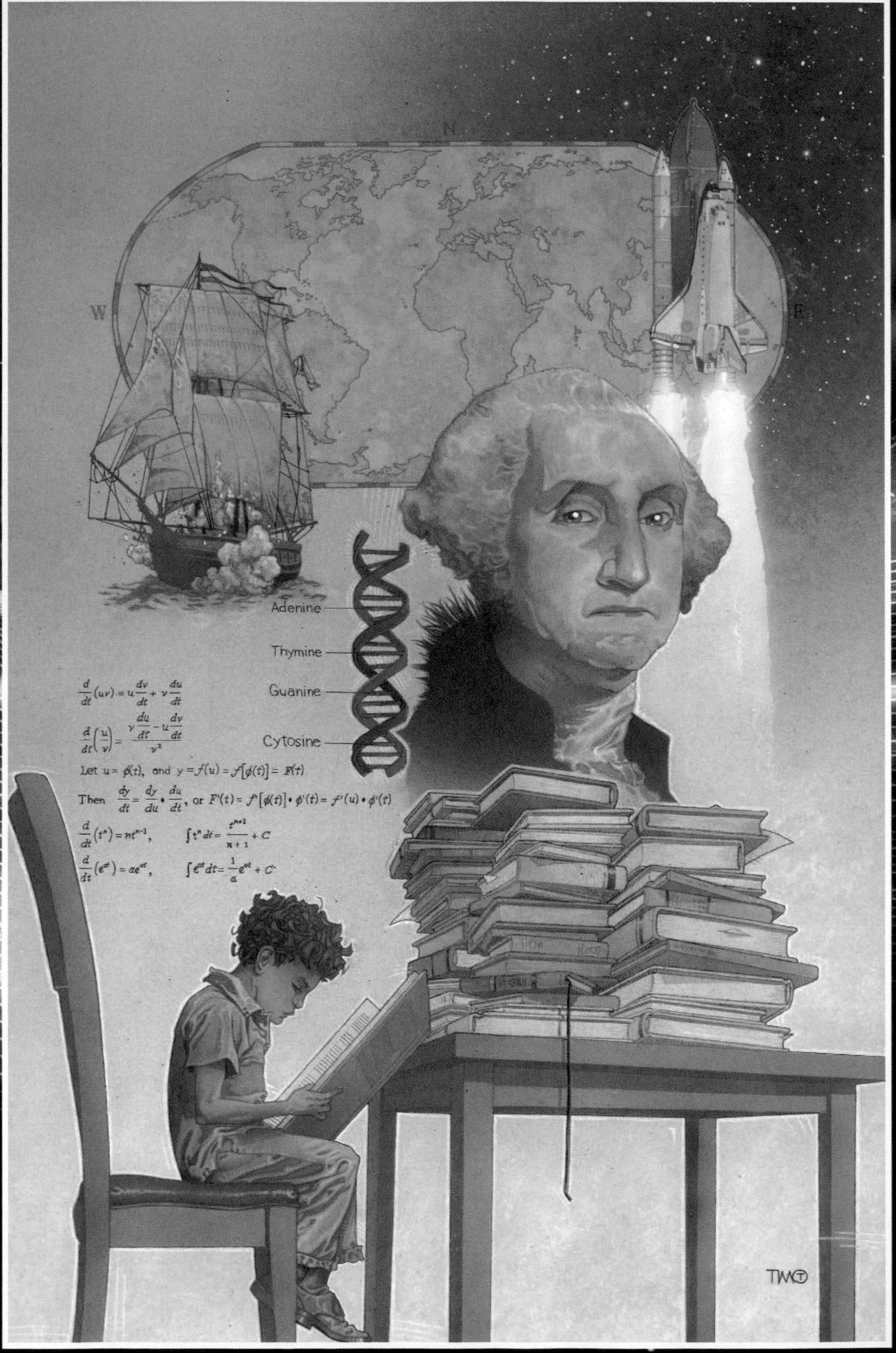
N
W
E
Adenine
Thymine
Guanine
Cytosine
$\frac{d}{dt}(uv) = u\frac{dv}{dt} + v\frac{du}{dt}$
$\frac{d}{dt}\left(\frac{u}{v}\right) = \frac{v\frac{du}{dt} - u\frac{dv}{dt}}{v^2}$
Let $u = \phi(t)$, and $y = f(u) = f[\phi(t)] = F(t)$
Then $\frac{dy}{dt} = \frac{dy}{du} \cdot \frac{du}{dt}$, or $F'(t) = f'[\phi(t)] \cdot \phi'(t) = f'(u) \cdot \phi'(t)$
$\frac{d}{dt}(t^n) = nt^{n-1}$, $\int t^n dt = \frac{t^{n+1}}{n+1} + C$
$\frac{d}{dt}(e^{at}) = ae^{at}$, $\int e^{at} dt = \frac{1}{a}e^{at} + C$
TWT

T W O

"I was mistaken about the first one. He tests well, but his character is not well suited to Battle School."

"I don't see that on the tests you've shown me."

"He's very sharp. He gives the right answers, but they aren't true."

"And what test did you use to determine this?"

"He committed murder."

"Well, that is a drawback. And the other one? A fish that small I'd generally throw back into the stream. He doesn't even have a name."

"Yes he does."

"Bean? That isn't a name. That's a joke."

"It won't be when he's done with it."

"Keep him until he's five. Do what you can with him, and show me your results then."

"I have other children to find."

"No, Sister Carlotta, you don't. Time's too short now. Bring this one up to snuff, and then..."

"Then what?"

"Then pray, I suppose. Let's all stick to our specialities."

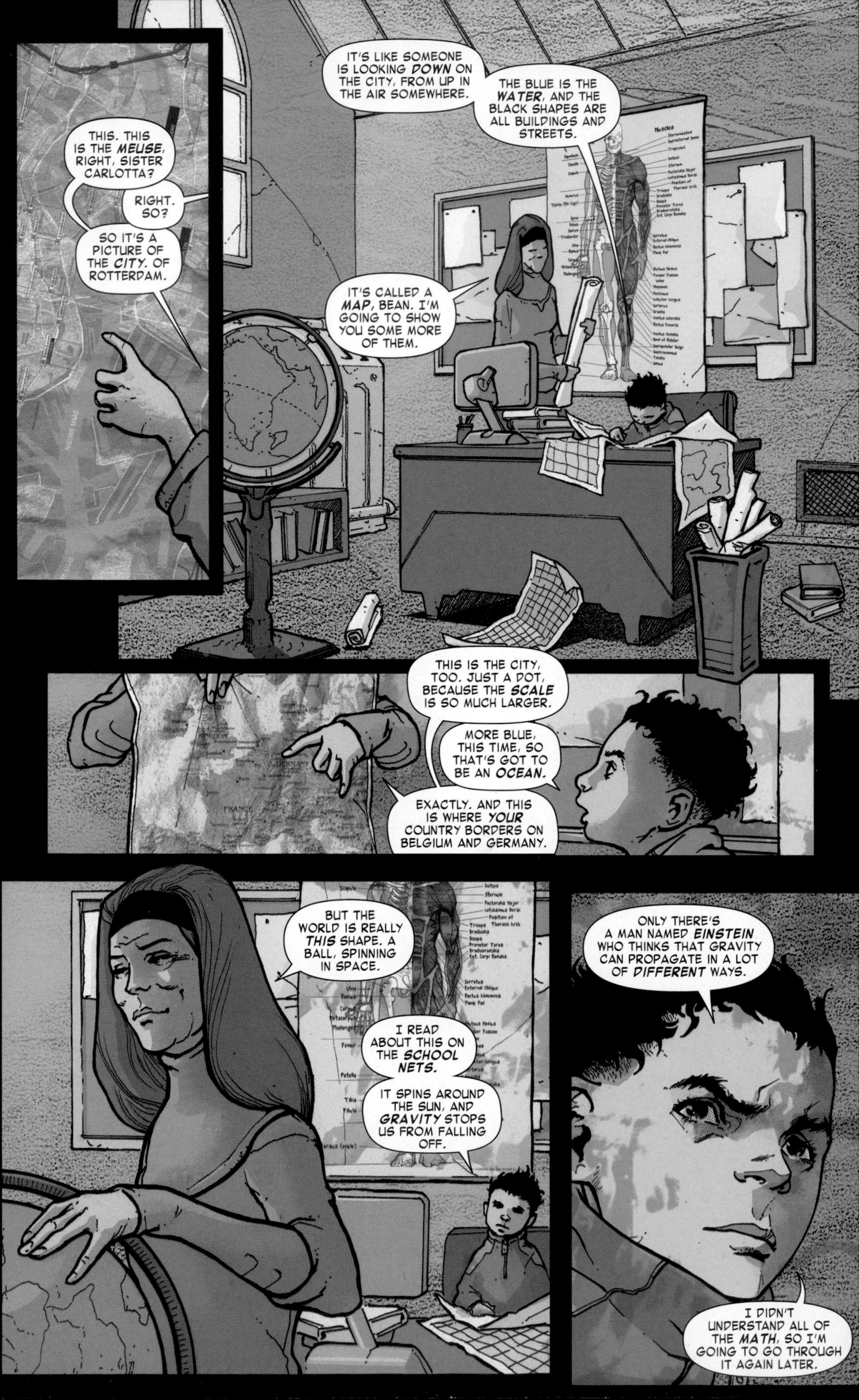
THIS. THIS IS THE MEUSE, RIGHT, SISTER CARLOTTA?
RIGHT. SO?
SO IT'S A PICTURE OF THE CITY. OF ROTTERDAM.
IT'S LIKE SOMEONE IS LOOKING DOWN ON THE CITY, FROM UP IN THE AIR SOMEWHERE.
THE BLUE IS THE WATER, AND THE BLACK SHAPES ARE ALL BUILDINGS AND STREETS.
IT'S CALLED A MAP, BEAN. I'M GOING TO SHOW YOU SOME MORE OF THEM.
THIS IS THE CITY, TOO. JUST A DOT, BECAUSE THE SCALE IS SO MUCH LARGER.
MORE BLUE, THIS TIME, SO THAT'S GOT TO BE AN OCEAN.
EXACTLY. AND THIS IS WHERE YOUR COUNTRY BORDERS ON BELGIUM AND GERMANY.
BUT THE WORLD IS REALLY THIS SHAPE. A BALL, SPINNING IN SPACE.
I READ ABOUT THIS ON THE SCHOOL NETS.
IT SPINS AROUND THE SUN, AND GRAVITY STOPS US FROM FALLING OFF.
ONLY THERE'S A MAN NAMED EINSTEIN WHO THINKS THAT GRAVITY CAN PROPAGATE IN A LOT OF DIFFERENT WAYS.
I DIDN'T UNDERSTAND ALL OF THE MATH, SO I'M GOING TO GO THROUGH IT AGAIN LATER.

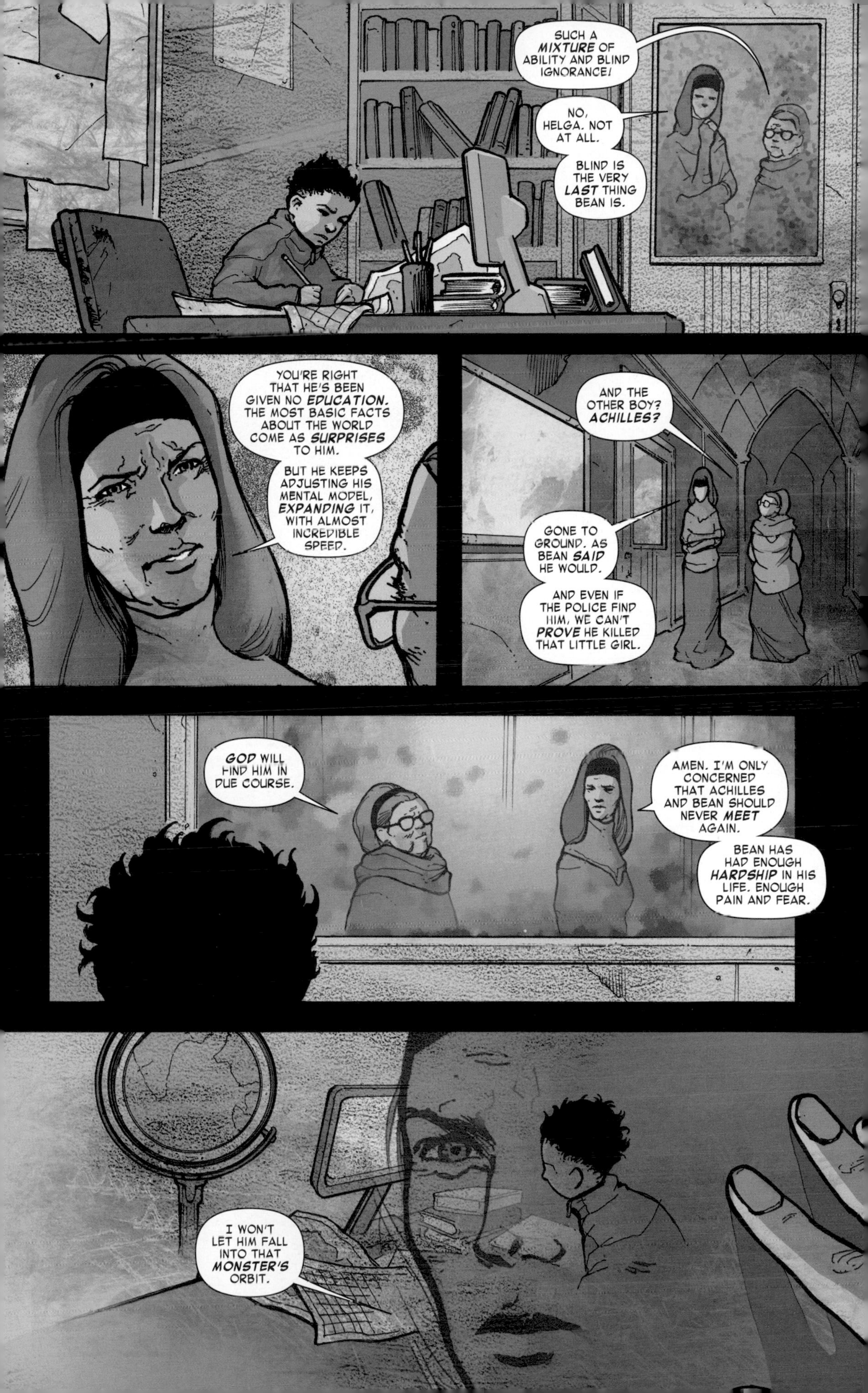
SUCH A MIXTURE OF ABILITY AND BLIND IGNORANCE!
NO, HELGA. NOT AT ALL.
BLIND IS THE VERY LAST THING BEAN IS.
YOU'RE RIGHT THAT HE'S BEEN GIVEN NO EDUCATION. THE MOST BASIC FACTS ABOUT THE WORLD COME AS SURPRISES TO HIM.
BUT HE KEEPS ADJUSTING HIS MENTAL MODEL, EXPANDING IT, WITH ALMOST INCREDIBLE SPEED.
AND THE OTHER BOY? ACHILLES?
GONE TO GROUND. AS BEAN SAID HE WOULD.
AND EVEN IF THE POLICE FIND HIM, WE CAN'T PROVE HE KILLED THAT LITTLE GIRL.
GOD WILL FIND HIM IN DUE COURSE.
AMEN. I'M ONLY CONCERNED THAT ACHILLES AND BEAN SHOULD NEVER MEET AGAIN.
BEAN HAS HAD ENOUGH HARDSHIP IN HIS LIFE. ENOUGH PAIN AND FEAR.
I WON'T LET HIM FALL INTO THAT MONSTER'S ORBIT.

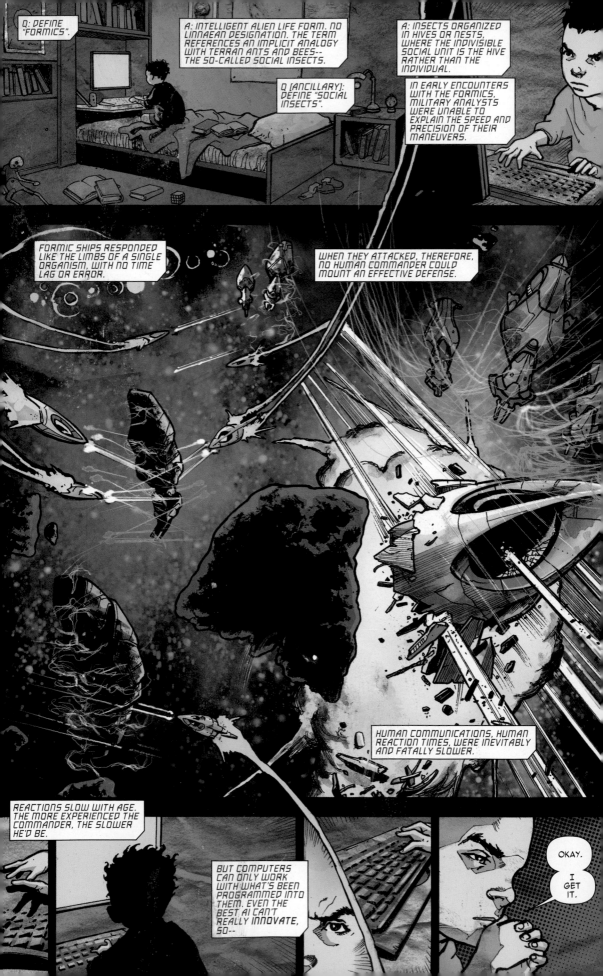

Q: DEFINE "FORMICS".

A: INTELLIGENT ALIEN LIFE FORM. NO LINNAEAN DESIGNATION. THE TERM REFERENCES AN IMPLICIT ANALOGY WITH TERRAN ANTS AND BEES-- THE SO-CALLED SOCIAL INSECTS.

A: INSECTS ORGANIZED IN HIVES OR NESTS, WHERE THE INDIVISIBLE SOCIAL UNIT IS THE HIVE RATHER THAN THE INDIVIDUAL.

Q [ANCILLARY]: DEFINE "SOCIAL INSECTS".

IN EARLY ENCOUNTERS WITH THE FORMICS, MILITARY ANALYSTS WERE UNABLE TO EXPLAIN THE SPEED AND PRECISION OF THEIR MANEUVERS.

FORMIC SHIPS RESPONDED LIKE THE LIMBS OF A SINGLE ORGANISM, WITH NO TIME LAG OR ERROR.

WHEN THEY ATTACKED, THEREFORE, NO HUMAN COMMANDER COULD MOUNT AN EFFECTIVE DEFENSE.

HUMAN COMMUNICATIONS, HUMAN REACTION TIMES, WERE INEVITABLY AND FATALLY SLOWER.

REACTIONS SLOW WITH AGE. THE MORE EXPERIENCED THE COMMANDER, THE SLOWER HE'D BE.

BUT COMPUTERS CAN ONLY WORK WITH WHAT'S BEEN PROGRAMMED INTO THEM. EVEN THE BEST AI CAN'T REALLY INNOVATE, SO--

OKAY. I GET IT.

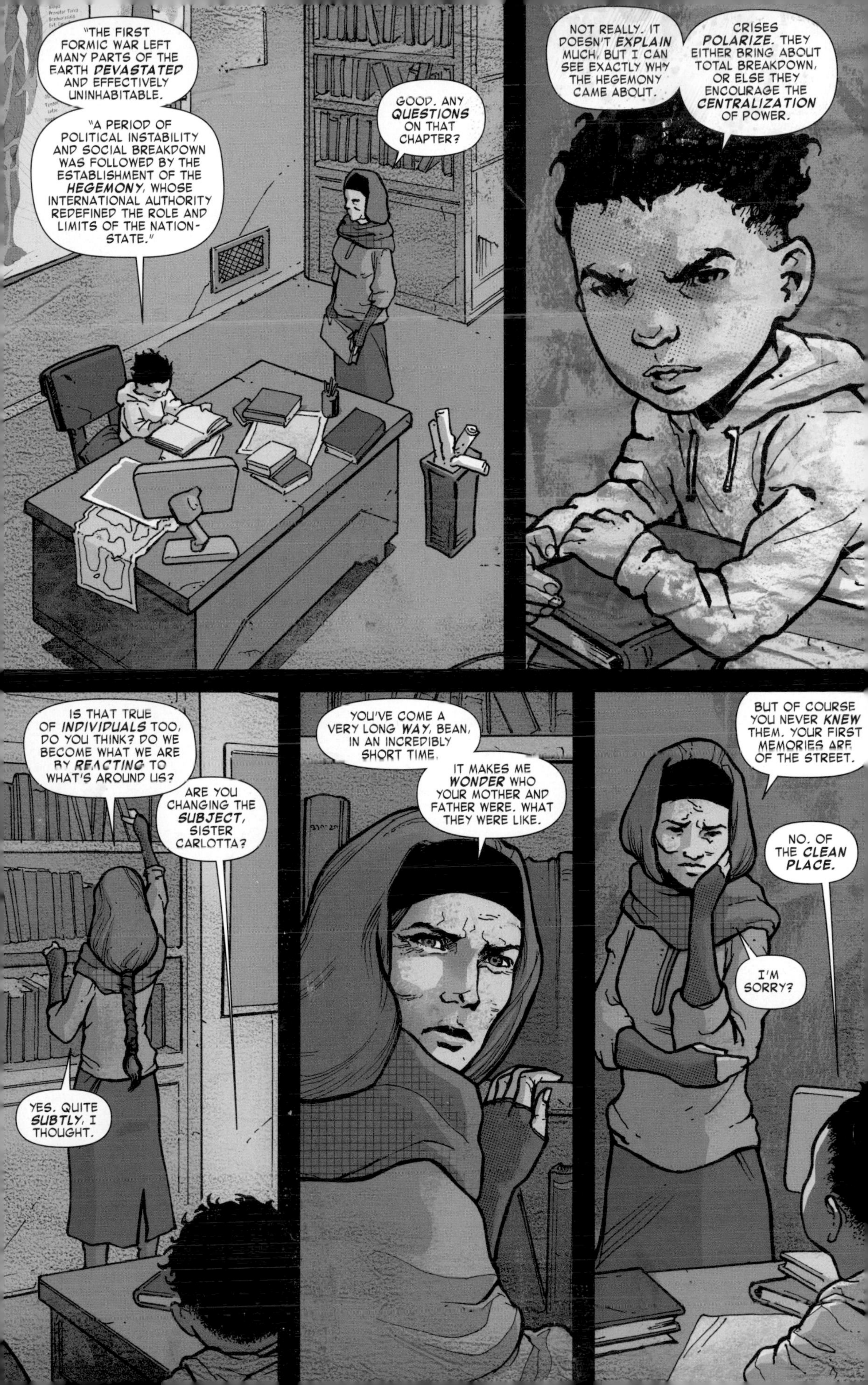
"THE FIRST FORMIC WAR LEFT MANY PARTS OF THE EARTH DEVASTATED AND EFFECTIVELY UNINHABITABLE.
"A PERIOD OF POLITICAL INSTABILITY AND SOCIAL BREAKDOWN WAS FOLLOWED BY THE ESTABLISHMENT OF THE HEGEMONY, WHOSE INTERNATIONAL AUTHORITY REDEFINED THE ROLE AND LIMITS OF THE NATION-STATE."
GOOD. ANY QUESTIONS ON THAT CHAPTER?
NOT REALLY. IT DOESN'T EXPLAIN MUCH, BUT I CAN SEE EXACTLY WHY THE HEGEMONY CAME ABOUT.
CRISES POLARIZE. THEY EITHER BRING ABOUT TOTAL BREAKDOWN, OR ELSE THEY ENCOURAGE THE CENTRALIZATION OF POWER.
IS THAT TRUE OF INDIVIDUALS TOO, DO YOU THINK? DO WE BECOME WHAT WE ARE BY REACTING TO WHAT'S AROUND US?
ARE YOU CHANGING THE SUBJECT, SISTER CARLOTTA?
YES. QUITE SUBTLY, I THOUGHT.
YOU'VE COME A VERY LONG WAY, BEAN, IN AN INCREDIBLY SHORT TIME.
IT MAKES ME WONDER WHO YOUR MOTHER AND FATHER WERE. WHAT THEY WERE LIKE.
BUT OF COURSE YOU NEVER KNEW THEM. YOUR FIRST MEMORIES ARE OF THE STREET.
NO. OF THE CLEAN PLACE.
I'M SORRY?

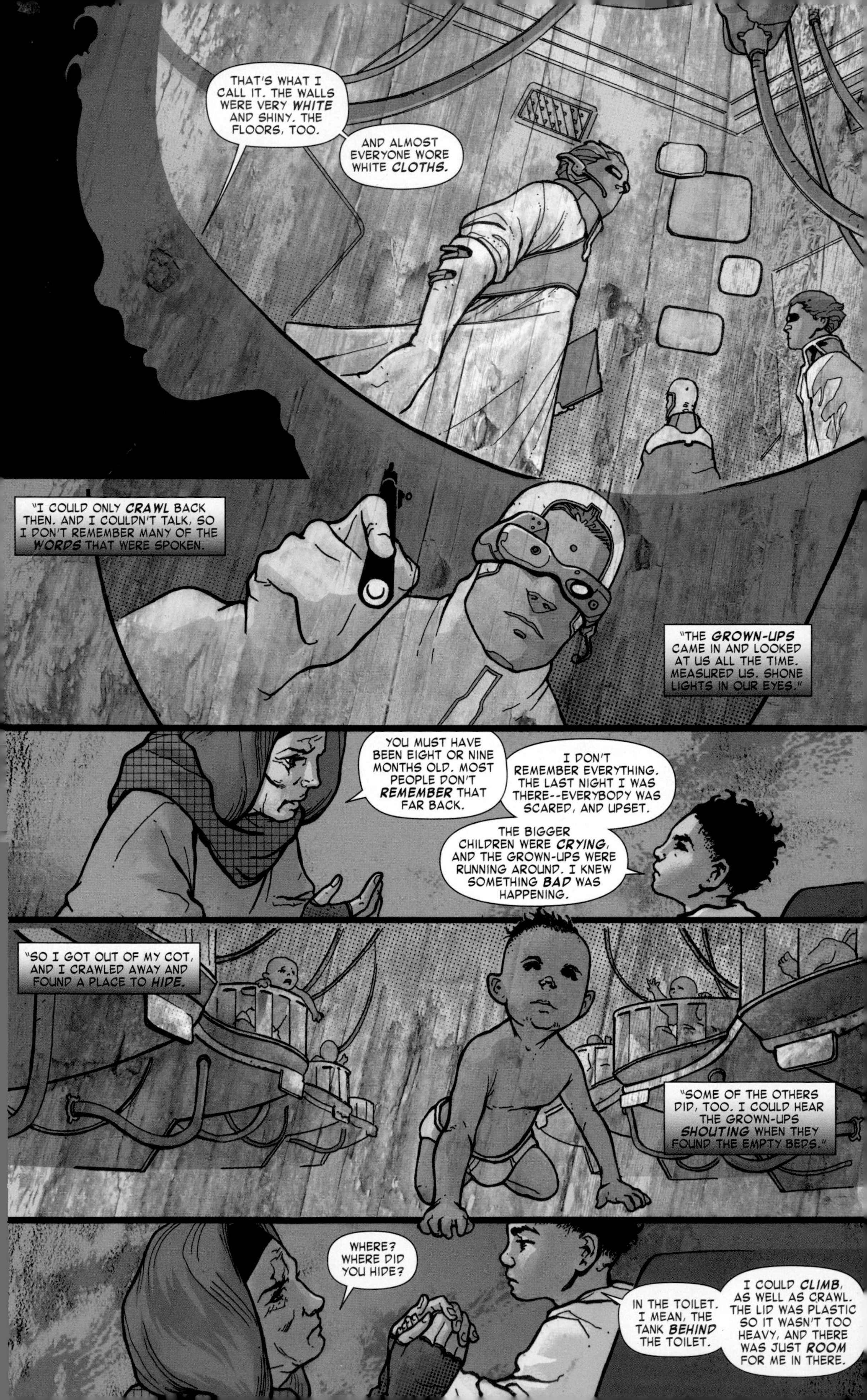
THAT'S WHAT I CALL IT. THE WALLS WERE VERY WHITE AND SHINY. THE FLOORS, TOO.
AND ALMOST EVERYONE WORE WHITE CLOTHS.
"I COULD ONLY CRAWL BACK THEN. AND I COULDN'T TALK, SO I DON'T REMEMBER MANY OF THE WORDS THAT WERE SPOKEN.
"THE GROWN-UPS CAME IN AND LOOKED AT US ALL THE TIME. MEASURED US. SHONE LIGHTS IN OUR EYES."
YOU MUST HAVE BEEN EIGHT OR NINE MONTHS OLD. MOST PEOPLE DON'T REMEMBER THAT FAR BACK.
I DON'T REMEMBER EVERYTHING. THE LAST NIGHT I WAS THERE--EVERYBODY WAS SCARED, AND UPSET.
THE BIGGER CHILDREN WERE CRYING, AND THE GROWN-UPS WERE RUNNING AROUND. I KNEW SOMETHING BAD WAS HAPPENING.
"SO I GOT OUT OF MY COT, AND I CRAWLED AWAY AND FOUND A PLACE TO HIDE.
"SOME OF THE OTHERS DID, TOO. I COULD HEAR THE GROWN-UPS SHOUTING WHEN THEY FOUND THE EMPTY BEDS."
WHERE? WHERE DID YOU HIDE?
IN THE TOILET. I MEAN, THE TANK BEHIND THE TOILET.
I COULD CLIMB, AS WELL AS CRAWL. THE LID WAS PLASTIC SO IT WASN'T TOO HEAVY, AND THERE WAS JUST ROOM FOR ME IN THERE.

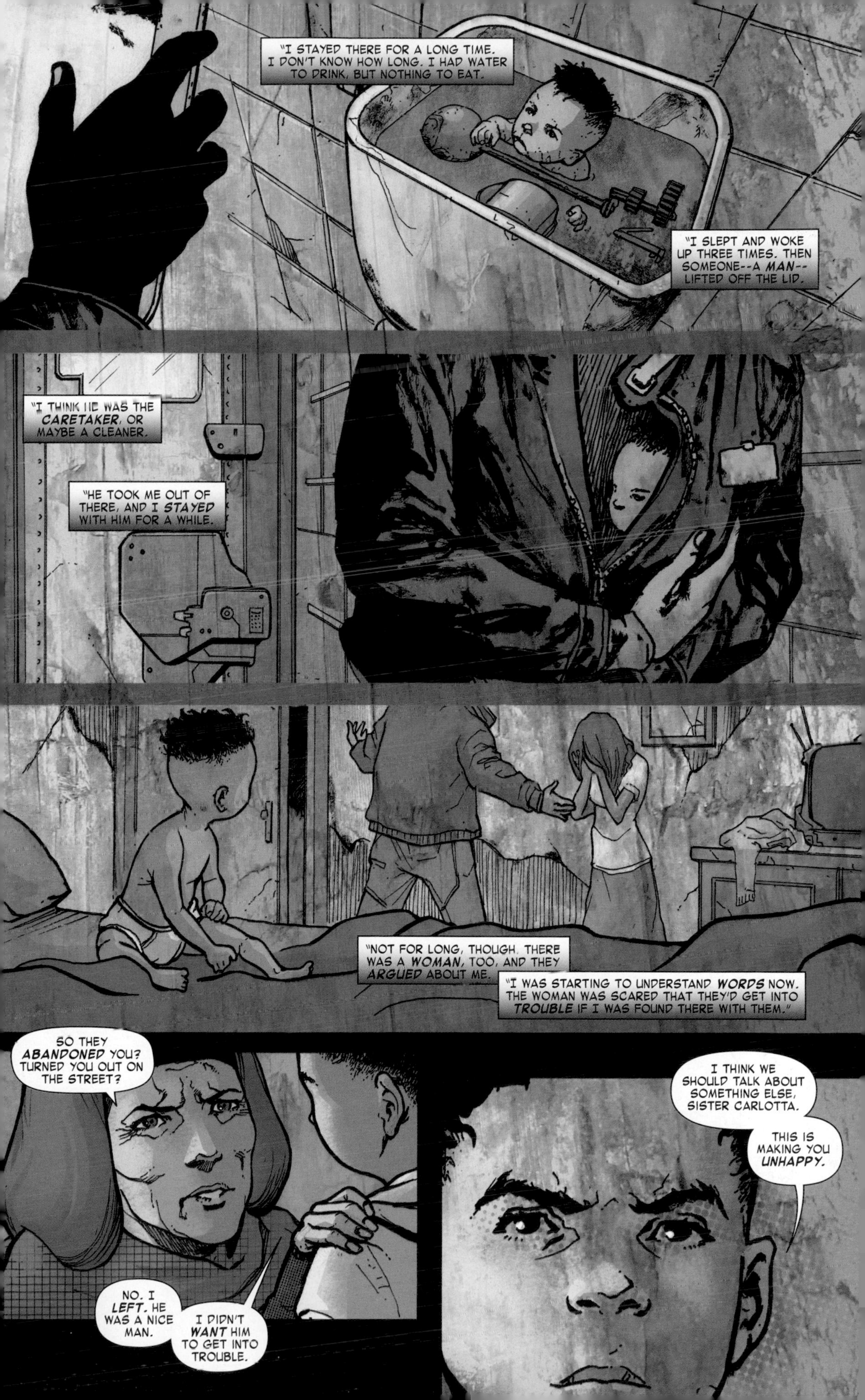
"I STAYED THERE FOR A LONG TIME. I DON'T KNOW HOW LONG. I HAD WATER TO DRINK, BUT NOTHING TO EAT.
"I SLEPT AND WOKE UP THREE TIMES. THEN SOMEONE--A MAN--LIFTED OFF THE LID.
"I THINK HE WAS THE CARETAKER, OR MAYBE A CLEANER.
"HE TOOK ME OUT OF THERE, AND I STAYED WITH HIM FOR A WHILE.
"NOT FOR LONG, THOUGH. THERE WAS A WOMAN, TOO, AND THEY ARGUED ABOUT ME.
"I WAS STARTING TO UNDERSTAND WORDS NOW. THE WOMAN WAS SCARED THAT THEY'D GET INTO TROUBLE IF I WAS FOUND THERE WITH THEM."
SO THEY ABANDONED YOU? TURNED YOU OUT ON THE STREET?
NO. I LEFT. HE WAS A NICE MAN.
I DIDN'T WANT HIM TO GET INTO TROUBLE.
I THINK WE SHOULD TALK ABOUT SOMETHING ELSE, SISTER CARLOTTA.
THIS IS MAKING YOU UNHAPPY.

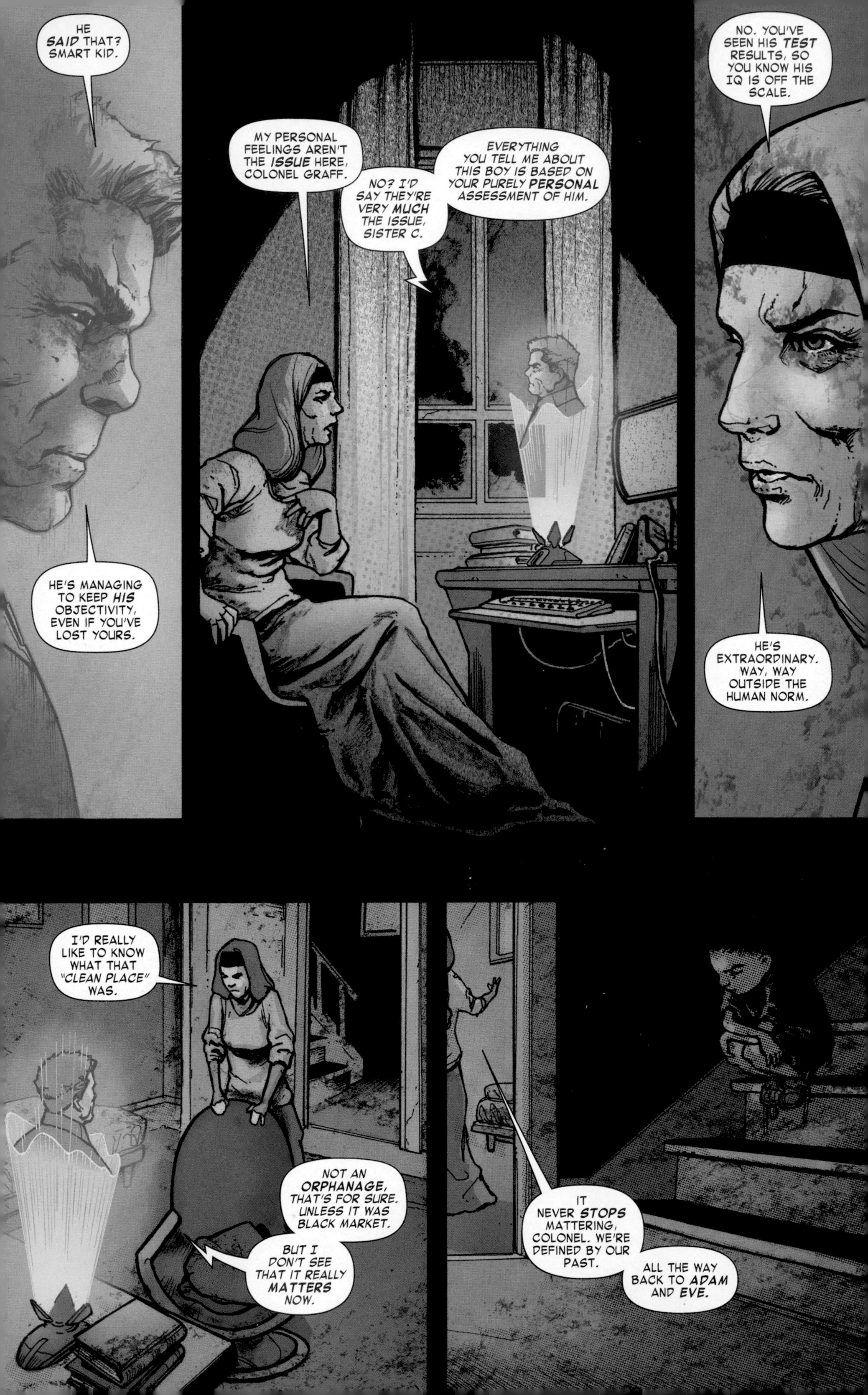

HE SAID THAT? SMART KID.
MY PERSONAL FEELINGS AREN'T THE ISSUE HERE, COLONEL GRAFF.
NO? I'D SAY THEY'RE VERY MUCH THE ISSUE, SISTER C.
EVERYTHING YOU TELL ME ABOUT THIS BOY IS BASED ON YOUR PURELY PERSONAL ASSESSMENT OF HIM.
HE'S MANAGING TO KEEP HIS OBJECTIVITY, EVEN IF YOU'VE LOST YOURS.
NO. YOU'VE SEEN HIS TEST RESULTS, SO YOU KNOW HIS IQ IS OFF THE SCALE.
HE'S EXTRAORDINARY. WAY, WAY OUTSIDE THE HUMAN NORM.
I'D REALLY LIKE TO KNOW WHAT THAT "CLEAN PLACE" WAS.
NOT AN ORPHANAGE, THAT'S FOR SURE. UNLESS IT WAS BLACK MARKET.
BUT I DON'T SEE THAT IT REALLY MATTERS NOW.
IT NEVER STOPS MATTERING, COLONEL. WE'RE DEFINED BY OUR PAST.
ALL THE WAY BACK TO ADAM AND EVE.

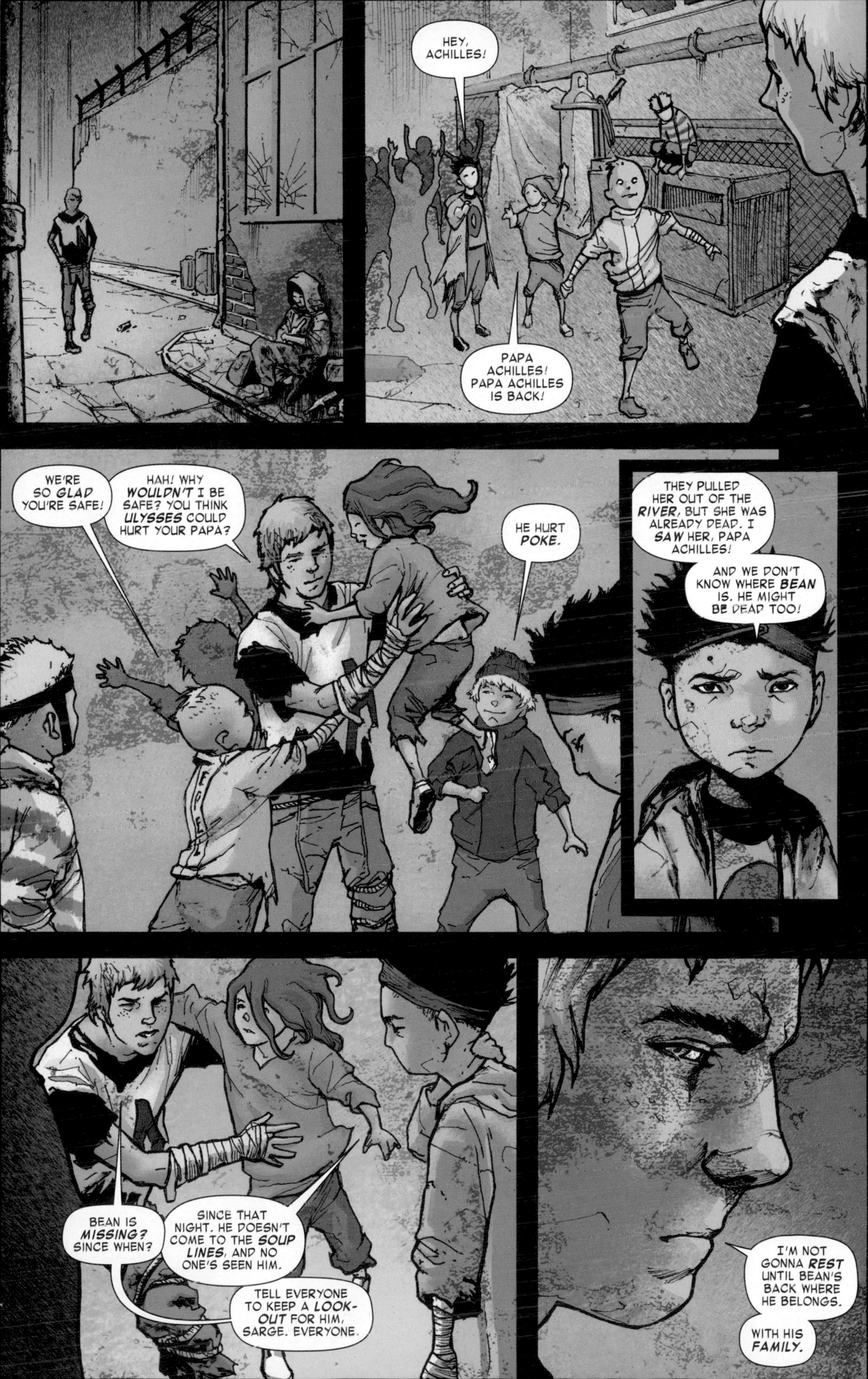
HEY, ACHILLES!
PAPA ACHILLES! PAPA ACHILLES IS BACK!
WE'RE SO GLAD YOU'RE SAFE!
HAH! WHY WOULDN'T I BE SAFE? YOU THINK ULYSSES COULD HURT YOUR PAPA?
HE HURT POKE.
THEY PULLED HER OUT OF THE RIVER, BUT SHE WAS ALREADY DEAD. I SAW HER, PAPA ACHILLES!
AND WE DON'T KNOW WHERE BEAN IS. HE MIGHT BE DEAD TOO!
BEAN IS MISSING? SINCE WHEN?
SINCE THAT NIGHT. HE DOESN'T COME TO THE SOUP LINES, AND NO ONE'S SEEN HIM.
TELL EVERYONE TO KEEP A LOOK-OUT FOR HIM, SARGE. EVERYONE.
I'M NOT GONNA REST UNTIL BEAN'S BACK WHERE HE BELONGS.
WITH HIS FAMILY.

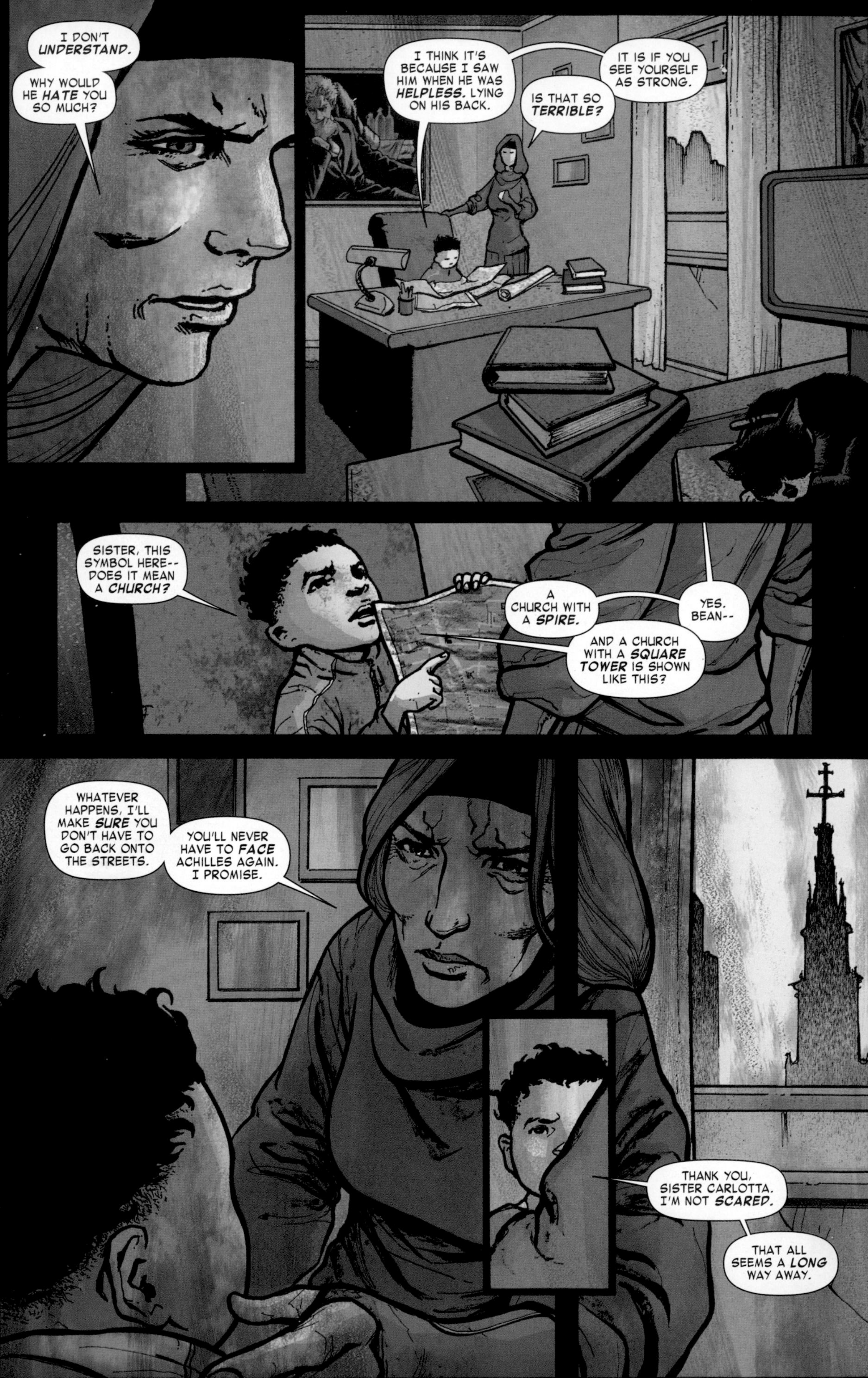
I DON'T UNDERSTAND.
WHY WOULD HE HATE YOU SO MUCH?
I THINK IT'S BECAUSE I SAW HIM WHEN HE WAS HELPLESS. LYING ON HIS BACK.
IS THAT SO TERRIBLE?
IT IS IF YOU SEE YOURSELF AS STRONG.
SISTER, THIS SYMBOL HERE-- DOES IT MEAN A CHURCH?
YES. BEAN--
A CHURCH WITH A SPIRE.
AND A CHURCH WITH A SQUARE TOWER IS SHOWN LIKE THIS?
WHATEVER HAPPENS, I'LL MAKE SURE YOU DON'T HAVE TO GO BACK ONTO THE STREETS.
YOU'LL NEVER HAVE TO FACE ACHILLES AGAIN. I PROMISE.
THANK YOU, SISTER CARLOTTA. I'M NOT SCARED.
THAT ALL SEEMS A LONG WAY AWAY.

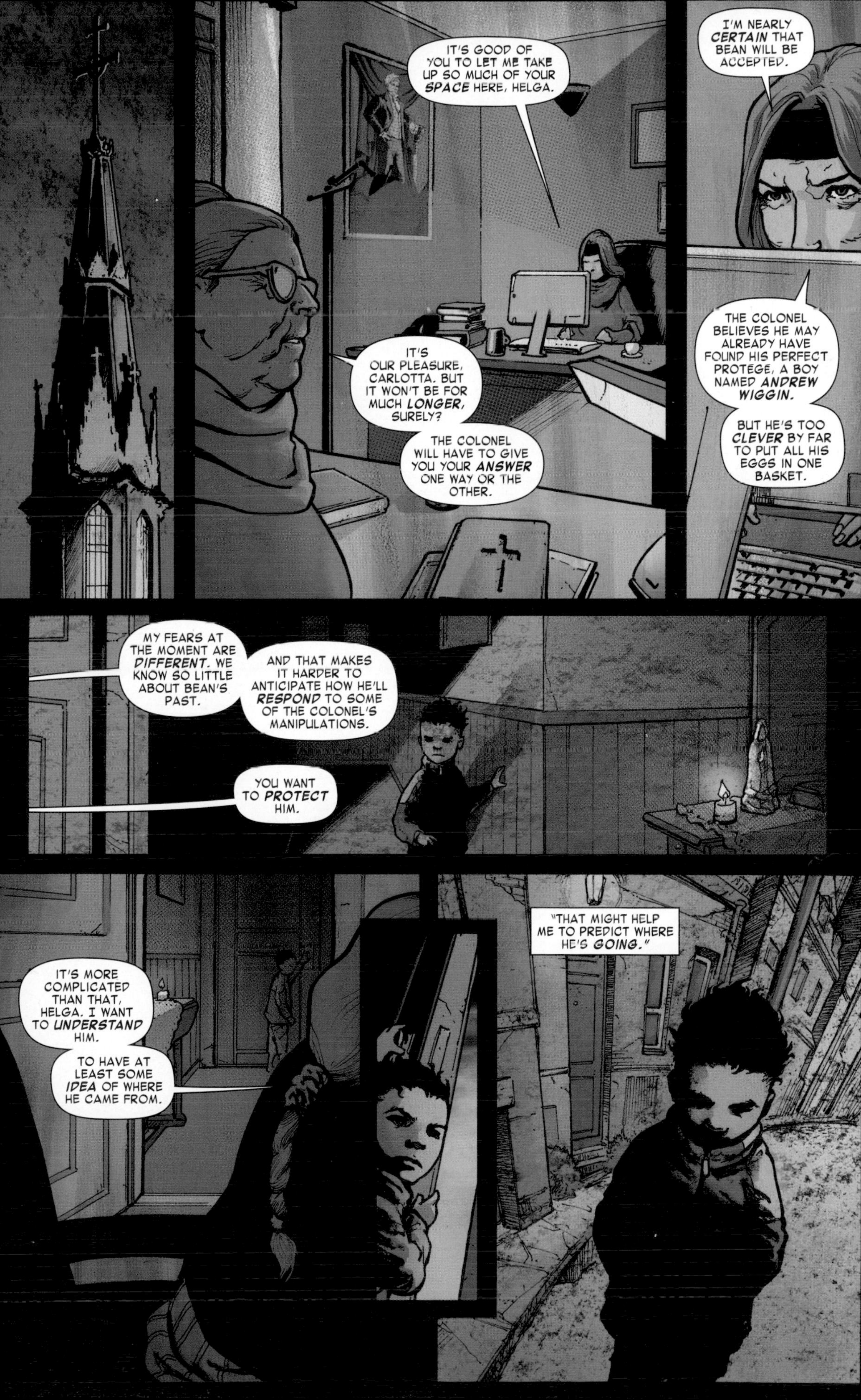
IT'S GOOD OF YOU TO LET ME TAKE UP SO MUCH OF YOUR SPACE HERE, HELGA.
IT'S OUR PLEASURE, CARLOTTA. BUT IT WON'T BE FOR MUCH LONGER, SURELY?
THE COLONEL WILL HAVE TO GIVE YOU YOUR ANSWER ONE WAY OR THE OTHER.
I'M NEARLY CERTAIN THAT BEAN WILL BE ACCEPTED.
THE COLONEL BELIEVES HE MAY ALREADY HAVE FOUND HIS PERFECT PROTEGE, A BOY NAMED ANDREW WIGGIN.
BUT HE'S TOO CLEVER BY FAR TO PUT ALL HIS EGGS IN ONE BASKET.
MY FEARS AT THE MOMENT ARE DIFFERENT. WE KNOW SO LITTLE ABOUT BEAN'S PAST.
AND THAT MAKES IT HARDER TO ANTICIPATE HOW HE'LL RESPOND TO SOME OF THE COLONEL'S MANIPULATIONS.
YOU WANT TO PROTECT HIM.
IT'S MORE COMPLICATED THAN THAT, HELGA. I WANT TO UNDERSTAND HIM.
TO HAVE AT LEAST SOME IDEA OF WHERE HE CAME FROM.
"THAT MIGHT HELP ME TO PREDICT WHERE HE'S GOING."

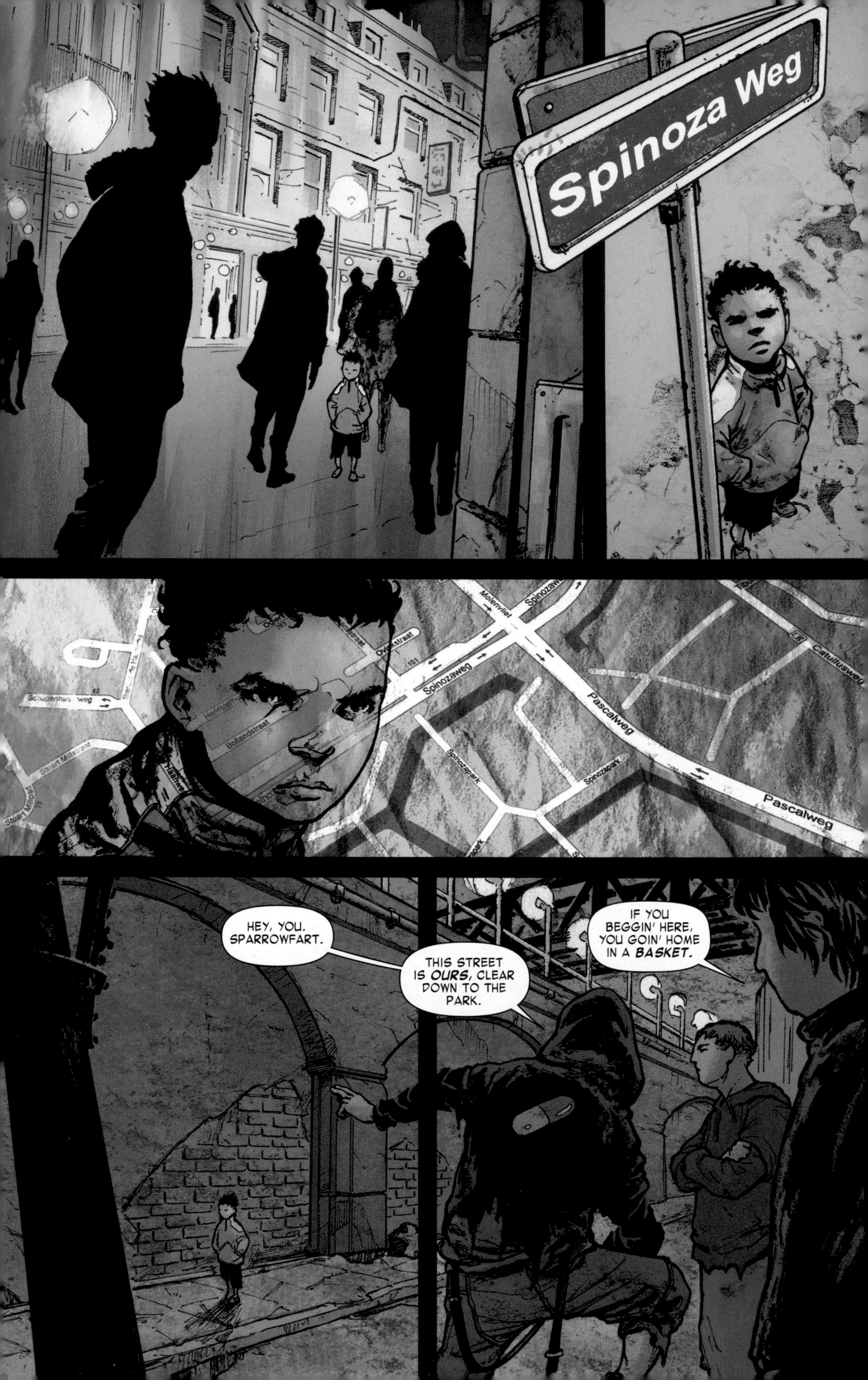

Spinoza Weg
Spinozaweg
Pascalweg
Catullusweg
Molenvliet
Spinozapark
Stuart Millstraat
HEY, YOU. SPARROWFART.
THIS STREET IS *OURS*, CLEAR DOWN TO THE PARK.
IF YOU BEGGIN' HERE, YOU GOIN' HOME IN A *BASKET*.

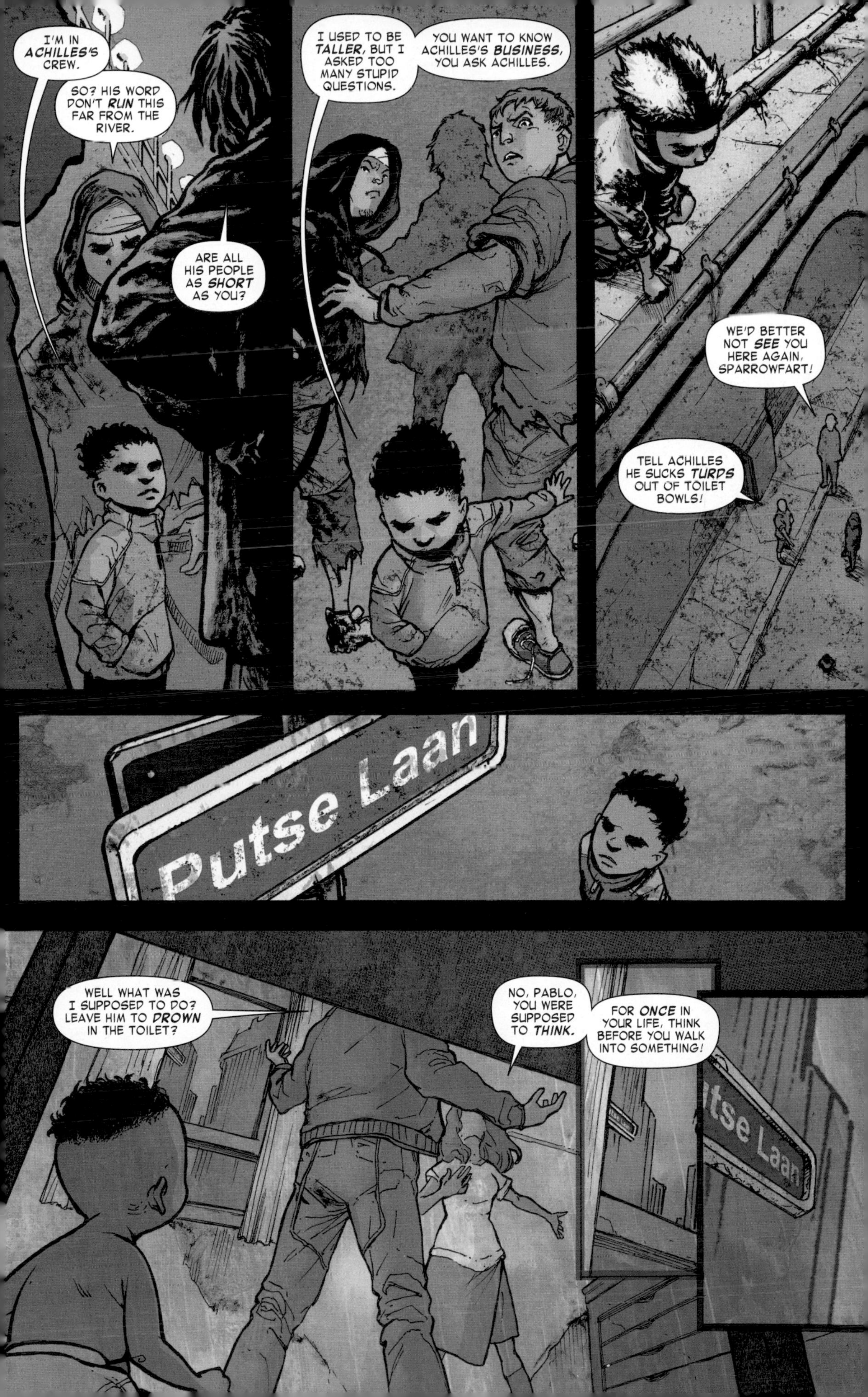
I'M IN ACHILLES'S CREW.
SO? HIS WORD DON'T RUN THIS FAR FROM THE RIVER.
ARE ALL HIS PEOPLE AS SHORT AS YOU?
I USED TO BE TALLER, BUT I ASKED TOO MANY STUPID QUESTIONS.
YOU WANT TO KNOW ACHILLES'S BUSINESS, YOU ASK ACHILLES.
WE'D BETTER NOT SEE YOU HERE AGAIN, SPARROWFART!
TELL ACHILLES HE SUCKS TURDS OUT OF TOILET BOWLS!
Putse Laan
WELL WHAT WAS I SUPPOSED TO DO? LEAVE HIM TO DROWN IN THE TOILET?
NO, PABLO, YOU WERE SUPPOSED TO THINK.
FOR ONCE IN YOUR LIFE, THINK BEFORE YOU WALK INTO SOMETHING!
tse Laan

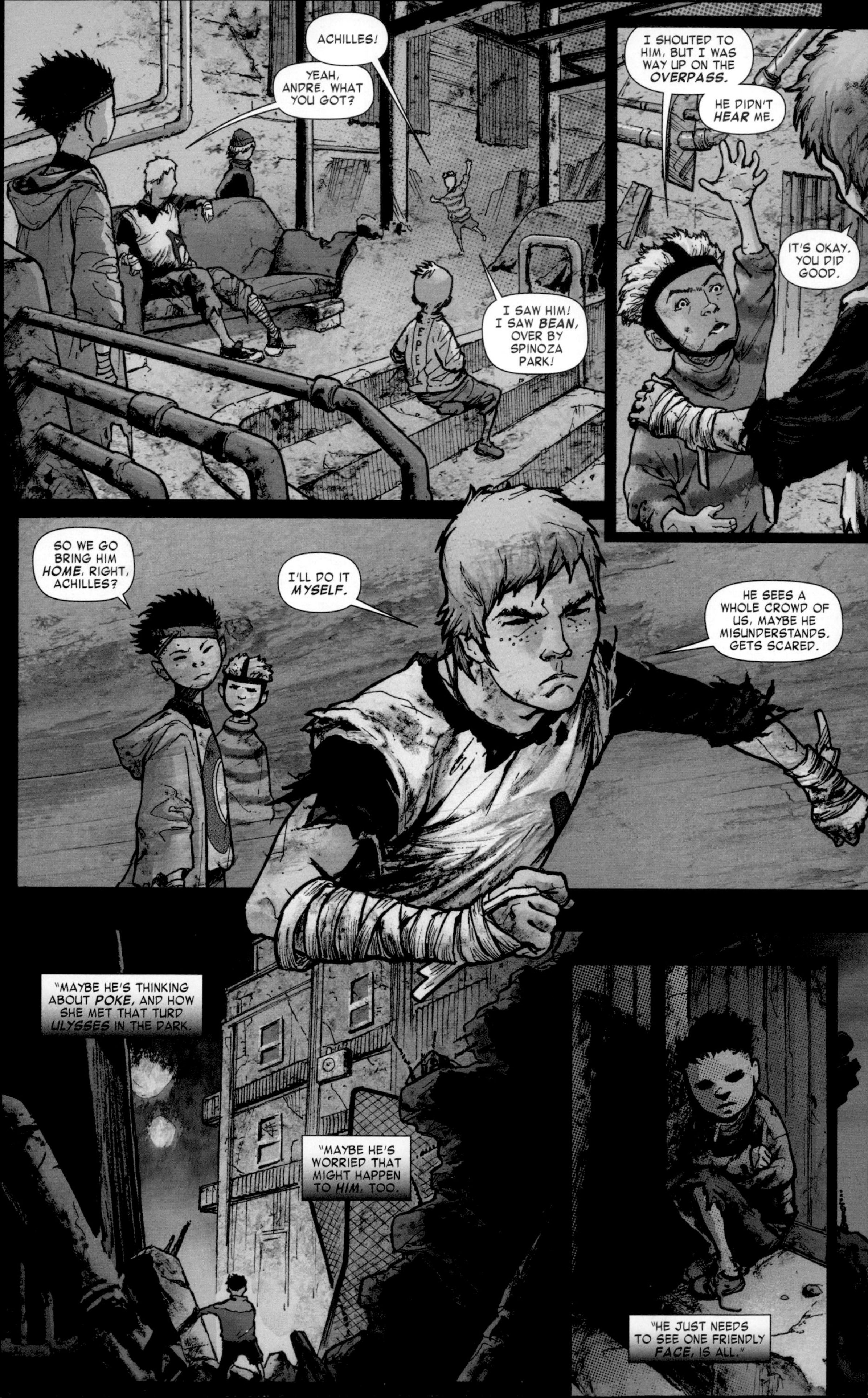
ACHILLES!
YEAH, ANDRÉ. WHAT YOU GOT?
I SAW HIM! I SAW BEAN, OVER BY SPINOZA PARK!
I SHOUTED TO HIM, BUT I WAS WAY UP ON THE OVERPASS.
HE DIDN'T HEAR ME.
IT'S OKAY. YOU DID GOOD.
SO WE GO BRING HIM HOME, RIGHT, ACHILLES?
I'LL DO IT MYSELF.
HE SEES A WHOLE CROWD OF US, MAYBE HE MISUNDERSTANDS. GETS SCARED.
"MAYBE HE'S THINKING ABOUT POKE, AND HOW SHE MET THAT TURD ULYSSES IN THE DARK.
"MAYBE HE'S WORRIED THAT MIGHT HAPPEN TO HIM, TOO.
"HE JUST NEEDS TO SEE ONE FRIENDLY FACE, IS ALL."

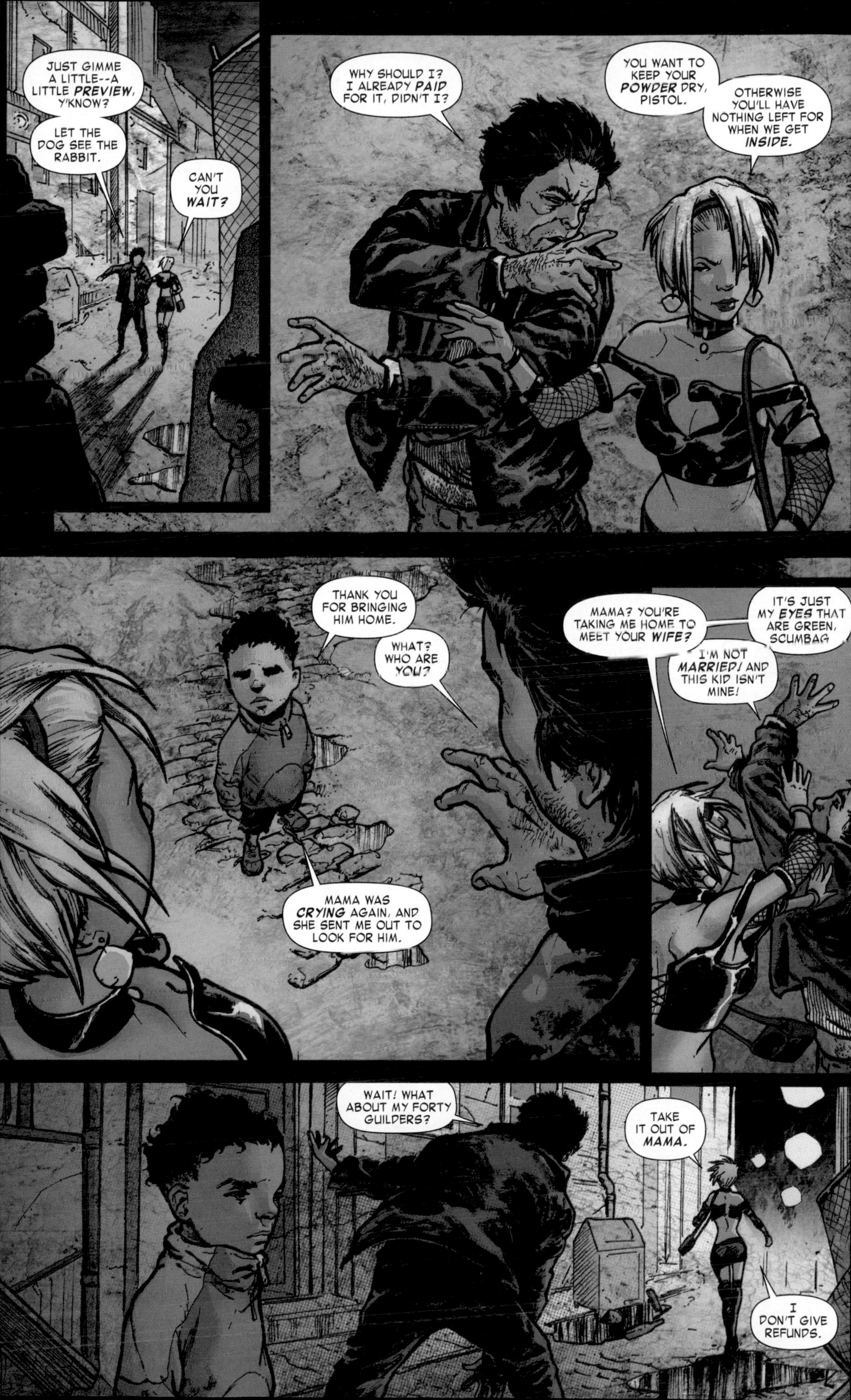
JUST GIMME A LITTLE--A LITTLE PREVIEW, Y'KNOW?
LET THE DOG SEE THE RABBIT.
CAN'T YOU WAIT?
WHY SHOULD I? I ALREADY PAID FOR IT, DIDN'T I?
YOU WANT TO KEEP YOUR POWDER DRY, PISTOL.
OTHERWISE YOU'LL HAVE NOTHING LEFT FOR WHEN WE GET INSIDE.
THANK YOU FOR BRINGING HIM HOME.
WHAT? WHO ARE YOU?
MAMA WAS CRYING AGAIN, AND SHE SENT ME OUT TO LOOK FOR HIM.
MAMA? YOU'RE TAKING ME HOME TO MEET YOUR WIFE?
IT'S JUST MY EYES THAT ARE GREEN, SCUMBAG
I'M NOT MARRIED! AND THIS KID ISN'T MINE!
WAIT! WHAT ABOUT MY FORTY GUILDERS?
TAKE IT OUT OF MAMA.
I DON'T GIVE REFUNDS.

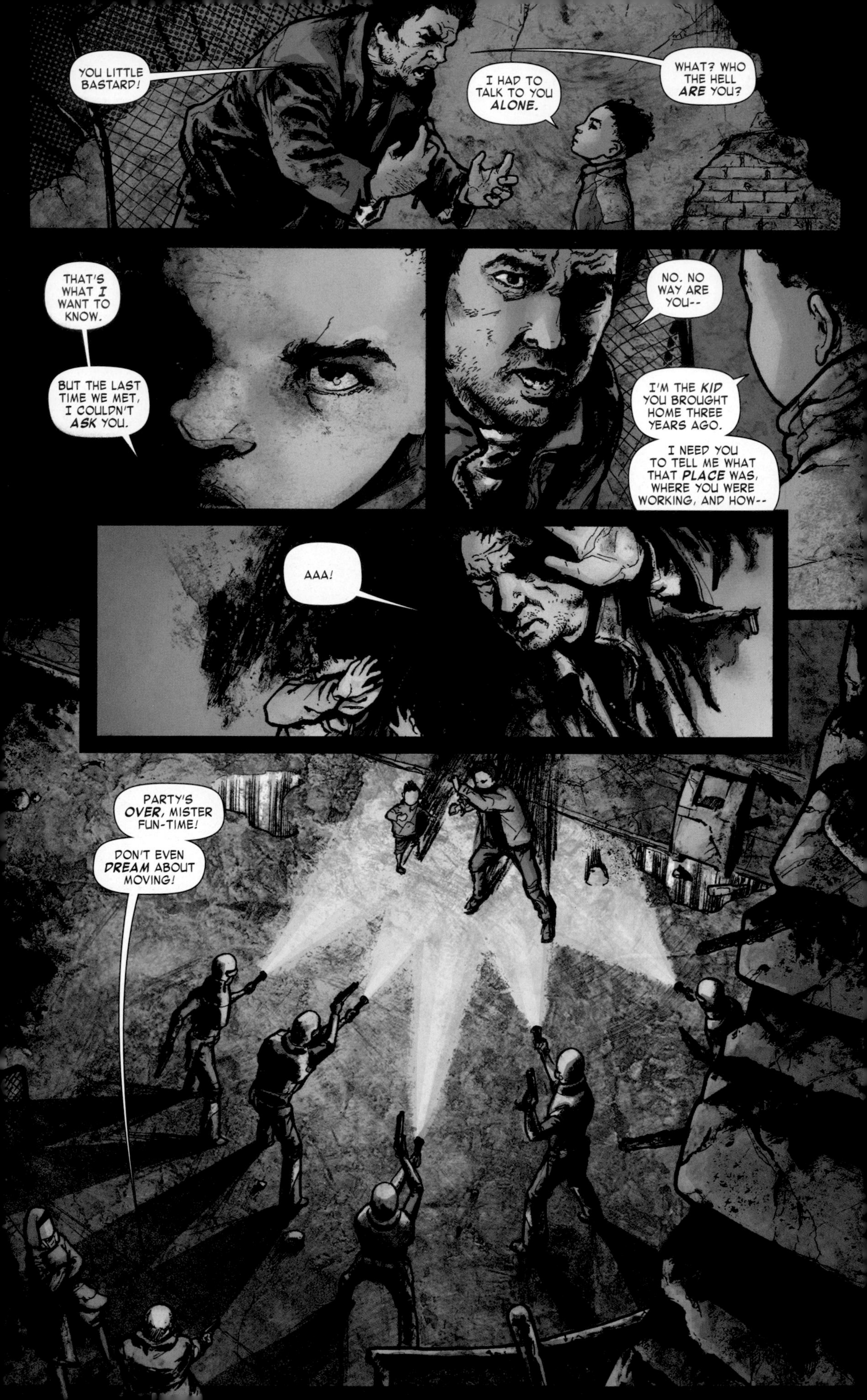
YOU LITTLE BASTARD!
I HAD TO TALK TO YOU ALONE.
WHAT? WHO THE HELL ARE YOU?
THAT'S WHAT I WANT TO KNOW.
BUT THE LAST TIME WE MET, I COULDN'T ASK YOU.
NO. NO WAY ARE YOU--
I'M THE KID YOU BROUGHT HOME THREE YEARS AGO.
I NEED YOU TO TELL ME WHAT THAT PLACE WAS, WHERE YOU WERE WORKING, AND HOW--
AAA!
PARTY'S OVER, MISTER FUN-TIME!
DON'T EVEN DREAM ABOUT MOVING!

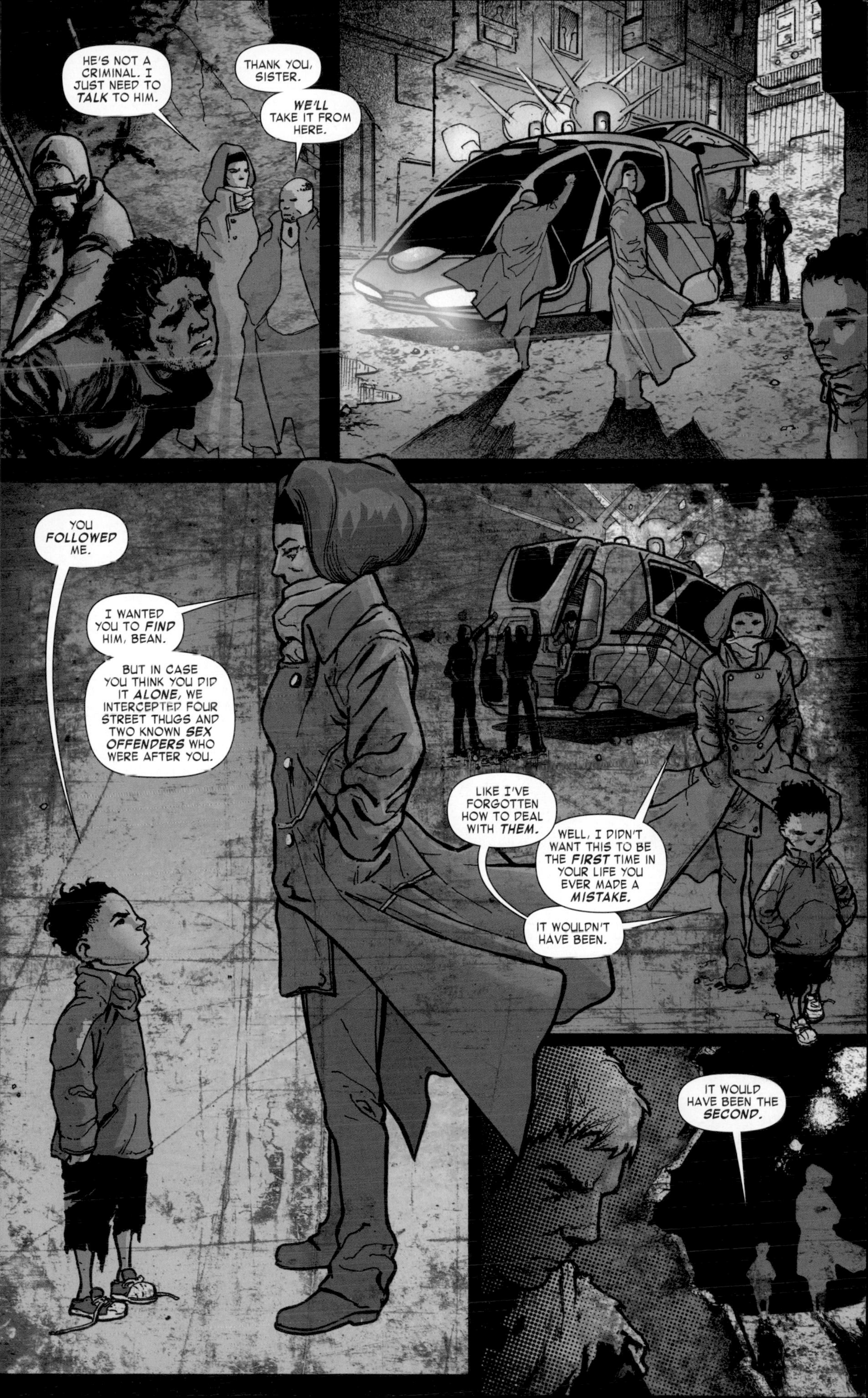
HE'S NOT A CRIMINAL. I JUST NEED TO TALK TO HIM.
THANK YOU, SISTER.
WE'LL TAKE IT FROM HERE.
YOU FOLLOWED ME.
I WANTED YOU TO FIND HIM, BEAN.
BUT IN CASE YOU THINK YOU DID IT ALONE, WE INTERCEPTED FOUR STREET THUGS AND TWO KNOWN SEX OFFENDERS WHO WERE AFTER YOU.
LIKE I'VE FORGOTTEN HOW TO DEAL WITH THEM.
WELL, I DIDN'T WANT THIS TO BE THE FIRST TIME IN YOUR LIFE YOU EVER MADE A MISTAKE.
IT WOULDN'T HAVE BEEN.
IT WOULD HAVE BEEN THE SECOND.

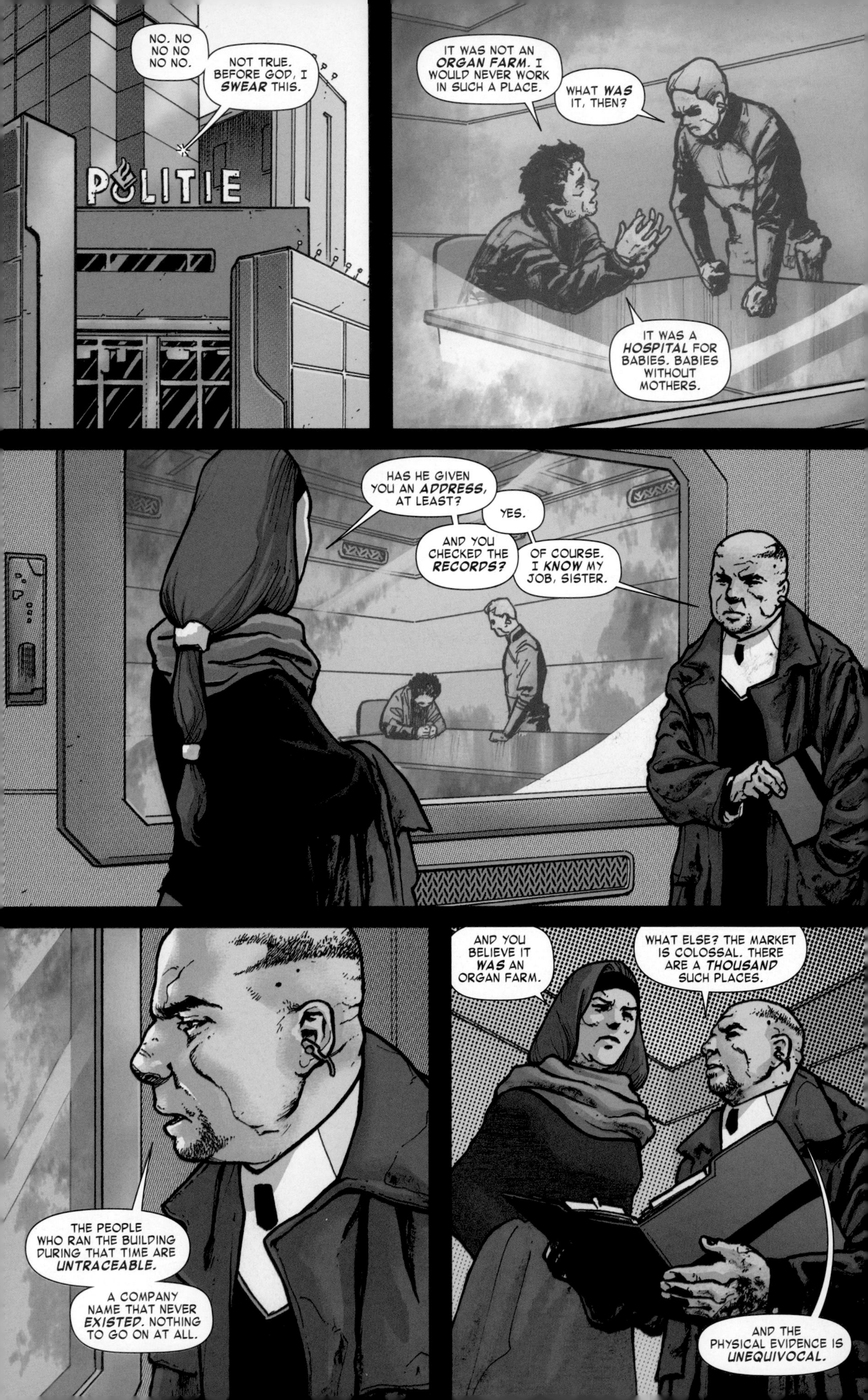
NO. NO NO NO NO NO.
NOT TRUE. BEFORE GOD, I SWEAR THIS.
POLITIE
IT WAS NOT AN ORGAN FARM. I WOULD NEVER WORK IN SUCH A PLACE.
WHAT WAS IT, THEN?
IT WAS A HOSPITAL FOR BABIES. BABIES WITHOUT MOTHERS.
HAS HE GIVEN YOU AN ADDRESS, AT LEAST?
YES.
AND YOU CHECKED THE RECORDS?
OF COURSE. I KNOW MY JOB, SISTER.
THE PEOPLE WHO RAN THE BUILDING DURING THAT TIME ARE UNTRACEABLE.
A COMPANY NAME THAT NEVER EXISTED. NOTHING TO GO ON AT ALL.
AND YOU BELIEVE IT WAS AN ORGAN FARM.
WHAT ELSE? THE MARKET IS COLOSSAL. THERE ARE A THOUSAND SUCH PLACES.
AND THE PHYSICAL EVIDENCE IS UNEQUIVOCAL.

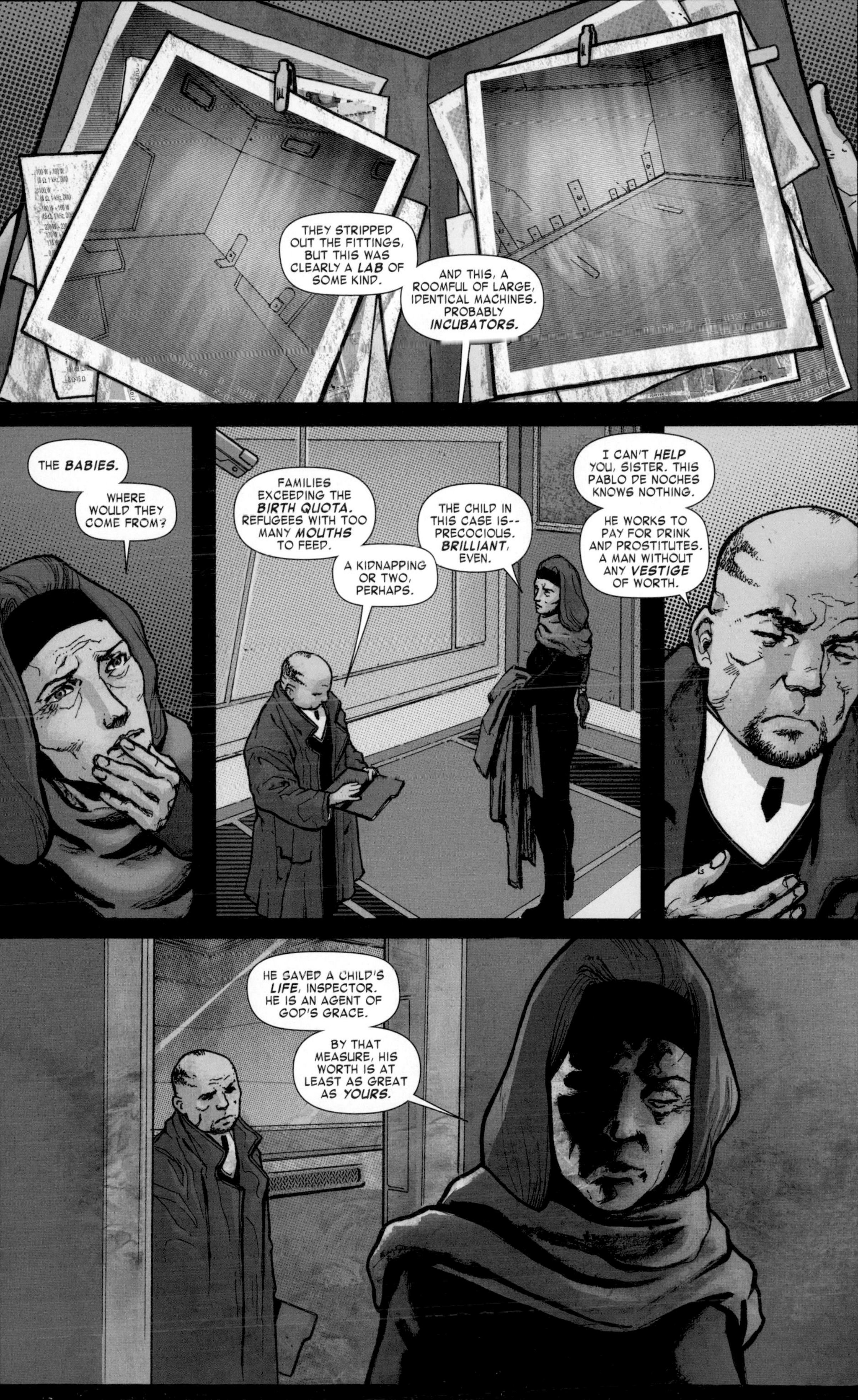
THEY STRIPPED OUT THE FITTINGS, BUT THIS WAS CLEARLY A LAB OF SOME KIND.
AND THIS, A ROOMFUL OF LARGE, IDENTICAL MACHINES. PROBABLY INCUBATORS.
THE BABIES.
WHERE WOULD THEY COME FROM?
FAMILIES EXCEEDING THE BIRTH QUOTA. REFUGEES WITH TOO MANY MOUTHS TO FEED.
A KIDNAPPING OR TWO, PERHAPS.
THE CHILD IN THIS CASE IS-- PRECOCIOUS. BRILLIANT, EVEN.
I CAN'T HELP YOU, SISTER. THIS PABLO DE NOCHES KNOWS NOTHING.
HE WORKS TO PAY FOR DRINK AND PROSTITUTES. A MAN WITHOUT ANY VESTIGE OF WORTH.
HE SAVED A CHILD'S LIFE, INSPECTOR. HE IS AN AGENT OF GOD'S GRACE.
BY THAT MEASURE, HIS WORTH IS AT LEAST AS GREAT AS YOURS.

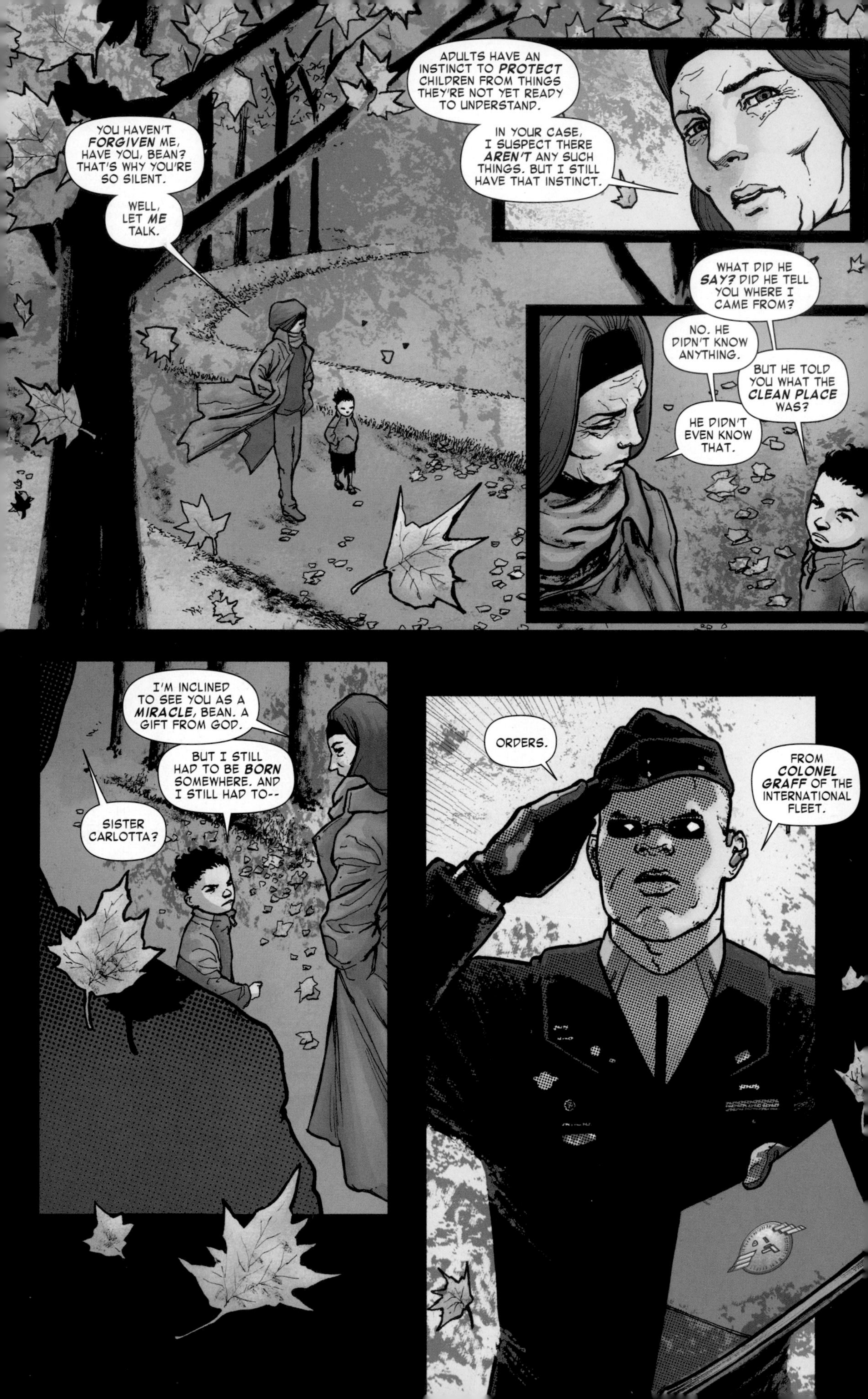
YOU HAVEN'T FORGIVEN ME, HAVE YOU, BEAN? THAT'S WHY YOU'RE SO SILENT.
WELL, LET ME TALK.
ADULTS HAVE AN INSTINCT TO PROTECT CHILDREN FROM THINGS THEY'RE NOT YET READY TO UNDERSTAND.
IN YOUR CASE, I SUSPECT THERE AREN'T ANY SUCH THINGS. BUT I STILL HAVE THAT INSTINCT.
WHAT DID HE SAY? DID HE TELL YOU WHERE I CAME FROM?
NO. HE DIDN'T KNOW ANYTHING.
BUT HE TOLD YOU WHAT THE CLEAN PLACE WAS?
HE DIDN'T EVEN KNOW THAT.
I'M INCLINED TO SEE YOU AS A MIRACLE, BEAN. A GIFT FROM GOD.
BUT I STILL HAD TO BE BORN SOMEWHERE. AND I STILL HAD TO--
SISTER CARLOTTA?
ORDERS.
FROM COLONEL GRAFF OF THE INTERNATIONAL FLEET.

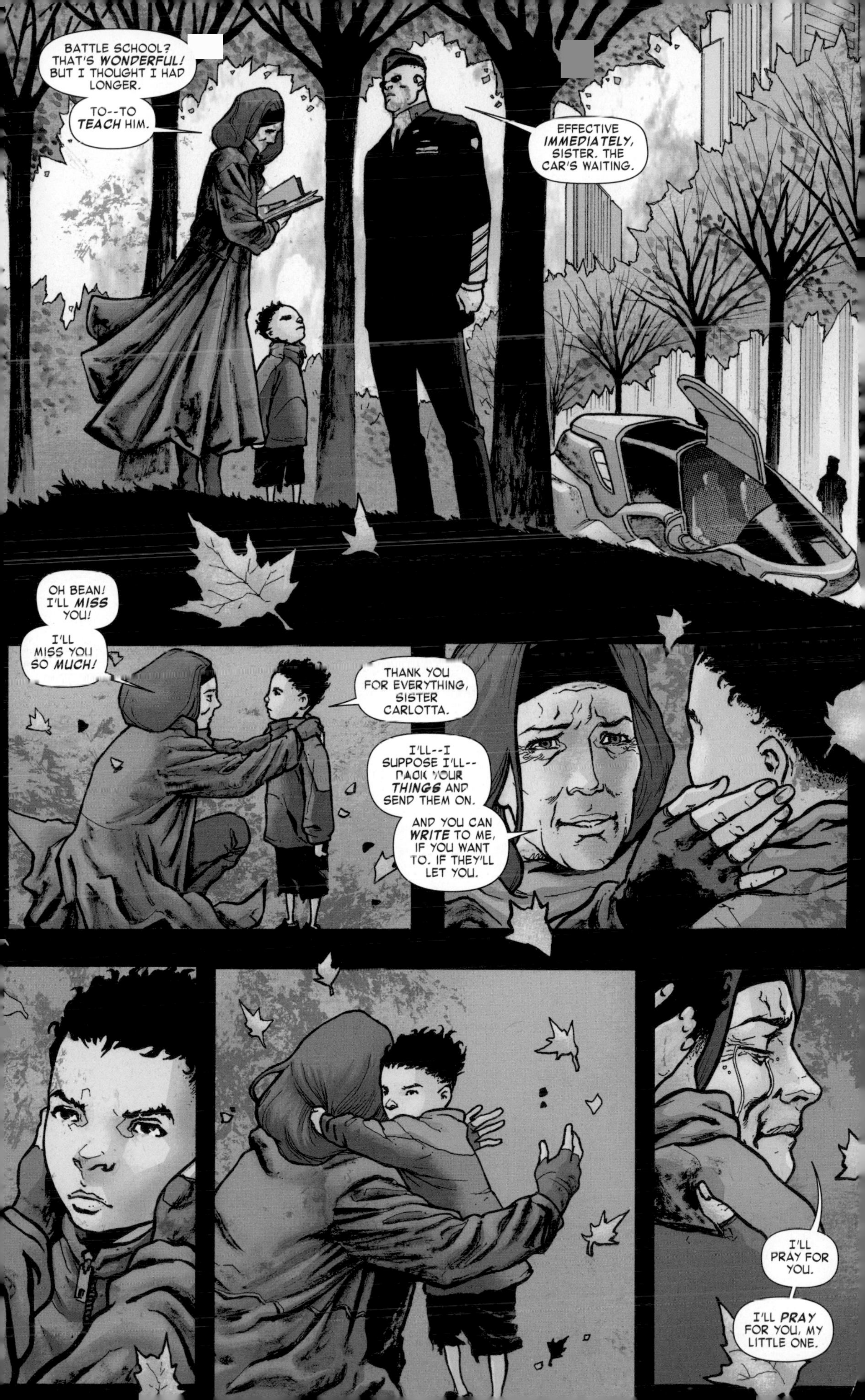
BATTLE SCHOOL? THAT'S WONDERFUL! BUT I THOUGHT I HAD LONGER.
TO--TO TEACH HIM.
EFFECTIVE IMMEDIATELY, SISTER. THE CAR'S WAITING.
OH BEAN! I'LL MISS YOU!
I'LL MISS YOU SO MUCH!
THANK YOU FOR EVERYTHING, SISTER CARLOTTA.
I'LL--I SUPPOSE I'LL--PACK YOUR THINGS AND SEND THEM ON.
AND YOU CAN WRITE TO ME, IF YOU WANT TO. IF THEY'LL LET YOU.
I'LL PRAY FOR YOU.
I'LL PRAY FOR YOU, MY LITTLE ONE.

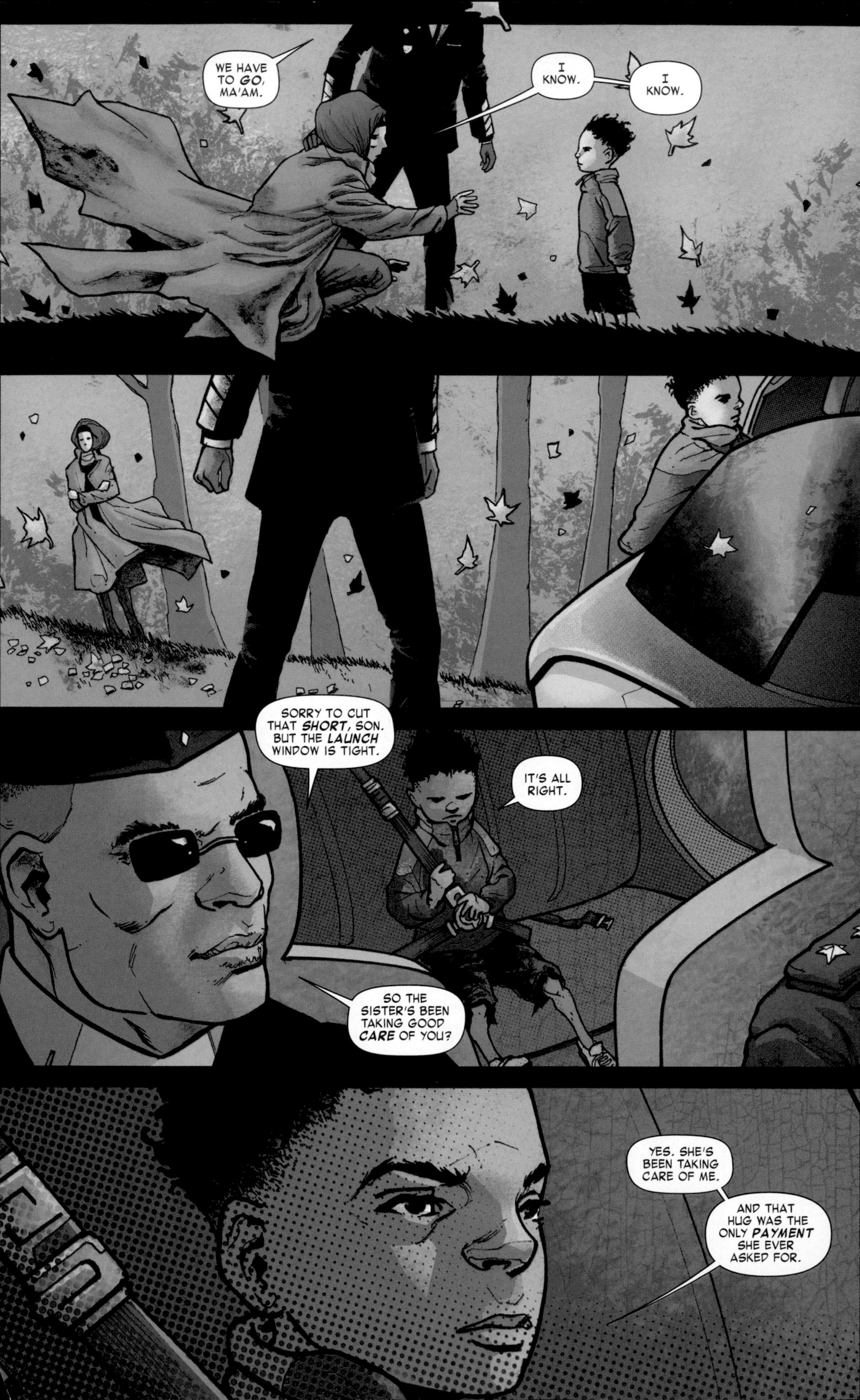
WE HAVE TO GO, MA'AM.
I KNOW.
I KNOW.
SORRY TO CUT THAT SHORT, SON. BUT THE LAUNCH WINDOW IS TIGHT.
IT'S ALL RIGHT.
SO THE SISTER'S BEEN TAKING GOOD CARE OF YOU?
YES. SHE'S BEEN TAKING CARE OF ME.
AND THAT HUG WAS THE ONLY PAYMENT SHE EVER ASKED FOR.

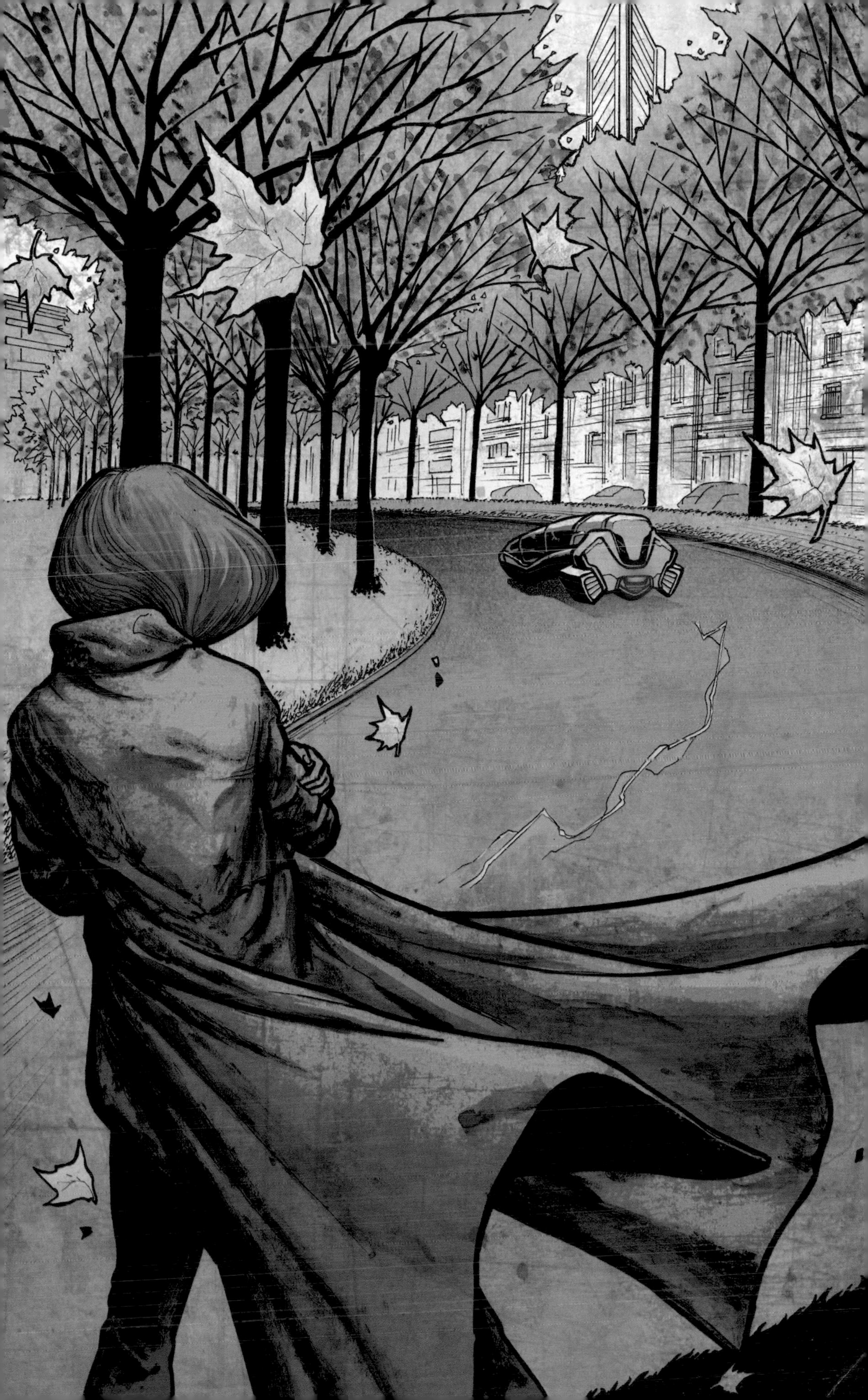

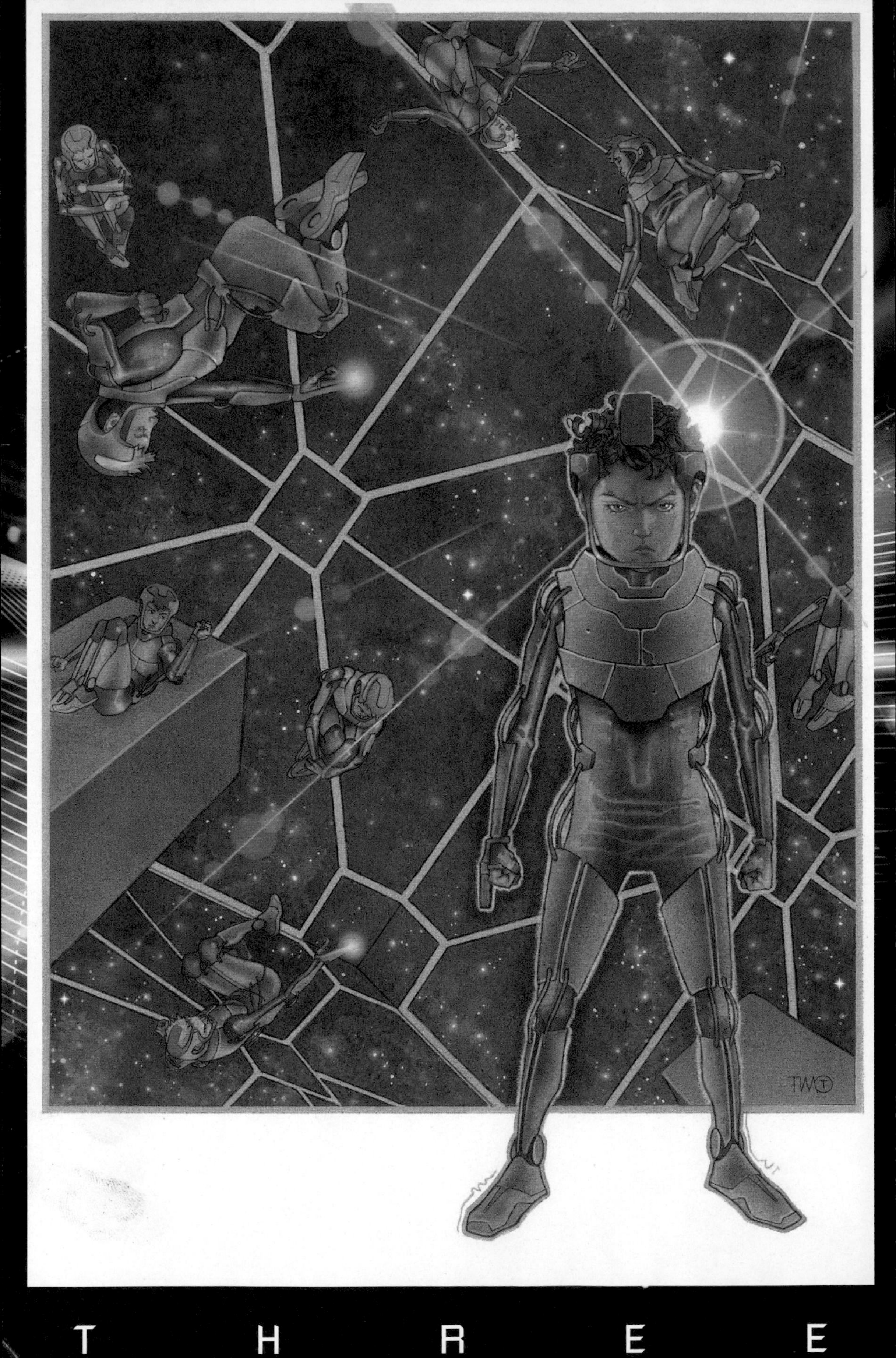

T H R E E

"Why are you giving me a five-year-old street urchin to tend?"

"You've seen the scores."

"Am I supposed to take those seriously?"

"Since the whole Battle School program is based on the reliability of our juvenile testing regime, yes, I think you should take his scores seriously. I did a little research. No child has ever done better. Not even your star pupil."

"It's not the validity of the tests that I doubt. It's the tester."

"If Sister Carlotta were inclined to fudge the scores, she would have pushed other children into the program long before now. I think you're annoyed because you've already decided to focus all your attention and energy on the Wiggin boy, and you don't want any distraction."

"When did I lie down on your couch?"

"If my analysis is wrong, do forgive me."

"Of course I'll give this Bean a chance. Even if I don't for one second believe his scores."

"Not just a chance. Advance him. Test him. Challenge him. Don't let him languish."

"We advance and test and challenge all our students. He's no different from anyone else."

"I'm making a note of the time."

"Why?"

"I want to know exactly how long it takes for you to eat those words..."

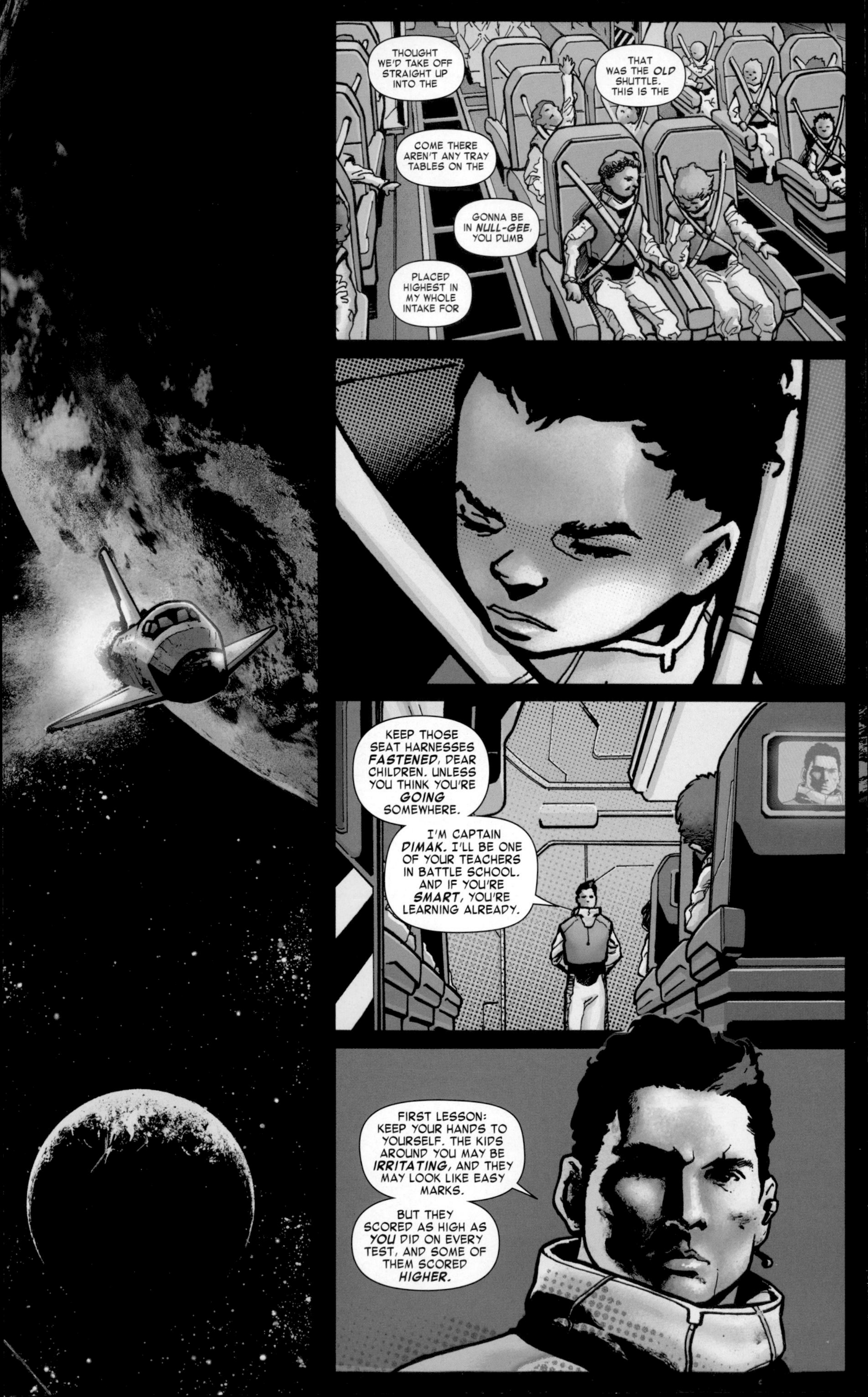
THOUGHT WE'D TAKE OFF STRAIGHT UP INTO THE
THAT WAS THE OLD SHUTTLE. THIS IS THE
COME THERE AREN'T ANY TRAY TABLES ON THE
GONNA BE IN NULL-GEE, YOU DUMB
PLACED HIGHEST IN MY WHOLE INTAKE FOR
KEEP THOSE SEAT HARNESSES FASTENED, DEAR CHILDREN. UNLESS YOU THINK YOU'RE GOING SOMEWHERE.
I'M CAPTAIN DIMAK. I'LL BE ONE OF YOUR TEACHERS IN BATTLE SCHOOL. AND IF YOU'RE SMART, YOU'RE LEARNING ALREADY.
FIRST LESSON: KEEP YOUR HANDS TO YOURSELF. THE KIDS AROUND YOU MAY BE IRRITATING, AND THEY MAY LOOK LIKE EASY MARKS.
BUT THEY SCORED AS HIGH AS YOU DID ON EVERY TEST, AND SOME OF THEM SCORED HIGHER.

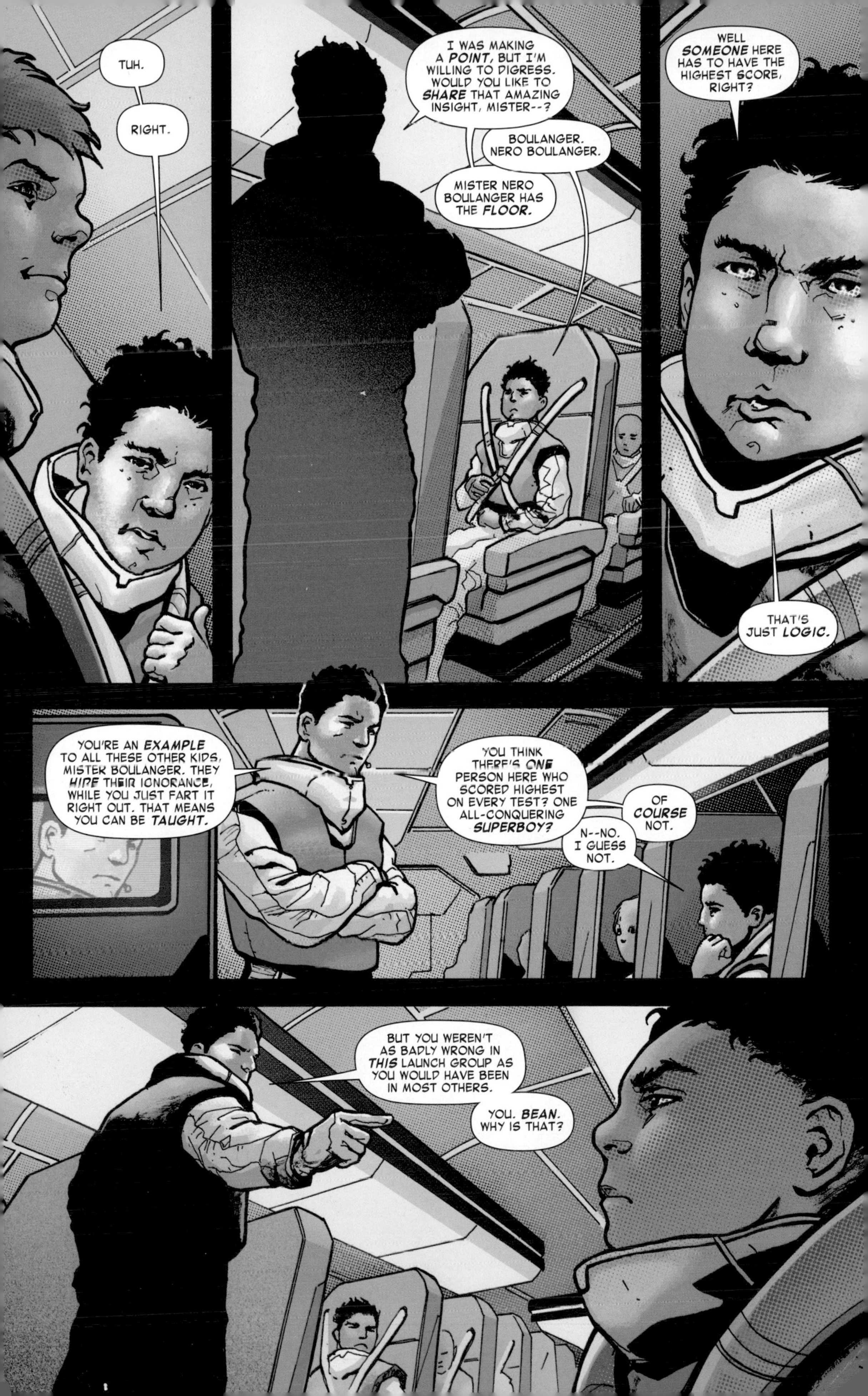
TUH.
RIGHT.
I WAS MAKING A POINT, BUT I'M WILLING TO DIGRESS. WOULD YOU LIKE TO SHARE THAT AMAZING INSIGHT, MISTER--?
BOULANGER. NERO BOULANGER.
MISTER NERO BOULANGER HAS THE FLOOR.
WELL SOMEONE HERE HAS TO HAVE THE HIGHEST SCORE, RIGHT?
THAT'S JUST LOGIC.
YOU'RE AN EXAMPLE TO ALL THESE OTHER KIDS, MISTER BOULANGER. THEY HIDE THEIR IGNORANCE, WHILE YOU JUST FART IT RIGHT OUT. THAT MEANS YOU CAN BE TAUGHT.
YOU THINK THERE'S ONE PERSON HERE WHO SCORED HIGHEST ON EVERY TEST? ONE ALL-CONQUERING SUPERBOY?
OF COURSE NOT.
N--NO. I GUESS NOT.
BUT YOU WEREN'T AS BADLY WRONG IN THIS LAUNCH GROUP AS YOU WOULD HAVE BEEN IN MOST OTHERS.
YOU. BEAN. WHY IS THAT?

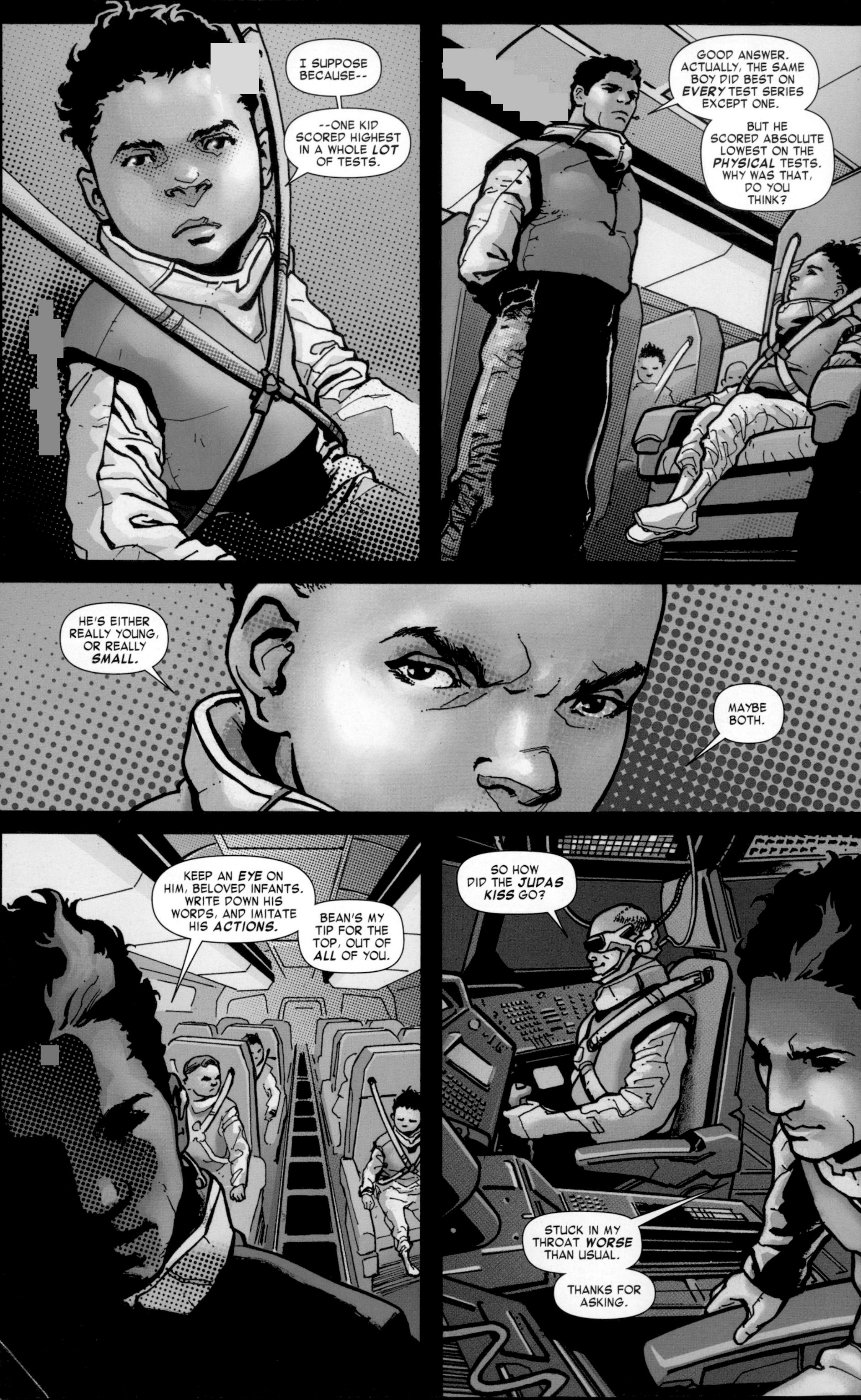
I SUPPOSE BECAUSE--
--ONE KID SCORED HIGHEST IN A WHOLE LOT OF TESTS.
GOOD ANSWER. ACTUALLY, THE SAME BOY DID BEST ON EVERY TEST SERIES EXCEPT ONE.
BUT HE SCORED ABSOLUTE LOWEST ON THE PHYSICAL TESTS. WHY WAS THAT, DO YOU THINK?
HE'S EITHER REALLY YOUNG, OR REALLY SMALL.
MAYBE BOTH.
KEEP AN EYE ON HIM, BELOVED INFANTS. WRITE DOWN HIS WORDS, AND IMITATE HIS ACTIONS.
BEAN'S MY TIP FOR THE TOP, OUT OF ALL OF YOU.
SO HOW DID THE JUDAS KISS GO?
STUCK IN MY THROAT WORSE THAN USUAL.
THANKS FOR ASKING.

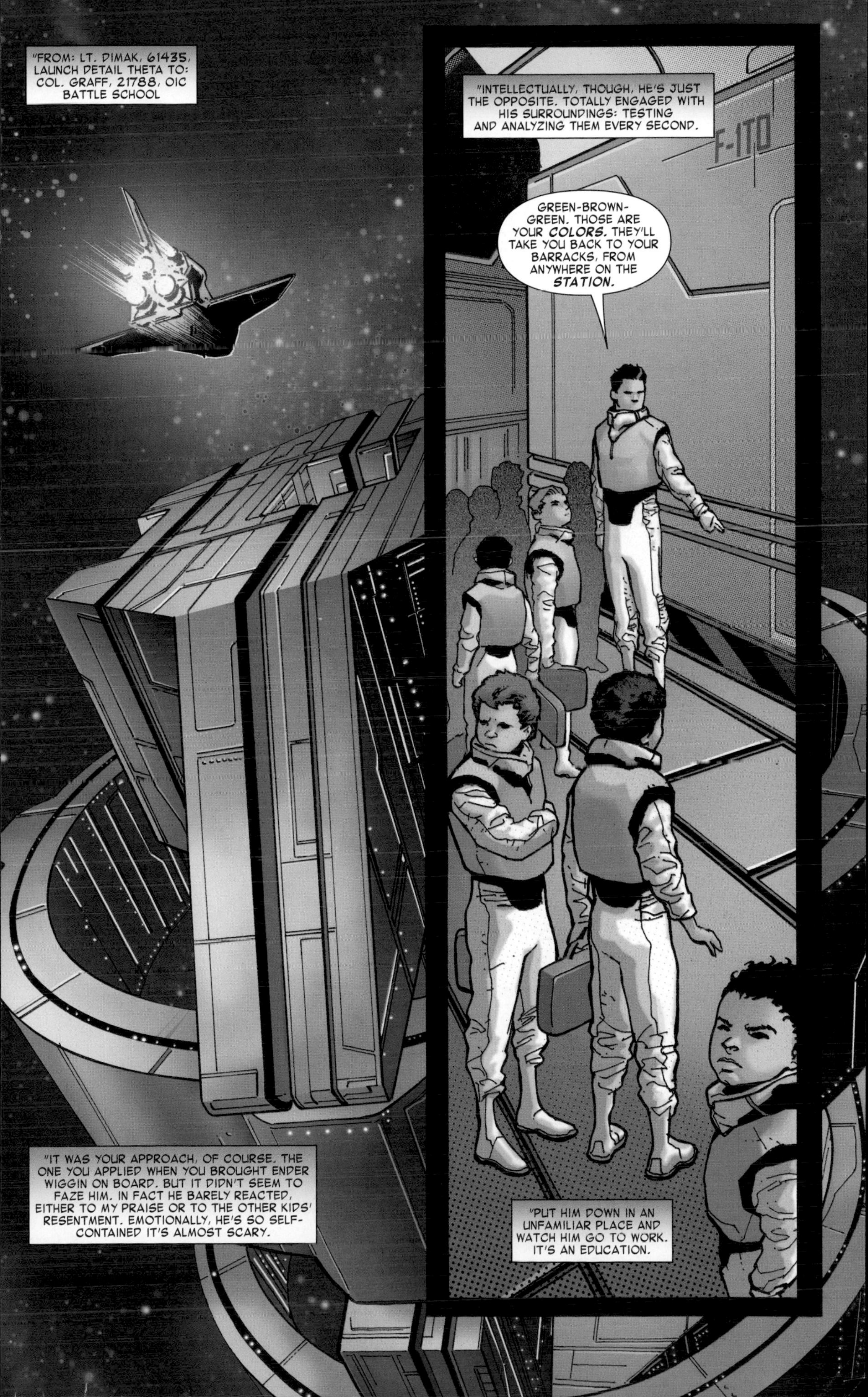
"FROM: LT. DIMAK, 61435, LAUNCH DETAIL THETA TO: COL. GRAFF, 21788, OIC BATTLE SCHOOL
"INTELLECTUALLY, THOUGH, HE'S JUST THE OPPOSITE. TOTALLY ENGAGED WITH HIS SURROUNDINGS: TESTING AND ANALYZING THEM EVERY SECOND.
F-1TO
GREEN-BROWN-GREEN. THOSE ARE YOUR COLORS. THEY'LL TAKE YOU BACK TO YOUR BARRACKS, FROM ANYWHERE ON THE STATION.
"IT WAS YOUR APPROACH, OF COURSE. THE ONE YOU APPLIED WHEN YOU BROUGHT ENDER WIGGIN ON BOARD. BUT IT DIDN'T SEEM TO FAZE HIM. IN FACT HE BARELY REACTED, EITHER TO MY PRAISE OR TO THE OTHER KIDS' RESENTMENT. EMOTIONALLY, HE'S SO SELF-CONTAINED IT'S ALMOST SCARY.
"PUT HIM DOWN IN AN UNFAMILIAR PLACE AND WATCH HIM GO TO WORK. IT'S AN EDUCATION.

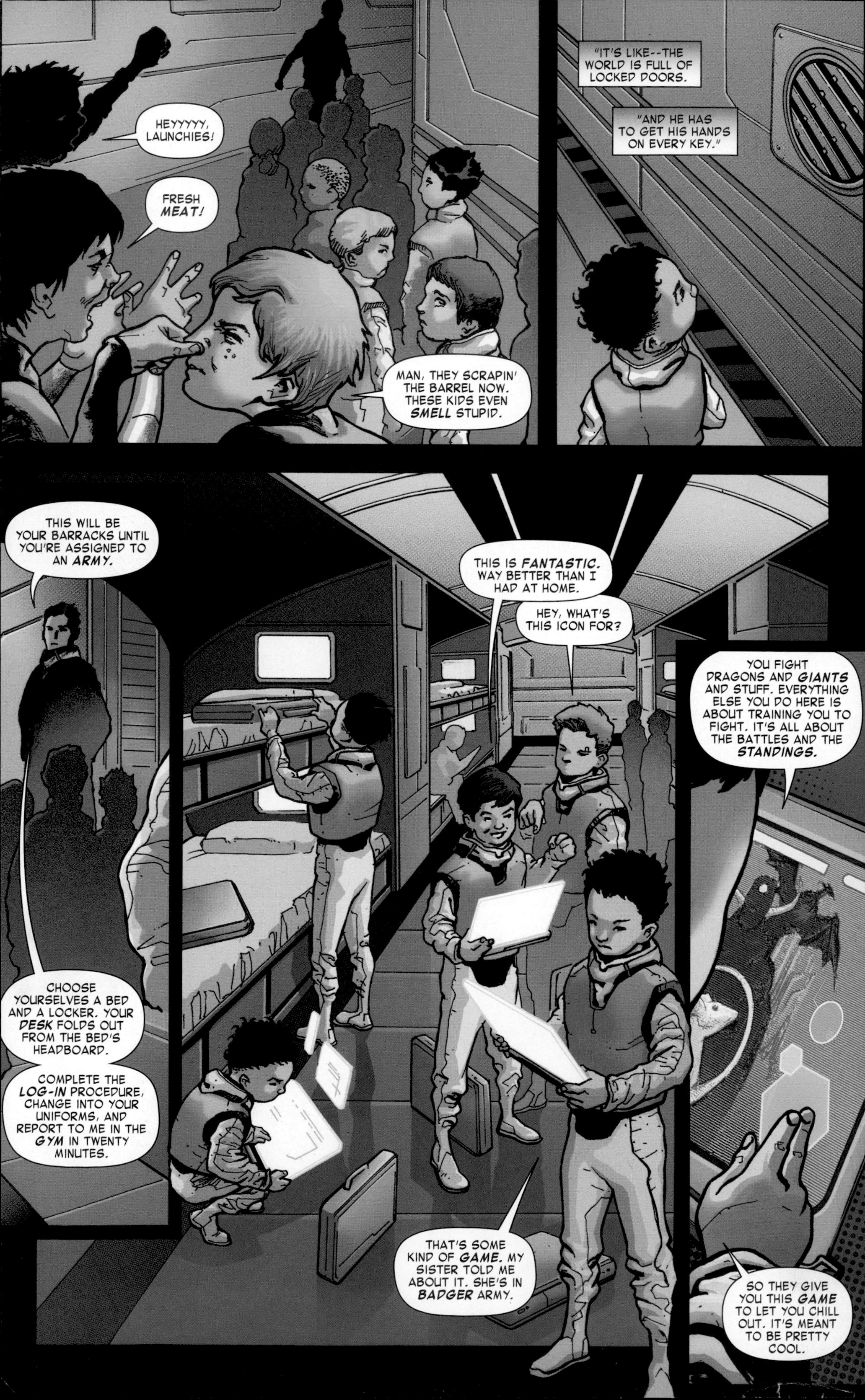
HEYYYYY, LAUNCHIES!
FRESH MEAT!
MAN, THEY SCRAPIN' THE BARREL NOW. THESE KIDS EVEN SMELL STUPID.
"IT'S LIKE--THE WORLD IS FULL OF LOCKED DOORS.
"AND HE HAS TO GET HIS HANDS ON EVERY KEY."
THIS WILL BE YOUR BARRACKS UNTIL YOU'RE ASSIGNED TO AN ARMY.
CHOOSE YOURSELVES A BED AND A LOCKER. YOUR DESK FOLDS OUT FROM THE BED'S HEADBOARD.
COMPLETE THE LOG-IN PROCEDURE, CHANGE INTO YOUR UNIFORMS, AND REPORT TO ME IN THE GYM IN TWENTY MINUTES.
THIS IS FANTASTIC. WAY BETTER THAN I HAD AT HOME.
HEY, WHAT'S THIS ICON FOR?
THAT'S SOME KIND OF GAME. MY SISTER TOLD ME ABOUT IT. SHE'S IN BADGER ARMY.
YOU FIGHT DRAGONS AND GIANTS AND STUFF. EVERYTHING ELSE YOU DO HERE IS ABOUT TRAINING YOU TO FIGHT. IT'S ALL ABOUT THE BATTLES AND THE STANDINGS.
SO THEY GIVE YOU THIS GAME TO LET YOU CHILL OUT. IT'S MEANT TO BE PRETTY COOL.

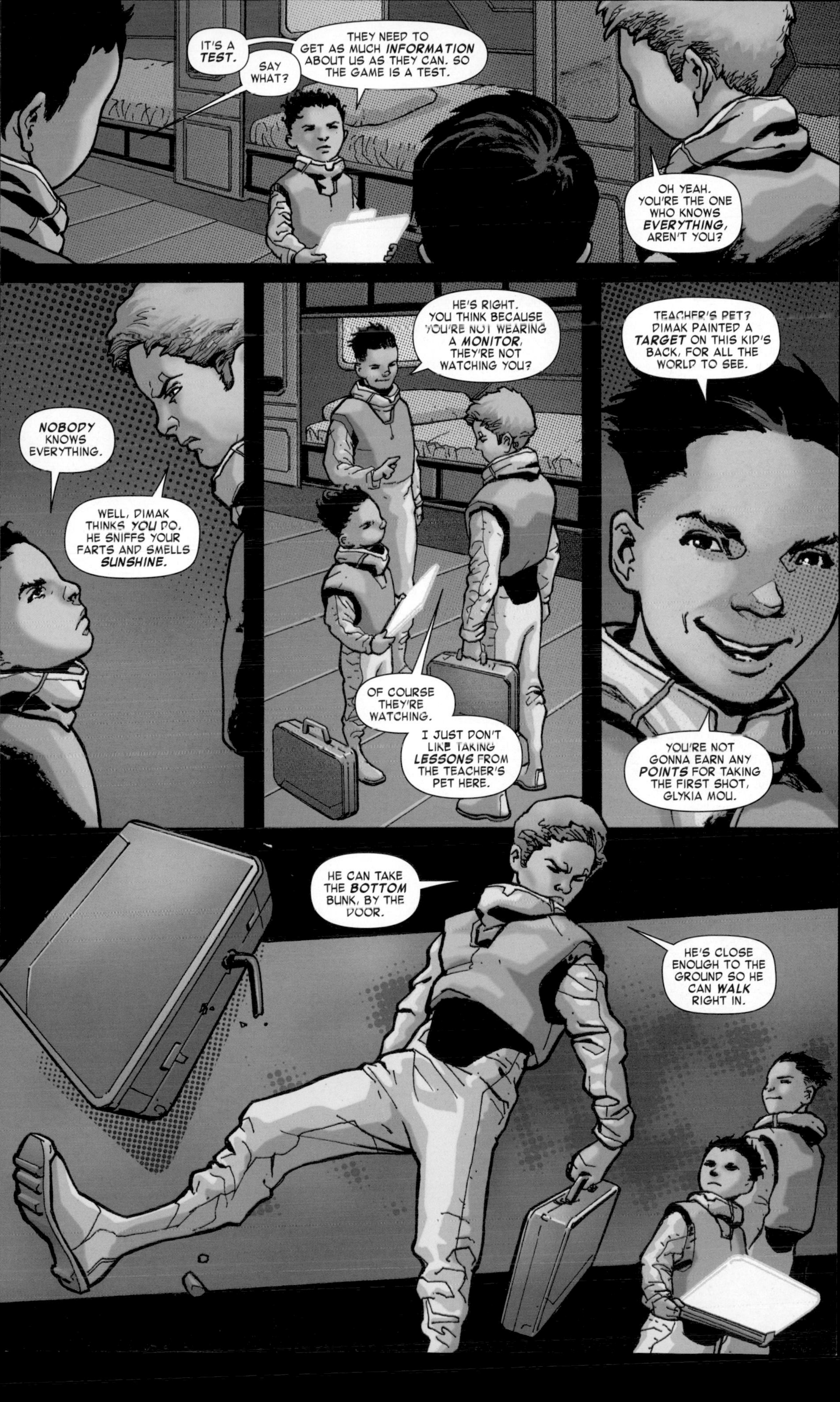
IT'S A TEST.
THEY NEED TO GET AS MUCH INFORMATION ABOUT US AS THEY CAN. SO THE GAME IS A TEST.
SAY WHAT?
OH YEAH. YOU'RE THE ONE WHO KNOWS EVERYTHING, AREN'T YOU?
NOBODY KNOWS EVERYTHING.
WELL, DIMAK THINKS YOU DO. HE SNIFFS YOUR FARTS AND SMELLS SUNSHINE.
HE'S RIGHT. YOU THINK BECAUSE YOU'RE NOT WEARING A MONITOR, THEY'RE NOT WATCHING YOU?
OF COURSE THEY'RE WATCHING.
I JUST DON'T LIKE TAKING LESSONS FROM THE TEACHER'S PET HERE.
TEACHER'S PET? DIMAK PAINTED A TARGET ON THIS KID'S BACK, FOR ALL THE WORLD TO SEE.
YOU'RE NOT GONNA EARN ANY POINTS FOR TAKING THE FIRST SHOT, GLYKIA MOU.
HE CAN TAKE THE BOTTOM BUNK, BY THE DOOR.
HE'S CLOSE ENOUGH TO THE GROUND SO HE CAN WALK RIGHT IN.

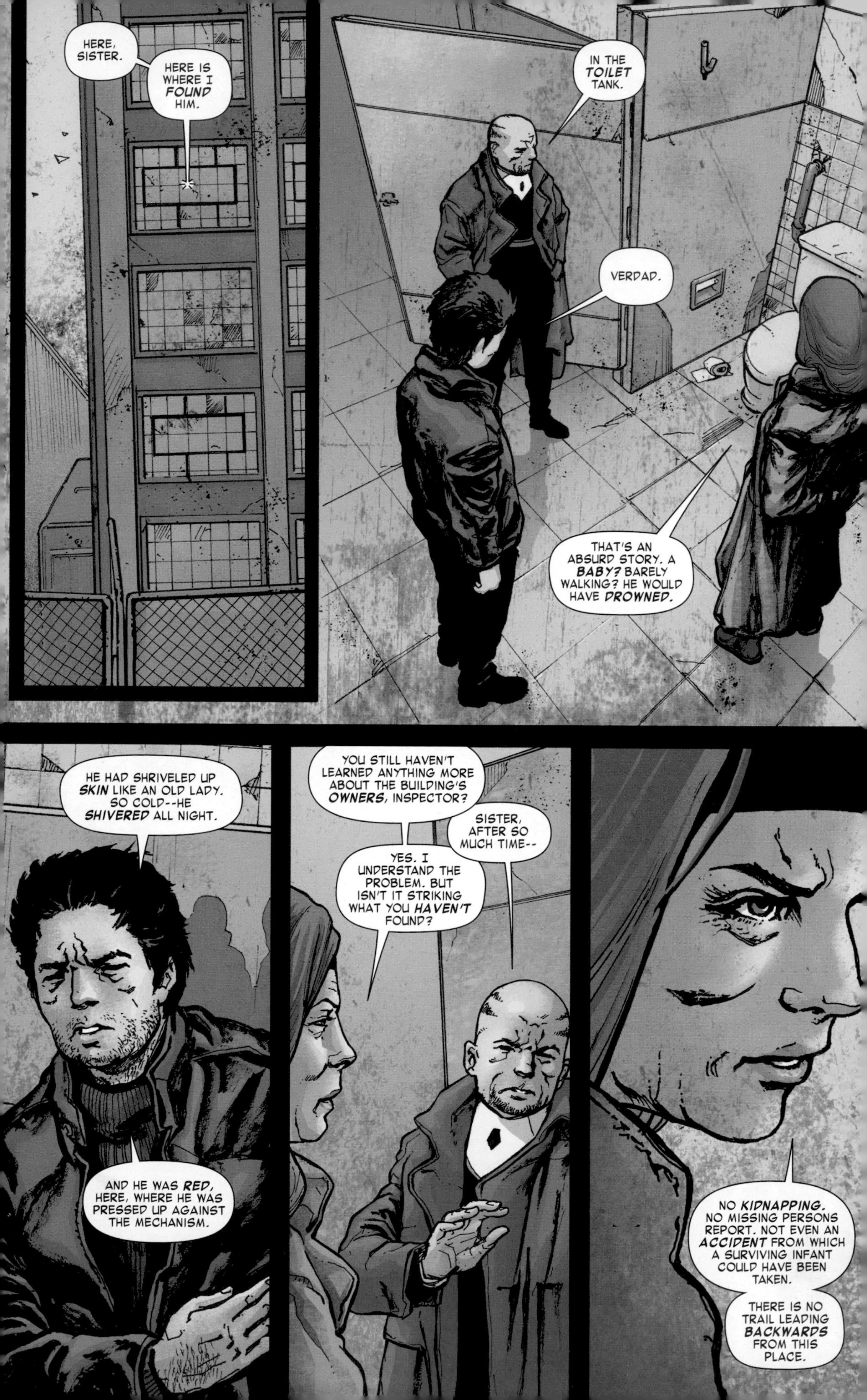
HERE, SISTER.
HERE IS WHERE I FOUND HIM.
IN THE TOILET TANK.
VERDAD.
THAT'S AN ABSURD STORY. A BABY? BARELY WALKING? HE WOULD HAVE DROWNED.
HE HAD SHRIVELED UP SKIN LIKE AN OLD LADY. SO COLD--HE SHIVERED ALL NIGHT.
AND HE WAS RED, HERE, WHERE HE WAS PRESSED UP AGAINST THE MECHANISM.
YOU STILL HAVEN'T LEARNED ANYTHING MORE ABOUT THE BUILDING'S OWNERS, INSPECTOR?
SISTER, AFTER SO MUCH TIME--
YES. I UNDERSTAND THE PROBLEM. BUT ISN'T IT STRIKING WHAT YOU HAVEN'T FOUND?
NO KIDNAPPING. NO MISSING PERSONS REPORT. NOT EVEN AN ACCIDENT FROM WHICH A SURVIVING INFANT COULD HAVE BEEN TAKEN.
THERE IS NO TRAIL LEADING BACKWARDS FROM THIS PLACE.

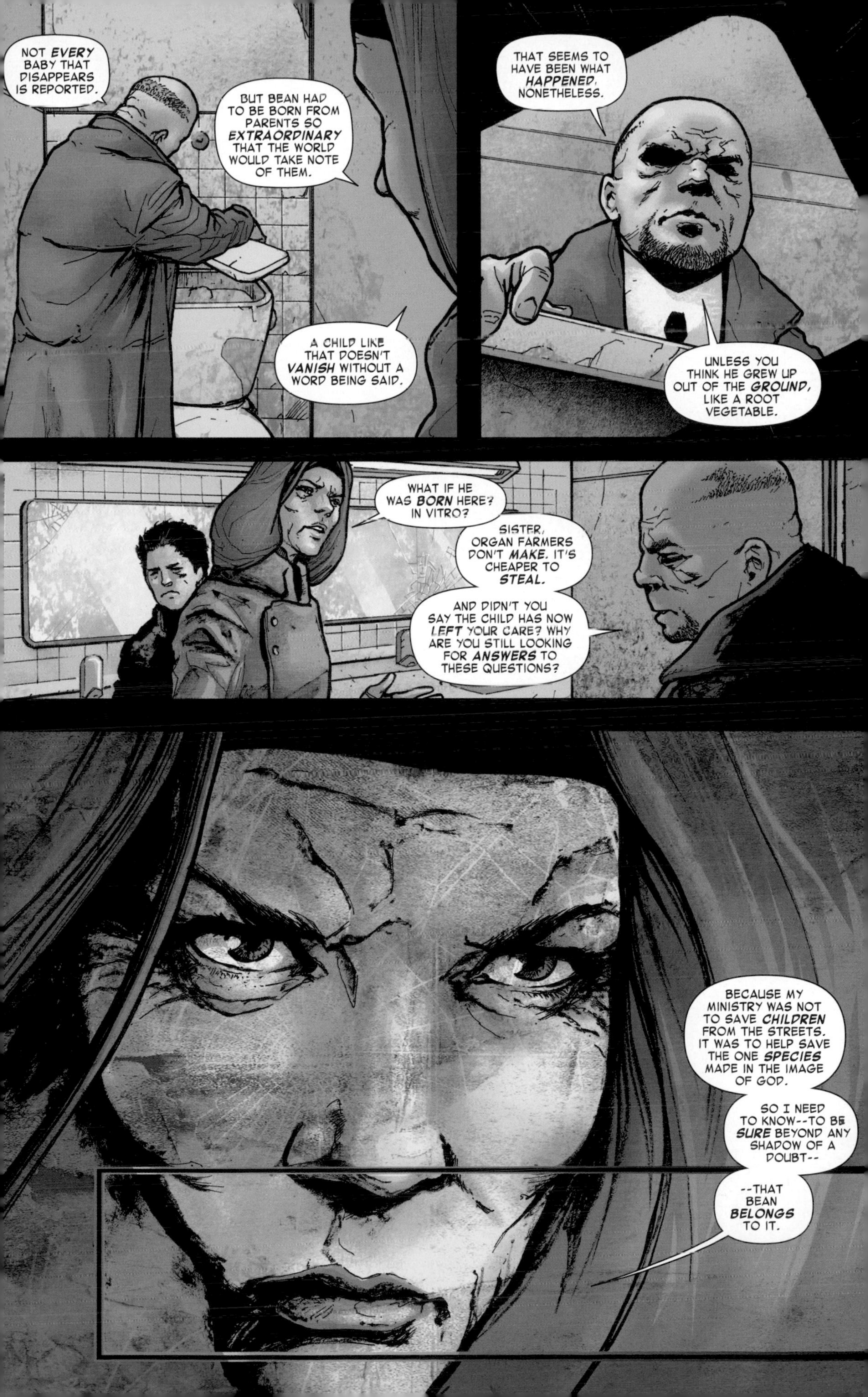
NOT EVERY BABY THAT DISAPPEARS IS REPORTED.
BUT BEAN HAD TO BE BORN FROM PARENTS SO EXTRAORDINARY THAT THE WORLD WOULD TAKE NOTE OF THEM.
A CHILD LIKE THAT DOESN'T VANISH WITHOUT A WORD BEING SAID.
THAT SEEMS TO HAVE BEEN WHAT HAPPENED, NONETHELESS.
UNLESS YOU THINK HE GREW UP OUT OF THE GROUND, LIKE A ROOT VEGETABLE.
WHAT IF HE WAS BORN HERE? IN VITRO?
SISTER, ORGAN FARMERS DON'T MAKE. IT'S CHEAPER TO STEAL.
AND DIDN'T YOU SAY THE CHILD HAS NOW LEFT YOUR CARE? WHY ARE YOU STILL LOOKING FOR ANSWERS TO THESE QUESTIONS?
BECAUSE MY MINISTRY WAS NOT TO SAVE CHILDREN FROM THE STREETS. IT WAS TO HELP SAVE THE ONE SPECIES MADE IN THE IMAGE OF GOD.
SO I NEED TO KNOW--TO BE SURE BEYOND ANY SHADOW OF A DOUBT--
--THAT BEAN BELONGS TO IT.

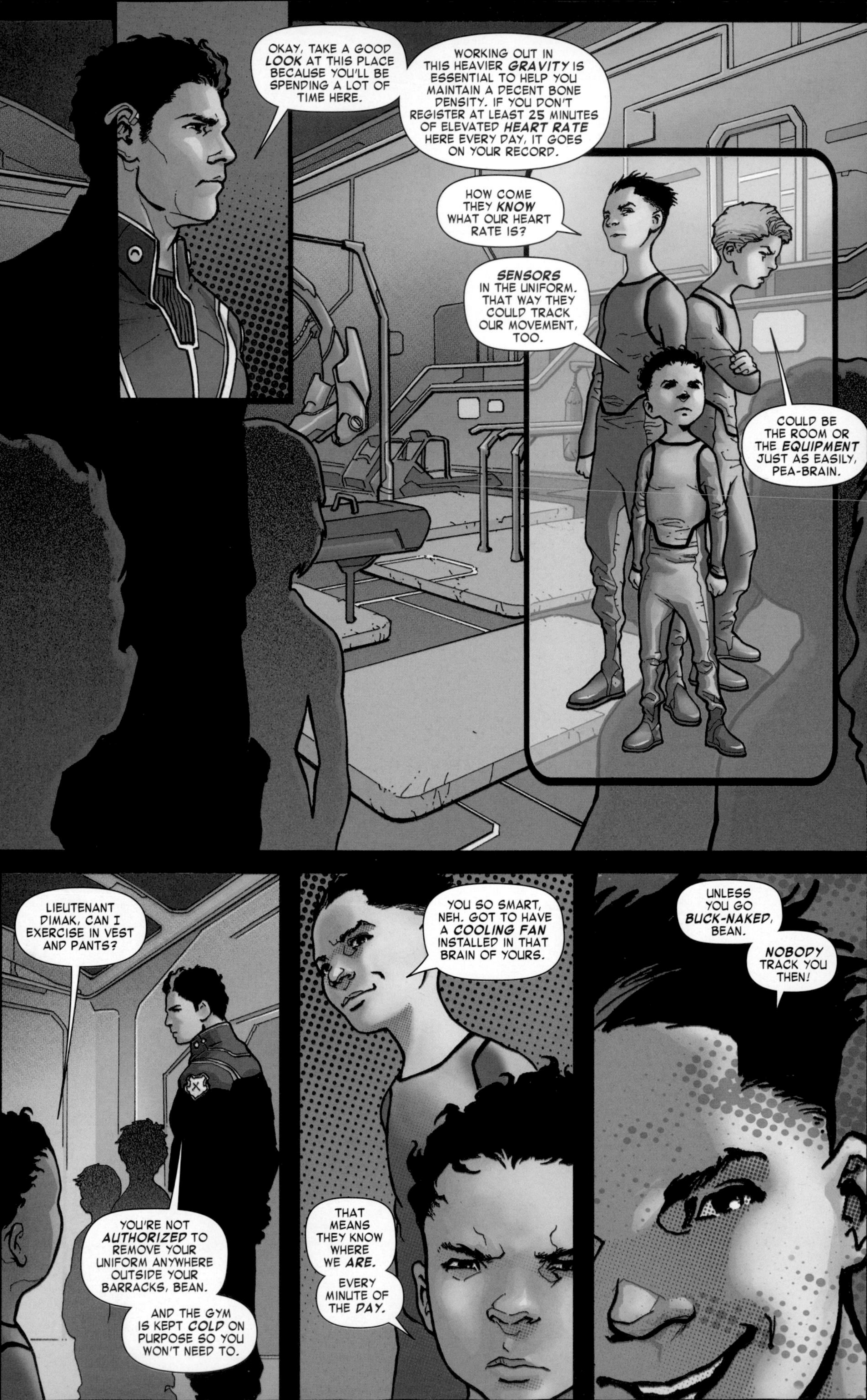
OKAY, TAKE A GOOD LOOK AT THIS PLACE BECAUSE YOU'LL BE SPENDING A LOT OF TIME HERE.
WORKING OUT IN THIS HEAVIER GRAVITY IS ESSENTIAL TO HELP YOU MAINTAIN A DECENT BONE DENSITY. IF YOU DON'T REGISTER AT LEAST 25 MINUTES OF ELEVATED HEART RATE HERE EVERY DAY, IT GOES ON YOUR RECORD.
HOW COME THEY KNOW WHAT OUR HEART RATE IS?
SENSORS IN THE UNIFORM. THAT WAY THEY COULD TRACK OUR MOVEMENT, TOO.
COULD BE THE ROOM OR THE EQUIPMENT JUST AS EASILY, PEA-BRAIN.
LIEUTENANT DIMAK, CAN I EXERCISE IN VEST AND PANTS?
YOU'RE NOT AUTHORIZED TO REMOVE YOUR UNIFORM ANYWHERE OUTSIDE YOUR BARRACKS, BEAN.
AND THE GYM IS KEPT COLD ON PURPOSE SO YOU WON'T NEED TO.
YOU SO SMART, NEH. GOT TO HAVE A COOLING FAN INSTALLED IN THAT BRAIN OF YOURS.
THAT MEANS THEY KNOW WHERE WE ARE.
EVERY MINUTE OF THE DAY.
UNLESS YOU GO BUCK-NAKED, BEAN.
NOBODY TRACK YOU THEN!

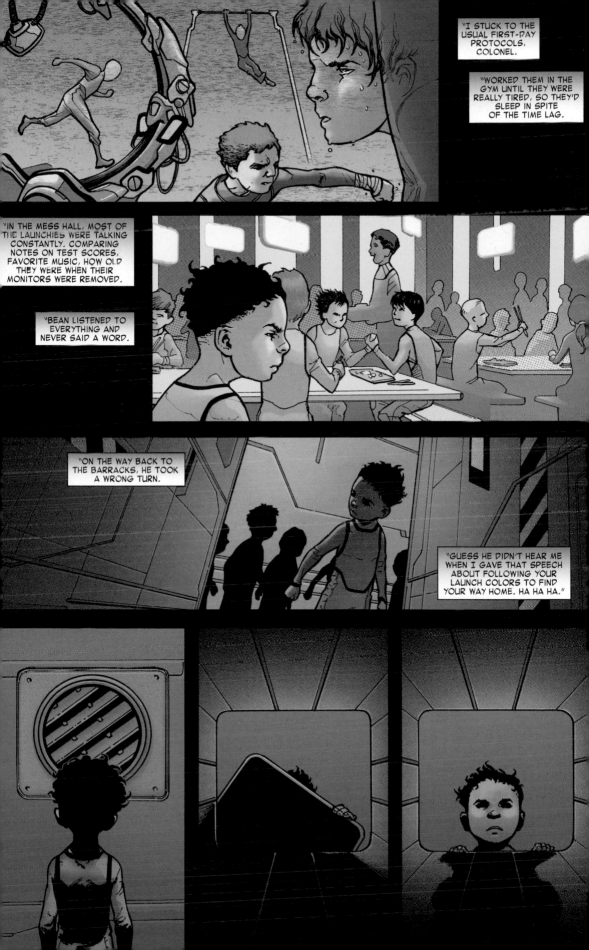

"I STUCK TO THE USUAL FIRST-DAY PROTOCOLS, COLONEL.

"WORKED THEM IN THE GYM UNTIL THEY WERE REALLY TIRED, SO THEY'D SLEEP IN SPITE OF THE TIME LAG.

"IN THE MESS HALL, MOST OF THE LAUNCHIES WERE TALKING CONSTANTLY. COMPARING NOTES ON TEST SCORES, FAVORITE MUSIC, HOW OLD THEY WERE WHEN THEIR MONITORS WERE REMOVED.

"BEAN LISTENED TO EVERYTHING AND NEVER SAID A WORD.

"ON THE WAY BACK TO THE BARRACKS, HE TOOK A WRONG TURN.

"GUESS HE DIDN'T HEAR ME WHEN I GAVE THAT SPEECH ABOUT FOLLOWING YOUR LAUNCH COLORS TO FIND YOUR WAY HOME. HA HA HA."

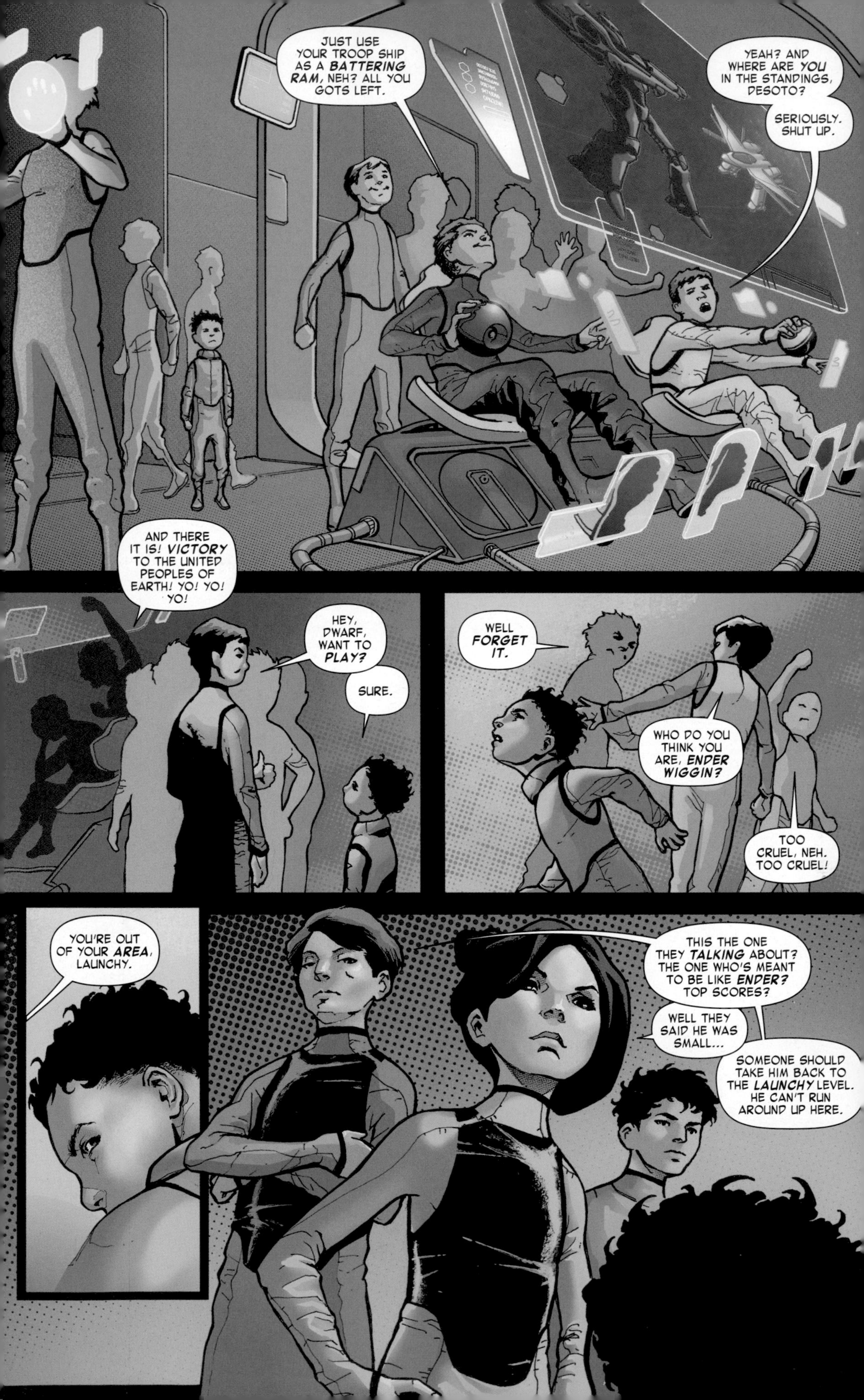

JUST USE YOUR TROOP SHIP AS A BATTERING RAM, NEH? ALL YOU GOTS LEFT.
YEAH? AND WHERE ARE YOU IN THE STANDINGS, DESOTO?
SERIOUSLY. SHUT UP.
AND THERE IT IS! VICTORY TO THE UNITED PEOPLES OF EARTH! YO! YO! YO!
HEY, DWARF, WANT TO PLAY?
SURE.
WELL FORGET IT.
WHO DO YOU THINK YOU ARE, ENDER WIGGIN?
TOO CRUEL, NEH. TOO CRUEL!
YOU'RE OUT OF YOUR AREA, LAUNCHY.
THIS THE ONE THEY TALKING ABOUT? THE ONE WHO'S MEANT TO BE LIKE ENDER? TOP SCORES?
WELL THEY SAID HE WAS SMALL...
SOMEONE SHOULD TAKE HIM BACK TO THE LAUNCHY LEVEL. HE CAN'T RUN AROUND UP HERE.

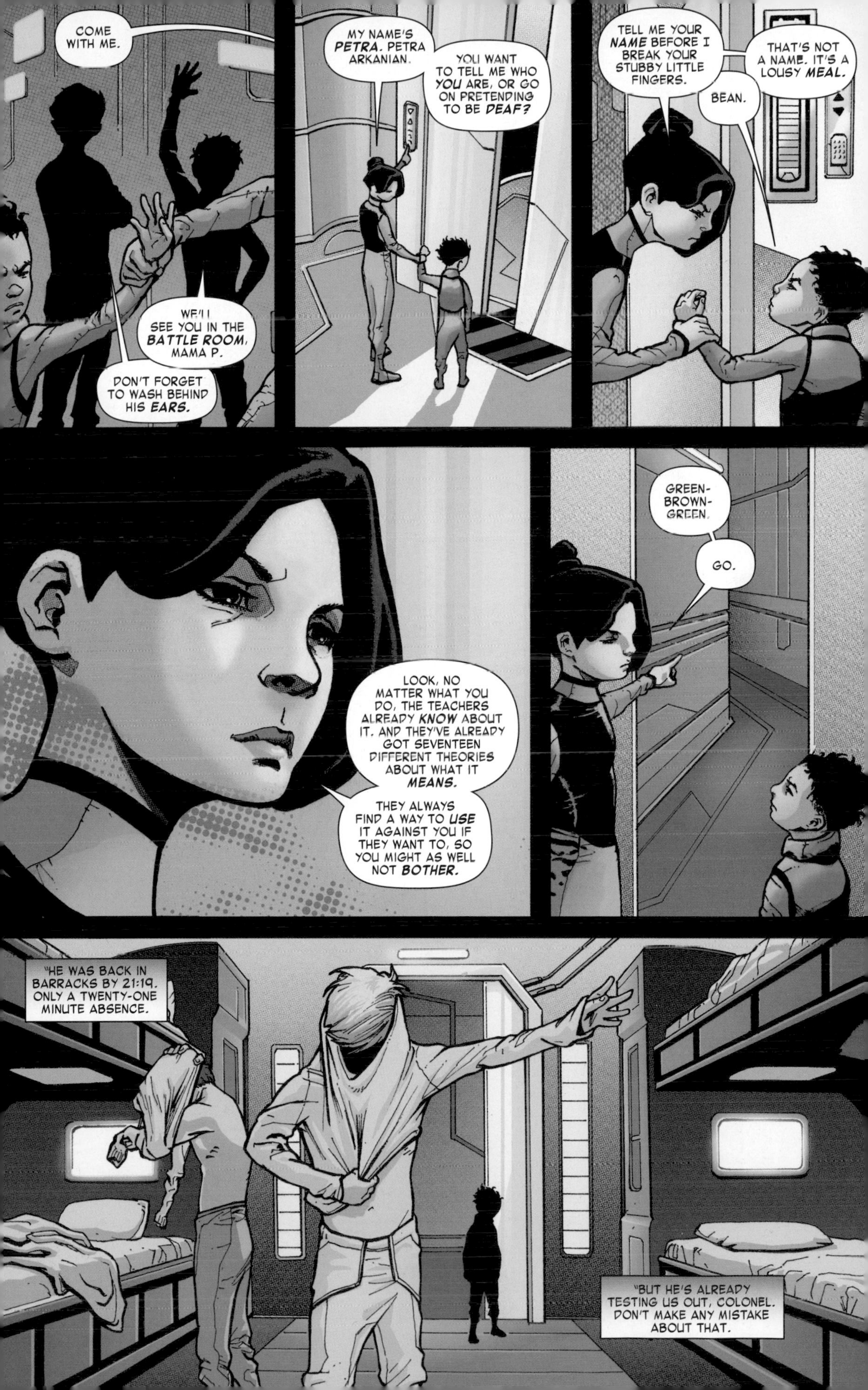
COME WITH ME.
WE'LL SEE YOU IN THE BATTLE ROOM, MAMA P.
DON'T FORGET TO WASH BEHIND HIS EARS.
MY NAME'S PETRA. PETRA ARKANIAN.
YOU WANT TO TELL ME WHO YOU ARE, OR GO ON PRETENDING TO BE DEAF?
TELL ME YOUR NAME BEFORE I BREAK YOUR STUBBY LITTLE FINGERS.
BEAN.
THAT'S NOT A NAME. IT'S A LOUSY MEAL.
LOOK, NO MATTER WHAT YOU DO, THE TEACHERS ALREADY KNOW ABOUT IT. AND THEY'VE ALREADY GOT SEVENTEEN DIFFERENT THEORIES ABOUT WHAT IT MEANS.
THEY ALWAYS FIND A WAY TO USE IT AGAINST YOU IF THEY WANT TO, SO YOU MIGHT AS WELL NOT BOTHER.
GREEN-BROWN-GREEN.
GO.
"HE WAS BACK IN BARRACKS BY 21:19. ONLY A TWENTY-ONE MINUTE ABSENCE.
"BUT HE'S ALREADY TESTING US OUT, COLONEL. DON'T MAKE ANY MISTAKE ABOUT THAT.

"WE'RE THE ONES ON THE MICROSCOPE SLIDE.

"AND IT'S BEAN'S BIG EYE THAT'S STARING DOWN AT US."

SNF! SNF!

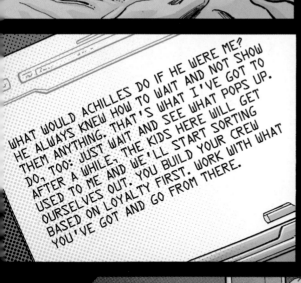

WHAT WOULD ACHILLES DO IF HE WERE ME? HE ALWAYS KNEW HOW TO WAIT AND NOT SHOW THEM ANYTHING. THAT'S WHAT I'VE GOT TO DO, TOO: JUST WAIT AND SEE WHAT POPS UP. AFTER A WHILE, THE KIDS HERE WILL GET USED TO ME AND WE'LL START SORTING OURSELVES OUT. YOU BUILD YOUR CREW BASED ON LOYALTY FIRST. WORK WITH WHAT YOU'VE GOT AND GO FROM THERE.

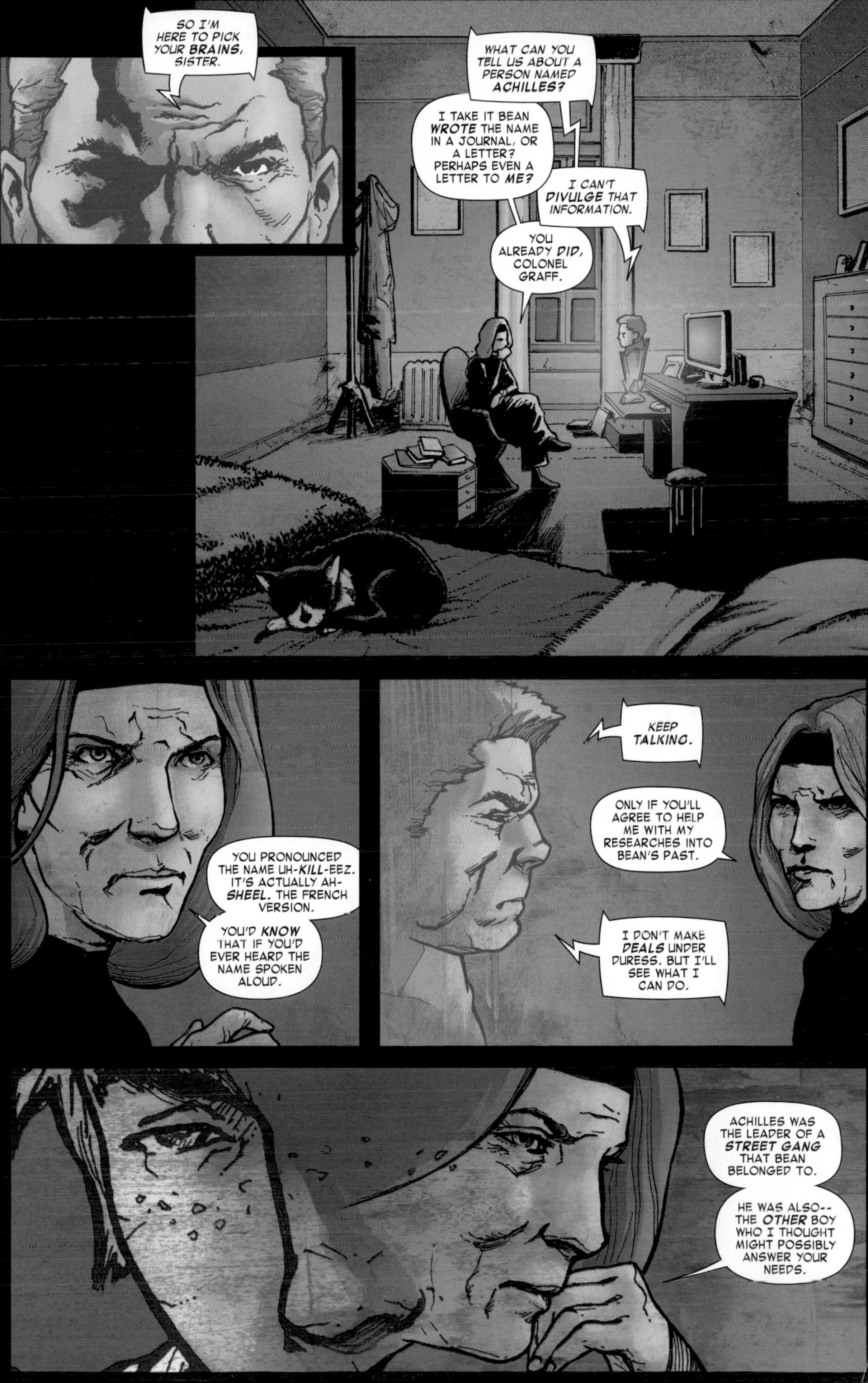
SO I'M HERE TO PICK YOUR BRAINS, SISTER.
WHAT CAN YOU TELL US ABOUT A PERSON NAMED ACHILLES?
I TAKE IT BEAN WROTE THE NAME IN A JOURNAL, OR A LETTER? PERHAPS EVEN A LETTER TO ME?
I CAN'T DIVULGE THAT INFORMATION.
YOU ALREADY DID, COLONEL GRAFF.
YOU PRONOUNCED THE NAME UH-KILL-EEZ. IT'S ACTUALLY AH-SHEEL. THE FRENCH VERSION.
YOU'D KNOW THAT IF YOU'D EVER HEARD THE NAME SPOKEN ALOUD.
KEEP TALKING.
ONLY IF YOU'LL AGREE TO HELP ME WITH MY RESEARCHES INTO BEAN'S PAST.
I DON'T MAKE DEALS UNDER DURESS. BUT I'LL SEE WHAT I CAN DO.
ACHILLES WAS THE LEADER OF A STREET GANG THAT BEAN BELONGED TO.
HE WAS ALSO-- THE OTHER BOY WHO I THOUGHT MIGHT POSSIBLY ANSWER YOUR NEEDS.

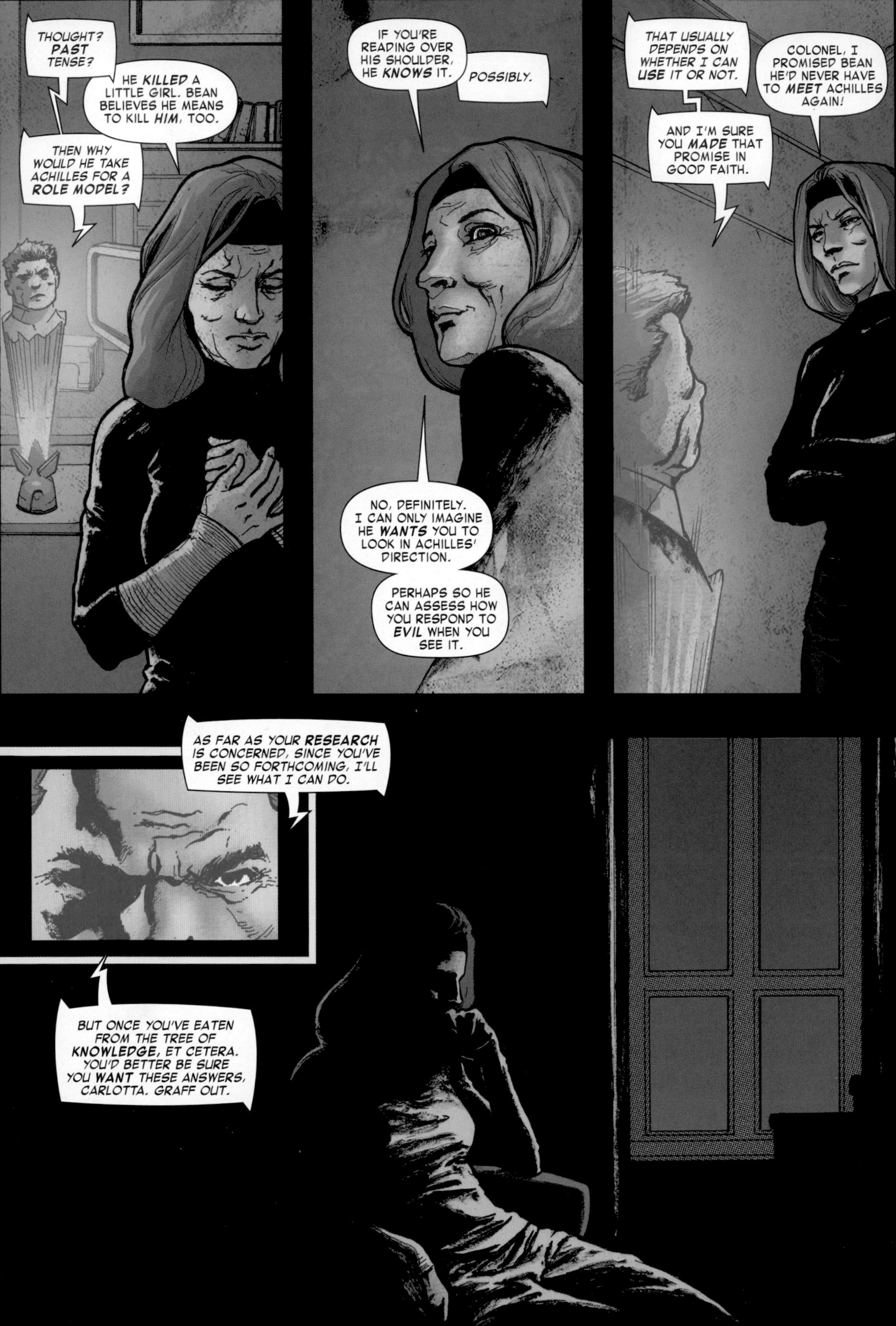
THOUGHT? PAST TENSE?
HE KILLED A LITTLE GIRL. BEAN BELIEVES HE MEANS TO KILL HIM, TOO.
THEN WHY WOULD HE TAKE ACHILLES FOR A ROLE MODEL?
IF YOU'RE READING OVER HIS SHOULDER, HE KNOWS IT.
POSSIBLY.
NO, DEFINITELY. I CAN ONLY IMAGINE HE WANTS YOU TO LOOK IN ACHILLES' DIRECTION.
PERHAPS SO HE CAN ASSESS HOW YOU RESPOND TO EVIL WHEN YOU SEE IT.
THAT USUALLY DEPENDS ON WHETHER I CAN USE IT OR NOT.
COLONEL, I PROMISED BEAN HE'D NEVER HAVE TO MEET ACHILLES AGAIN!
AND I'M SURE YOU MADE THAT PROMISE IN GOOD FAITH.
AS FAR AS YOUR RESEARCH IS CONCERNED, SINCE YOU'VE BEEN SO FORTHCOMING, I'LL SEE WHAT I CAN DO.
BUT ONCE YOU'VE EATEN FROM THE TREE OF KNOWLEDGE, ET CETERA. YOU'D BETTER BE SURE YOU WANT THESE ANSWERS, CARLOTTA. GRAFF OUT.

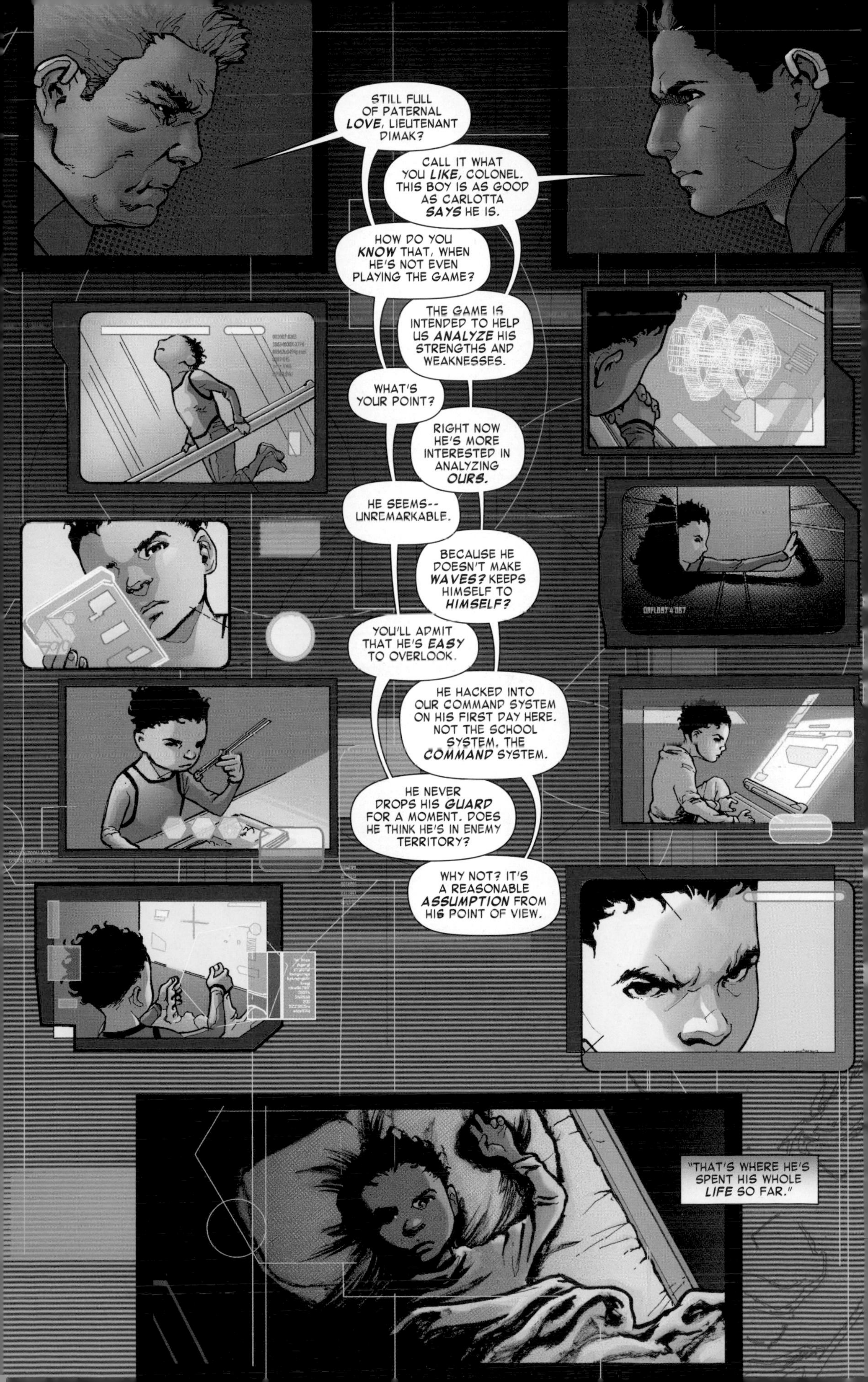

STILL FULL OF PATERNAL LOVE, LIEUTENANT DIMAK?
CALL IT WHAT YOU LIKE, COLONEL. THIS BOY IS AS GOOD AS CARLOTTA SAYS HE IS.
HOW DO YOU KNOW THAT, WHEN HE'S NOT EVEN PLAYING THE GAME?
THE GAME IS INTENDED TO HELP US ANALYZE HIS STRENGTHS AND WEAKNESSES.
WHAT'S YOUR POINT?
RIGHT NOW HE'S MORE INTERESTED IN ANALYZING OURS.
HE SEEMS--UNREMARKABLE.
BECAUSE HE DOESN'T MAKE WAVES? KEEPS HIMSELF TO HIMSELF?
YOU'LL ADMIT THAT HE'S EASY TO OVERLOOK.
HE HACKED INTO OUR COMMAND SYSTEM ON HIS FIRST DAY HERE. NOT THE SCHOOL SYSTEM. THE COMMAND SYSTEM.
HE NEVER DROPS HIS GUARD FOR A MOMENT. DOES HE THINK HE'S IN ENEMY TERRITORY?
WHY NOT? IT'S A REASONABLE ASSUMPTION FROM HIS POINT OF VIEW.
"THAT'S WHERE HE'S SPENT HIS WHOLE LIFE SO FAR."

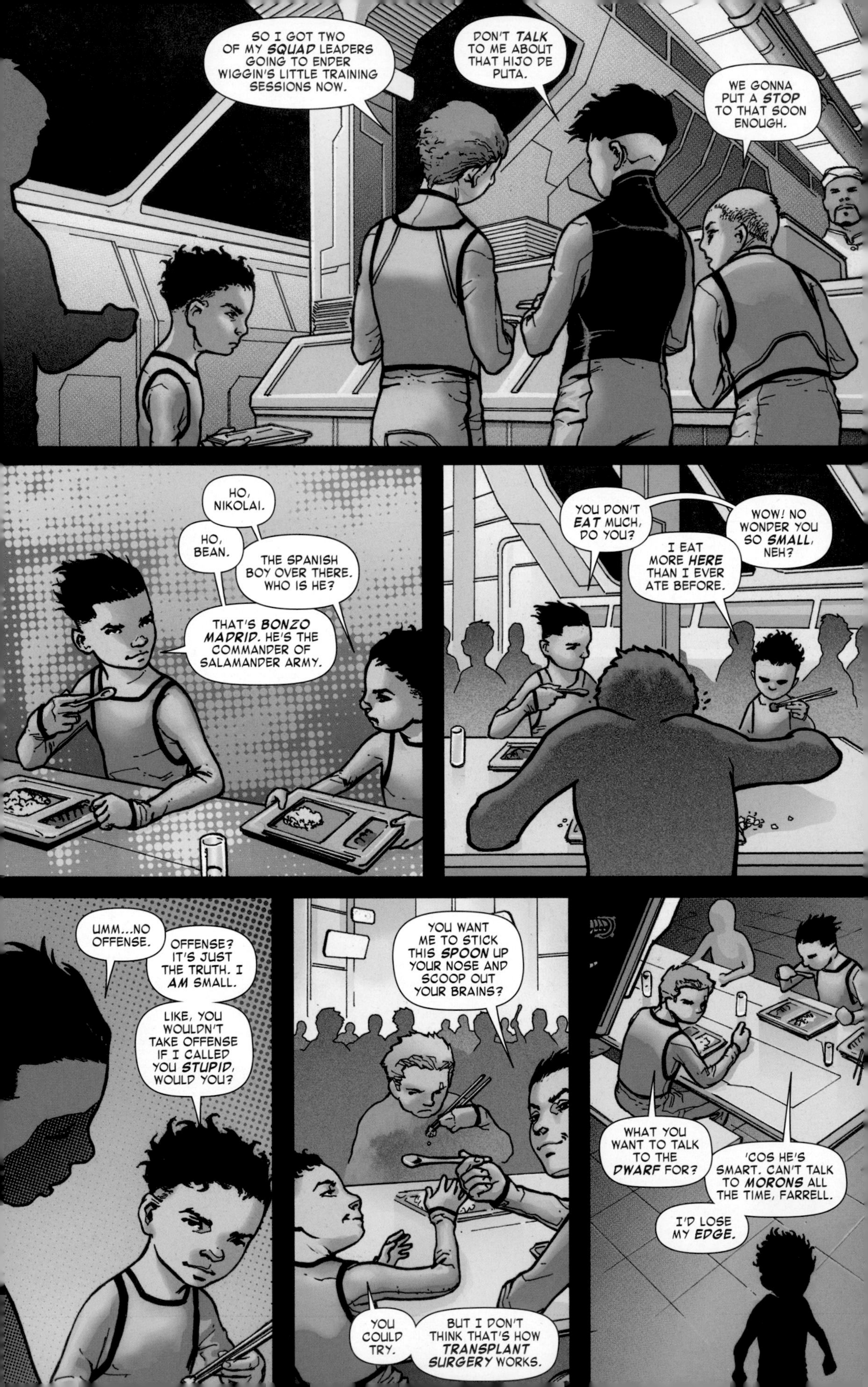
SO I GOT TWO OF MY SQUAD LEADERS GOING TO ENDER WIGGIN'S LITTLE TRAINING SESSIONS NOW.
DON'T TALK TO ME ABOUT THAT HIJO DE PUTA.
WE GONNA PUT A STOP TO THAT SOON ENOUGH.
HO, NIKOLAI.
HO, BEAN.
THE SPANISH BOY OVER THERE. WHO IS HE?
THAT'S BONZO MADRID. HE'S THE COMMANDER OF SALAMANDER ARMY.
YOU DON'T EAT MUCH, DO YOU?
I EAT MORE HERE THAN I EVER ATE BEFORE.
WOW! NO WONDER YOU SO SMALL, NEH?
UMM...NO OFFENSE.
OFFENSE? IT'S JUST THE TRUTH. I AM SMALL.
LIKE, YOU WOULDN'T TAKE OFFENSE IF I CALLED YOU STUPID, WOULD YOU?
YOU WANT ME TO STICK THIS SPOON UP YOUR NOSE AND SCOOP OUT YOUR BRAINS?
YOU COULD TRY.
BUT I DON'T THINK THAT'S HOW TRANSPLANT SURGERY WORKS.
WHAT YOU WANT TO TALK TO THE DWARF FOR?
'COS HE'S SMART. CAN'T TALK TO MORONS ALL THE TIME, FARRELL.
I'D LOSE MY EDGE.

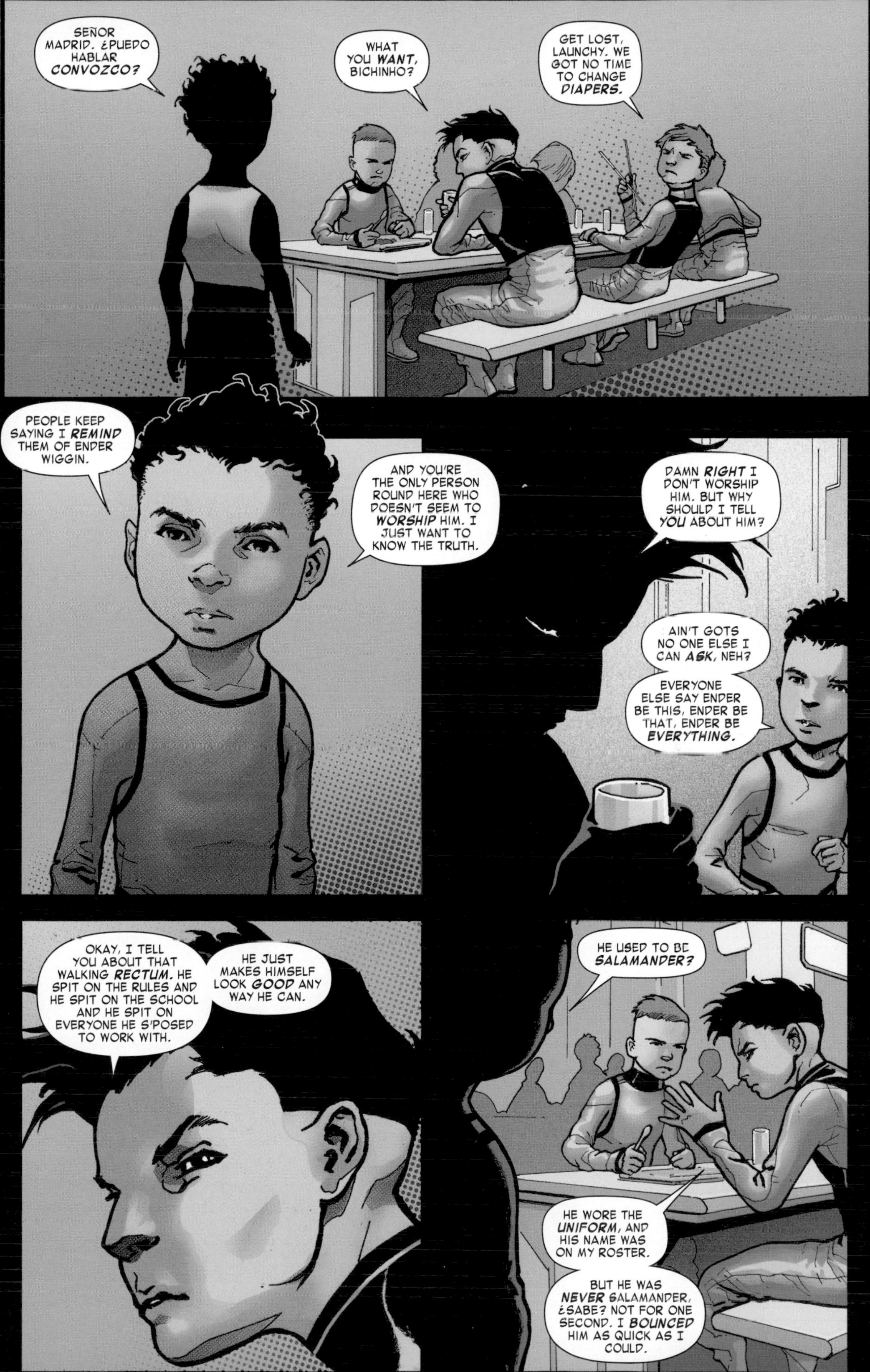
SEÑOR MADRID. ¿PUEDO HABLAR CONVOZCO?
WHAT YOU WANT, BICHINHO?
GET LOST, LAUNCHY. WE GOT NO TIME TO CHANGE DIAPERS.
PEOPLE KEEP SAYING I REMIND THEM OF ENDER WIGGIN.
AND YOU'RE THE ONLY PERSON ROUND HERE WHO DOESN'T SEEM TO WORSHIP HIM. I JUST WANT TO KNOW THE TRUTH.
DAMN RIGHT I DON'T WORSHIP HIM. BUT WHY SHOULD I TELL YOU ABOUT HIM?
AIN'T GOTS NO ONE ELSE I CAN ASK, NEH?
EVERYONE ELSE SAY ENDER BE THIS, ENDER BE THAT, ENDER BE EVERYTHING.
OKAY, I TELL YOU ABOUT THAT WALKING RECTUM. HE SPIT ON THE RULES AND HE SPIT ON THE SCHOOL AND HE SPIT ON EVERYONE HE S'POSED TO WORK WITH.
HE JUST MAKES HIMSELF LOOK GOOD ANY WAY HE CAN.
HE USED TO BE SALAMANDER?
HE WORE THE UNIFORM, AND HIS NAME WAS ON MY ROSTER.
BUT HE WAS NEVER SALAMANDER, ¿SABE? NOT FOR ONE SECOND. I BOUNCED HIM AS QUICK AS I COULD.

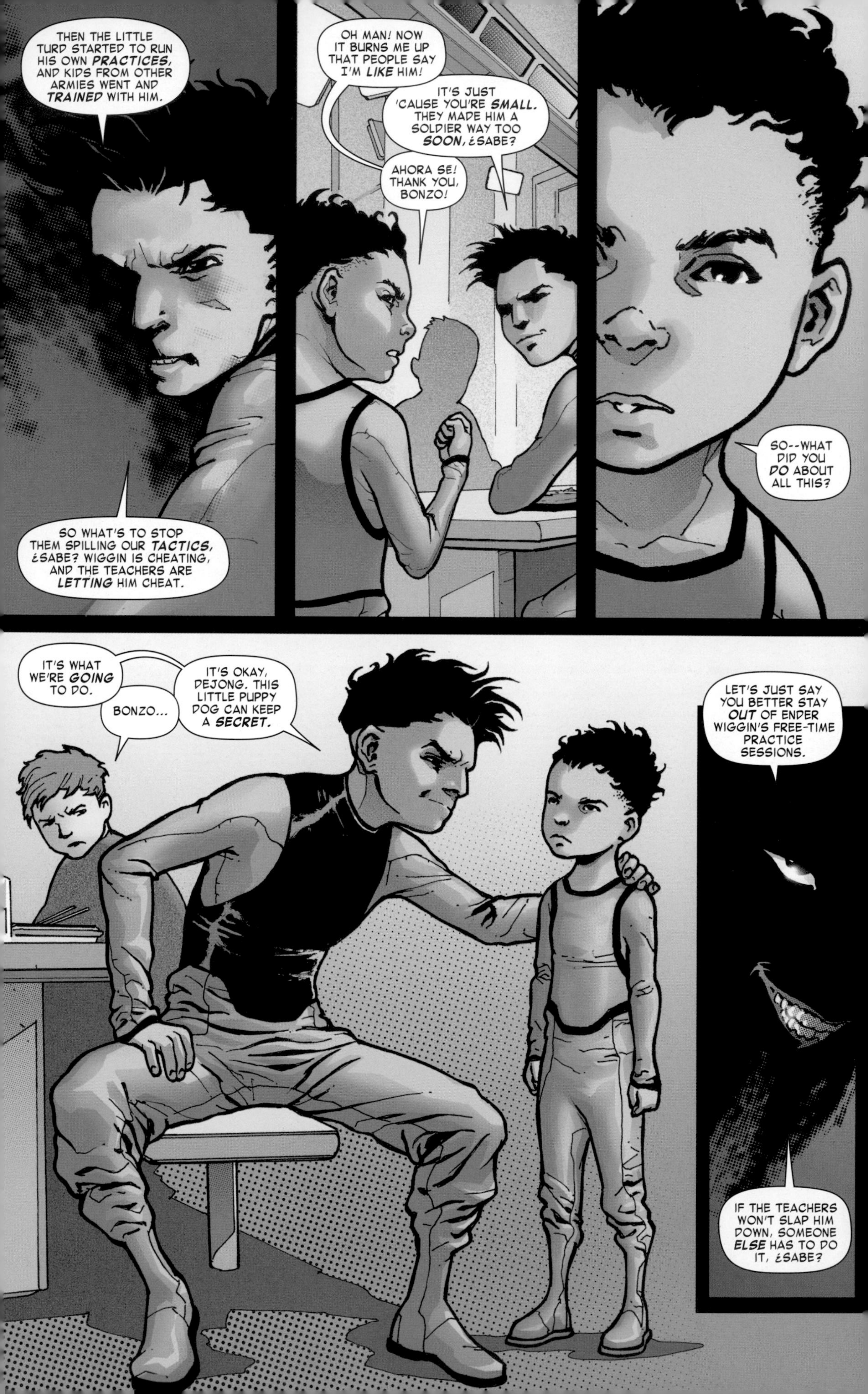
THEN THE LITTLE TURD STARTED TO RUN HIS OWN PRACTICES, AND KIDS FROM OTHER ARMIES WENT AND TRAINED WITH HIM.
SO WHAT'S TO STOP THEM SPILLING OUR TACTICS, ¿SABE? WIGGIN IS CHEATING, AND THE TEACHERS ARE LETTING HIM CHEAT.
OH MAN! NOW IT BURNS ME UP THAT PEOPLE SAY I'M LIKE HIM!
IT'S JUST 'CAUSE YOU'RE SMALL. THEY MADE HIM A SOLDIER WAY TOO SOON, ¿SABE?
AHORA SE! THANK YOU, BONZO!
SO--WHAT DID YOU DO ABOUT ALL THIS?
IT'S WHAT WE'RE GOING TO DO.
BONZO...
IT'S OKAY, DEJONG. THIS LITTLE PUPPY DOG CAN KEEP A SECRET.
LET'S JUST SAY YOU BETTER STAY OUT OF ENDER WIGGIN'S FREE-TIME PRACTICE SESSIONS.
IF THE TEACHERS WON'T SLAP HIM DOWN, SOMEONE ELSE HAS TO DO IT, ¿SABE?

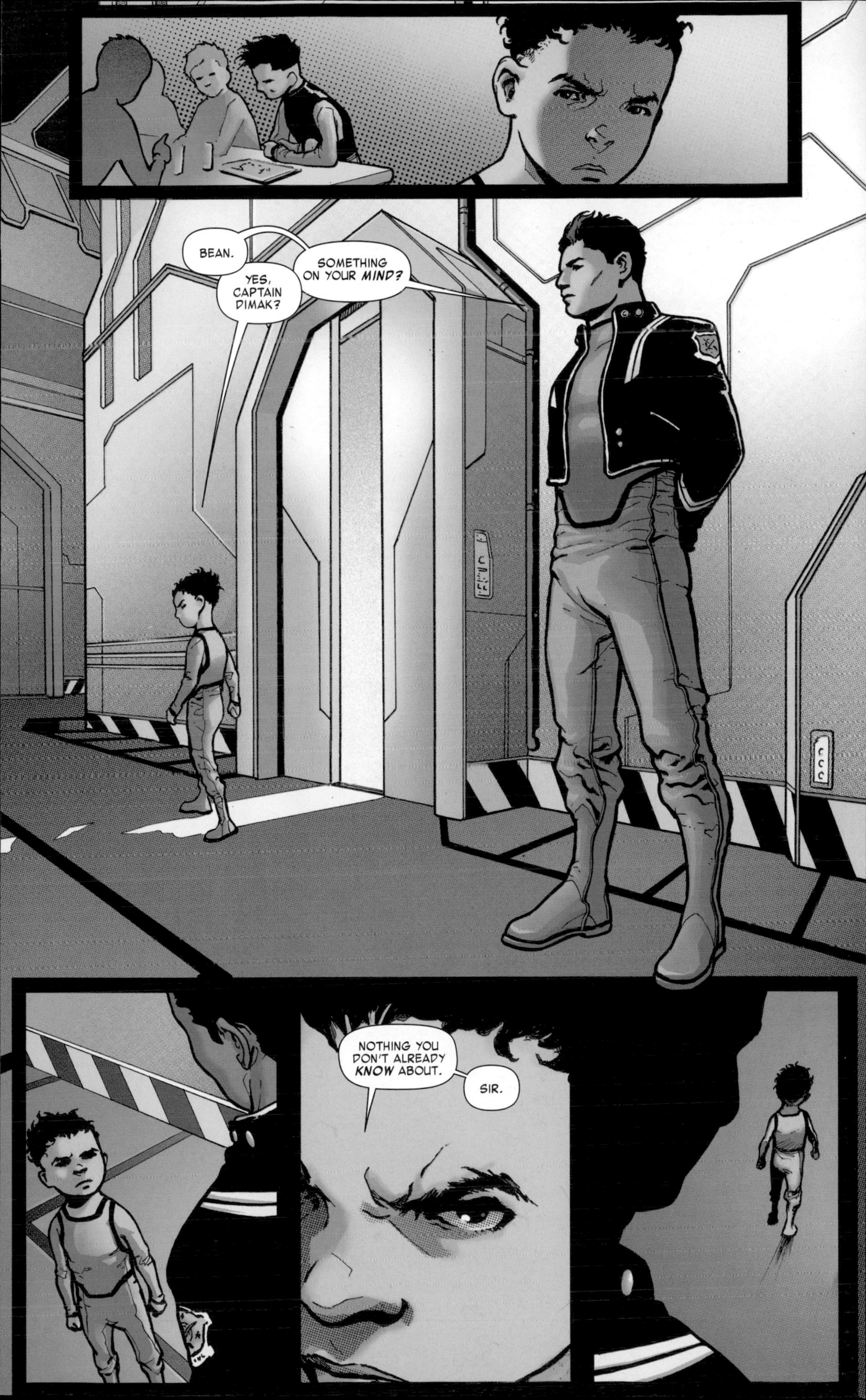
BEAN.
YES, CAPTAIN DIMAK?
SOMETHING ON YOUR *MIND?*
NOTHING YOU DON'T ALREADY *KNOW* ABOUT.
SIR.

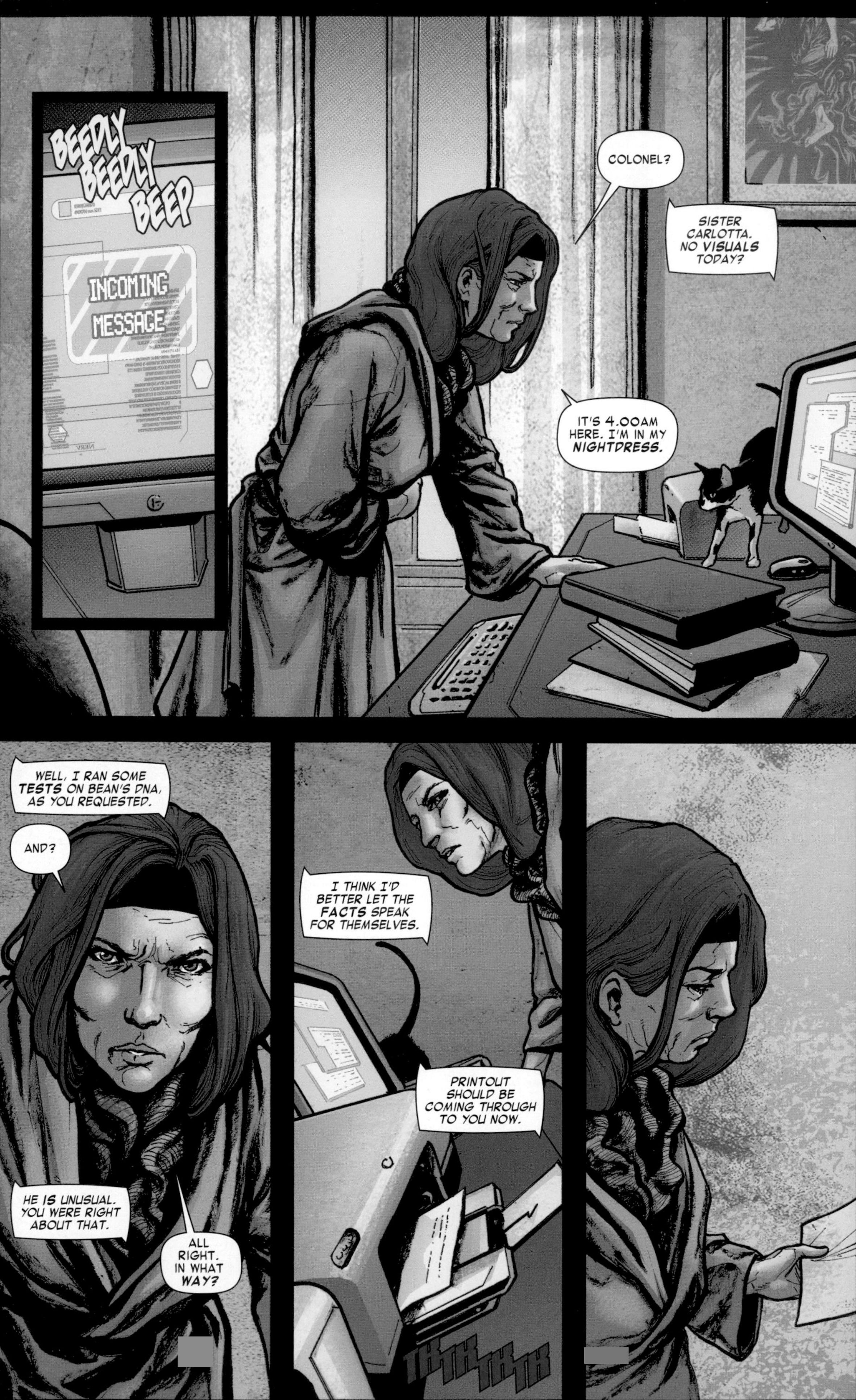
BEEDLY BEEDLY BEEP
INCOMING MESSAGE
COLONEL?
SISTER CARLOTTA. NO VISUALS TODAY?
IT'S 4.00AM HERE. I'M IN MY NIGHTDRESS.
WELL, I RAN SOME TESTS ON BEAN'S DNA, AS YOU REQUESTED.
AND?
HE IS UNUSUAL. YOU WERE RIGHT ABOUT THAT.
ALL RIGHT. IN WHAT WAY?
I THINK I'D BETTER LET THE FACTS SPEAK FOR THEMSELVES.
PRINTOUT SHOULD BE COMING THROUGH TO YOU NOW.
TKTK TKTK

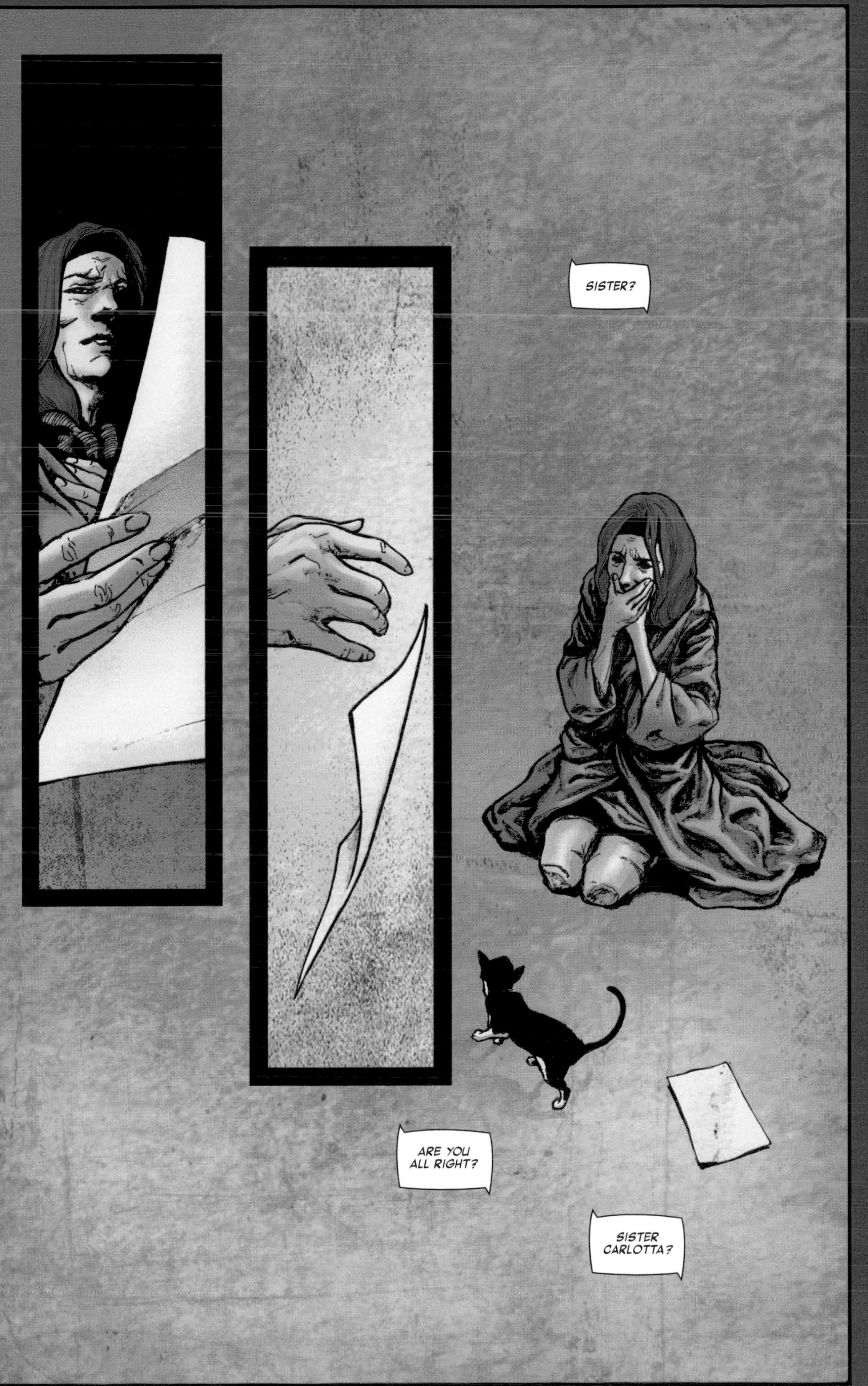
SISTER?
ARE YOU ALL RIGHT?
SISTER CARLOTTA?

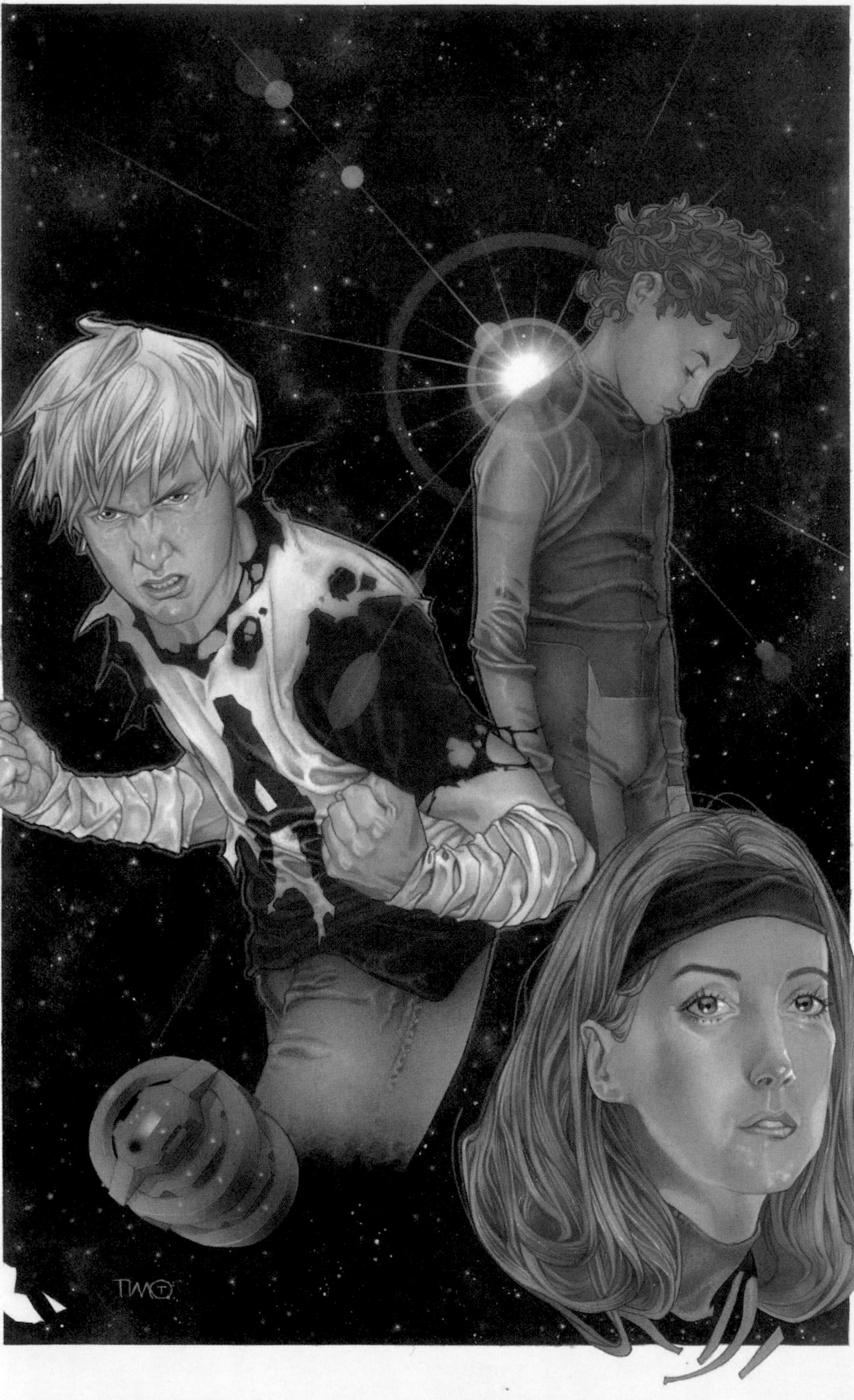

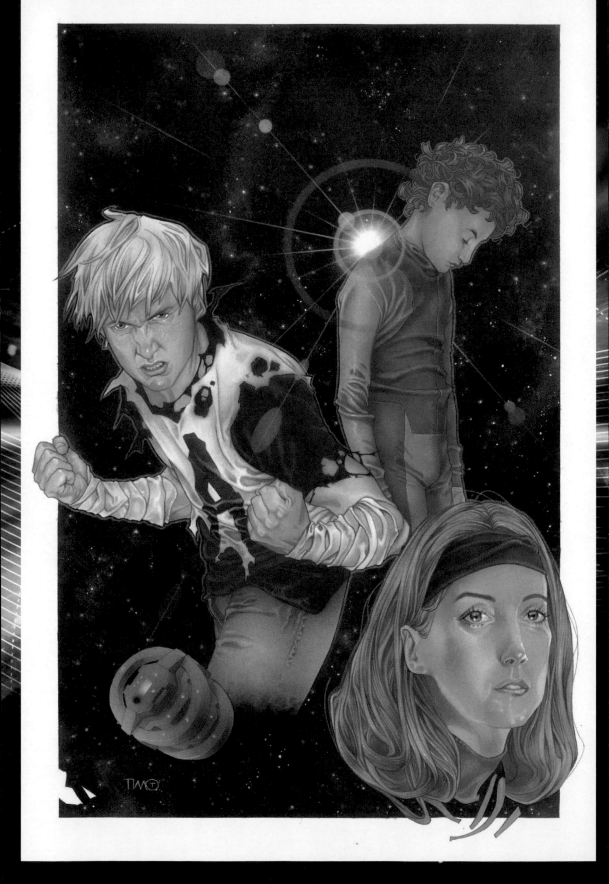

F O U R

"He doesn't play the fantasy game at all?"

"He's never so much as chosen a figure."

"It's not possible that he hasn't discovered it."

"He reset the preferences on his desk so that the invitation no longer pops up."

"From which you conclude..."

"He knows it isn't a game. He doesn't want us analyzing the workings of his mind."

"And yet he wants us to advance him."

"I don't know that. He buries himself in his studies. For three months he's been getting perfect scores on every test."

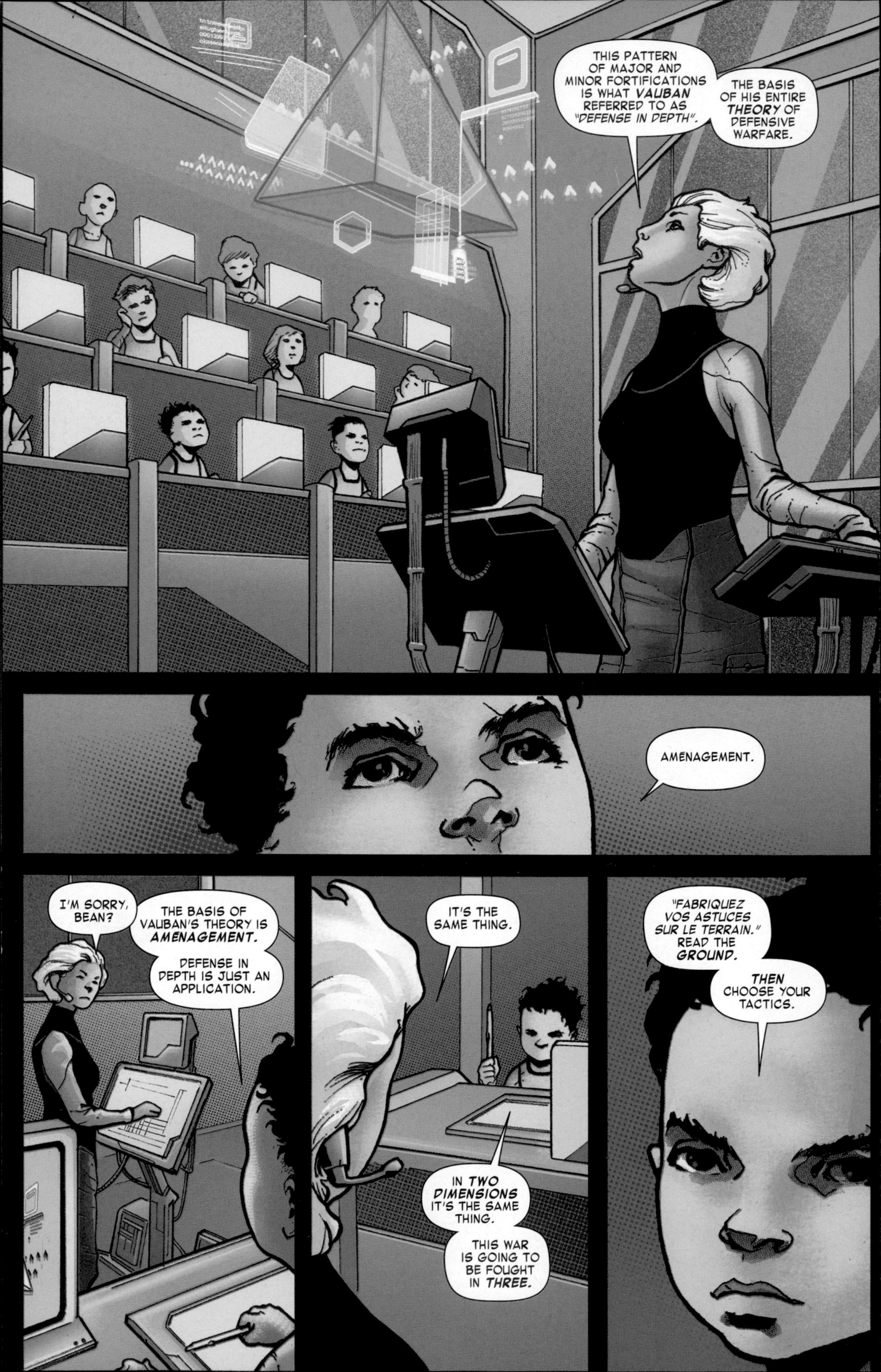

THIS PATTERN OF MAJOR AND MINOR FORTIFICATIONS IS WHAT VAUBAN REFERRED TO AS "DEFENSE IN DEPTH".
THE BASIS OF HIS ENTIRE THEORY OF DEFENSIVE WARFARE.
AMENAGEMENT.
I'M SORRY, BEAN?
THE BASIS OF VAUBAN'S THEORY IS AMENAGEMENT.
DEFENSE IN DEPTH IS JUST AN APPLICATION.
IT'S THE SAME THING.
IN TWO DIMENSIONS IT'S THE SAME THING.
THIS WAR IS GOING TO BE FOUGHT IN THREE.
"FABRIQUEZ VOS ASTUCES SUR LE TERRAIN." READ THE GROUND.
THEN CHOOSE YOUR TACTICS.

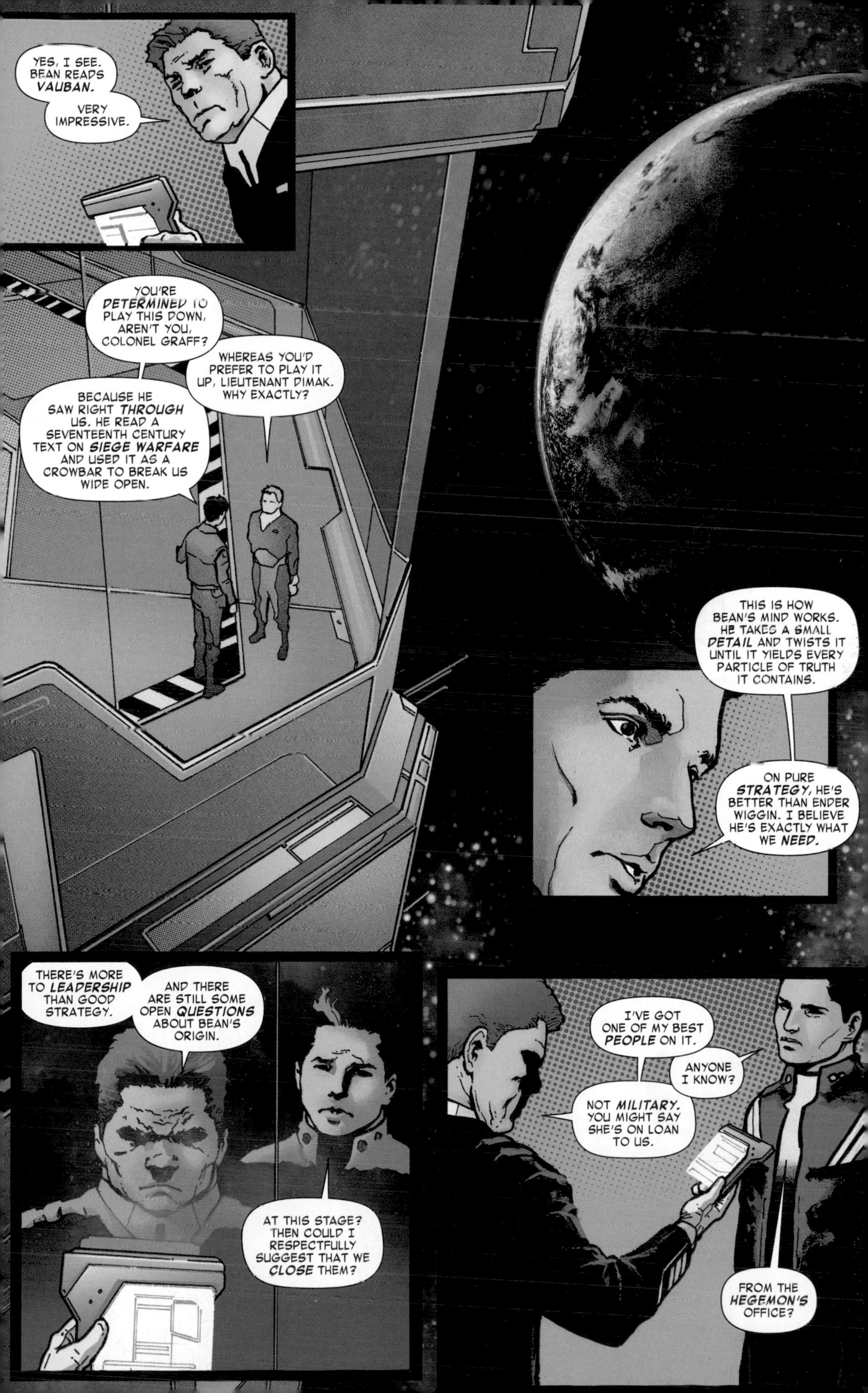

YES, I SEE. BEAN READS VAUBAN.
VERY IMPRESSIVE.
YOU'RE DETERMINED TO PLAY THIS DOWN, AREN'T YOU, COLONEL GRAFF?
WHEREAS YOU'D PREFER TO PLAY IT UP, LIEUTENANT DIMAK. WHY EXACTLY?
BECAUSE HE SAW RIGHT THROUGH US. HE READ A SEVENTEENTH CENTURY TEXT ON SIEGE WARFARE AND USED IT AS A CROWBAR TO BREAK US WIDE OPEN.
THIS IS HOW BEAN'S MIND WORKS. HE TAKES A SMALL DETAIL AND TWISTS IT UNTIL IT YIELDS EVERY PARTICLE OF TRUTH IT CONTAINS.
ON PURE STRATEGY, HE'S BETTER THAN ENDER WIGGIN. I BELIEVE HE'S EXACTLY WHAT WE NEED.
THERE'S MORE TO LEADERSHIP THAN GOOD STRATEGY.
AND THERE ARE STILL SOME OPEN QUESTIONS ABOUT BEAN'S ORIGIN.
AT THIS STAGE? THEN COULD I RESPECTFULLY SUGGEST THAT WE CLOSE THEM?
I'VE GOT ONE OF MY BEST PEOPLE ON IT.
ANYONE I KNOW?
NOT MILITARY. YOU MIGHT SAY SHE'S ON LOAN TO US.
FROM THE HEGEMON'S OFFICE?

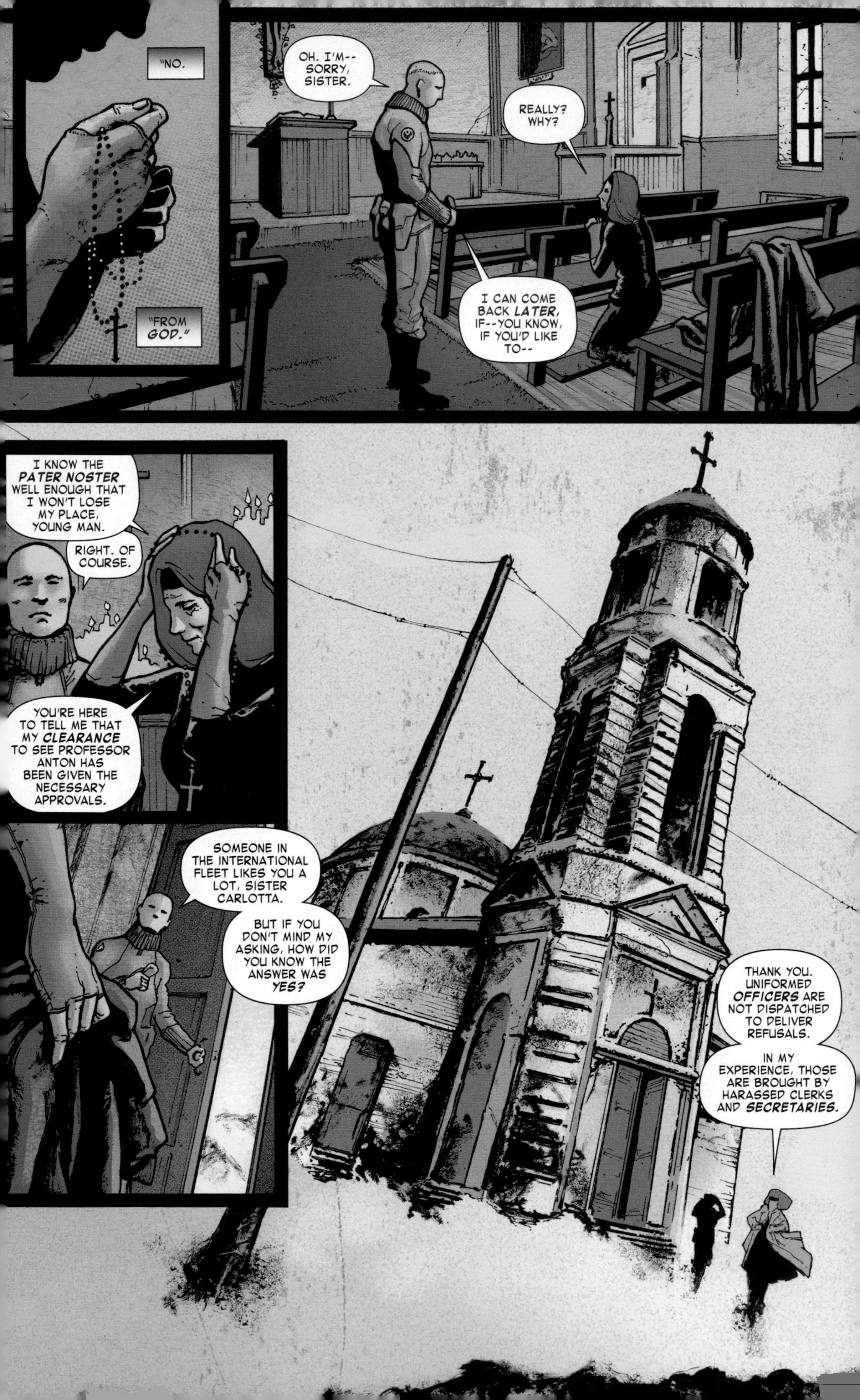
"NO.
"FROM GOD."
OH. I'M-- SORRY, SISTER.
REALLY? WHY?
I CAN COME BACK LATER, IF--YOU KNOW, IF YOU'D LIKE TO--
I KNOW THE PATER NOSTER WELL ENOUGH THAT I WON'T LOSE MY PLACE, YOUNG MAN.
RIGHT. OF COURSE.
YOU'RE HERE TO TELL ME THAT MY CLEARANCE TO SEE PROFESSOR ANTON HAS BEEN GIVEN THE NECESSARY APPROVALS.
SOMEONE IN THE INTERNATIONAL FLEET LIKES YOU A LOT, SISTER CARLOTTA.
BUT IF YOU DON'T MIND MY ASKING, HOW DID YOU KNOW THE ANSWER WAS YES?
THANK YOU. UNIFORMED OFFICERS ARE NOT DISPATCHED TO DELIVER REFUSALS.
IN MY EXPERIENCE, THOSE ARE BROUGHT BY HARASSED CLERKS AND SECRETARIES.

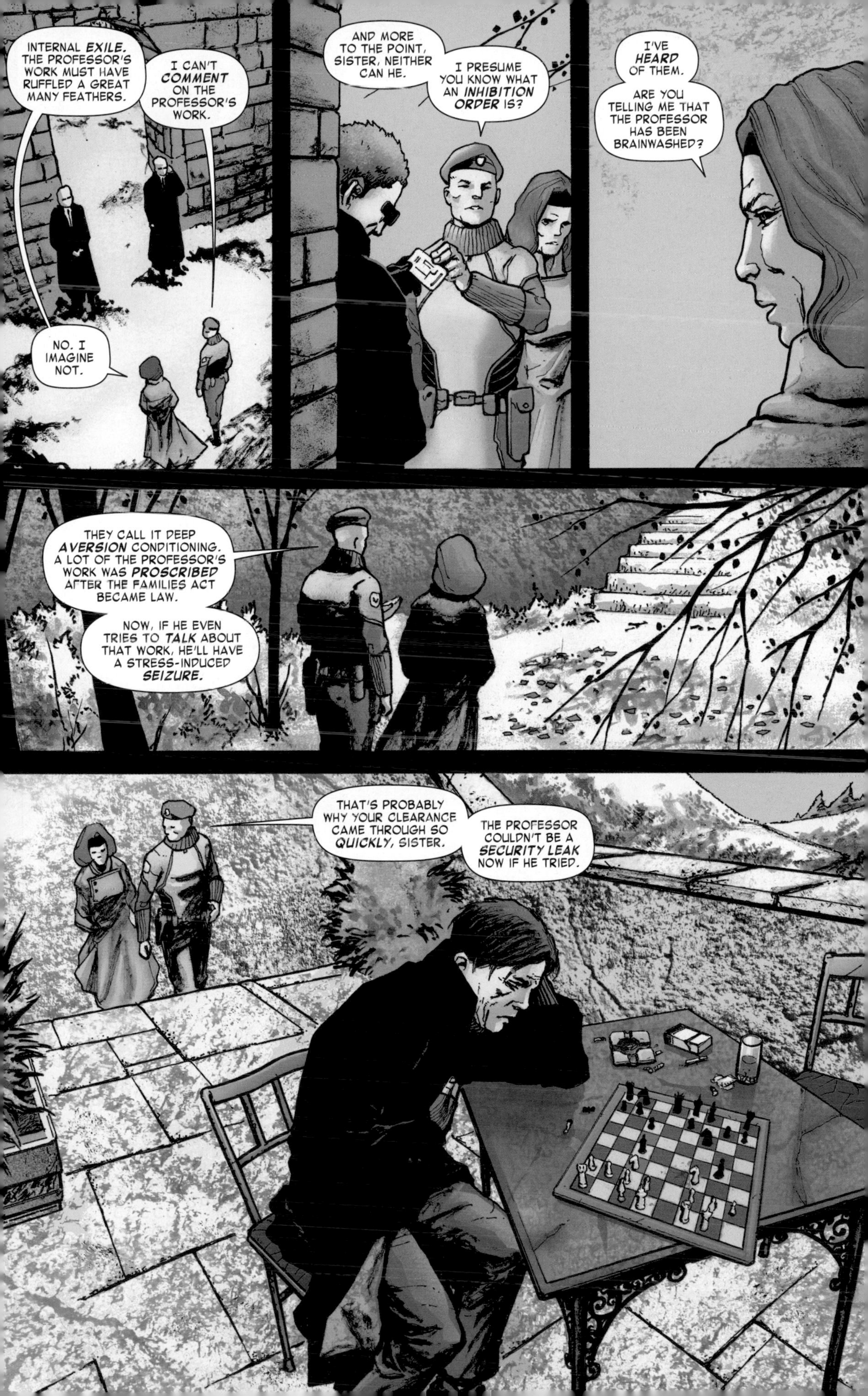
INTERNAL EXILE. THE PROFESSOR'S WORK MUST HAVE RUFFLED A GREAT MANY FEATHERS.
I CAN'T COMMENT ON THE PROFESSOR'S WORK.
NO. I IMAGINE NOT.
AND MORE TO THE POINT, SISTER, NEITHER CAN HE.
I PRESUME YOU KNOW WHAT AN INHIBITION ORDER IS?
I'VE HEARD OF THEM.
ARE YOU TELLING ME THAT THE PROFESSOR HAS BEEN BRAINWASHED?
THEY CALL IT DEEP AVERSION CONDITIONING. A LOT OF THE PROFESSOR'S WORK WAS PROSCRIBED AFTER THE FAMILIES ACT BECAME LAW.
NOW, IF HE EVEN TRIES TO TALK ABOUT THAT WORK, HE'LL HAVE A STRESS-INDUCED SEIZURE.
THAT'S PROBABLY WHY YOUR CLEARANCE CAME THROUGH SO QUICKLY, SISTER.
THE PROFESSOR COULDN'T BE A SECURITY LEAK NOW IF HE TRIED.

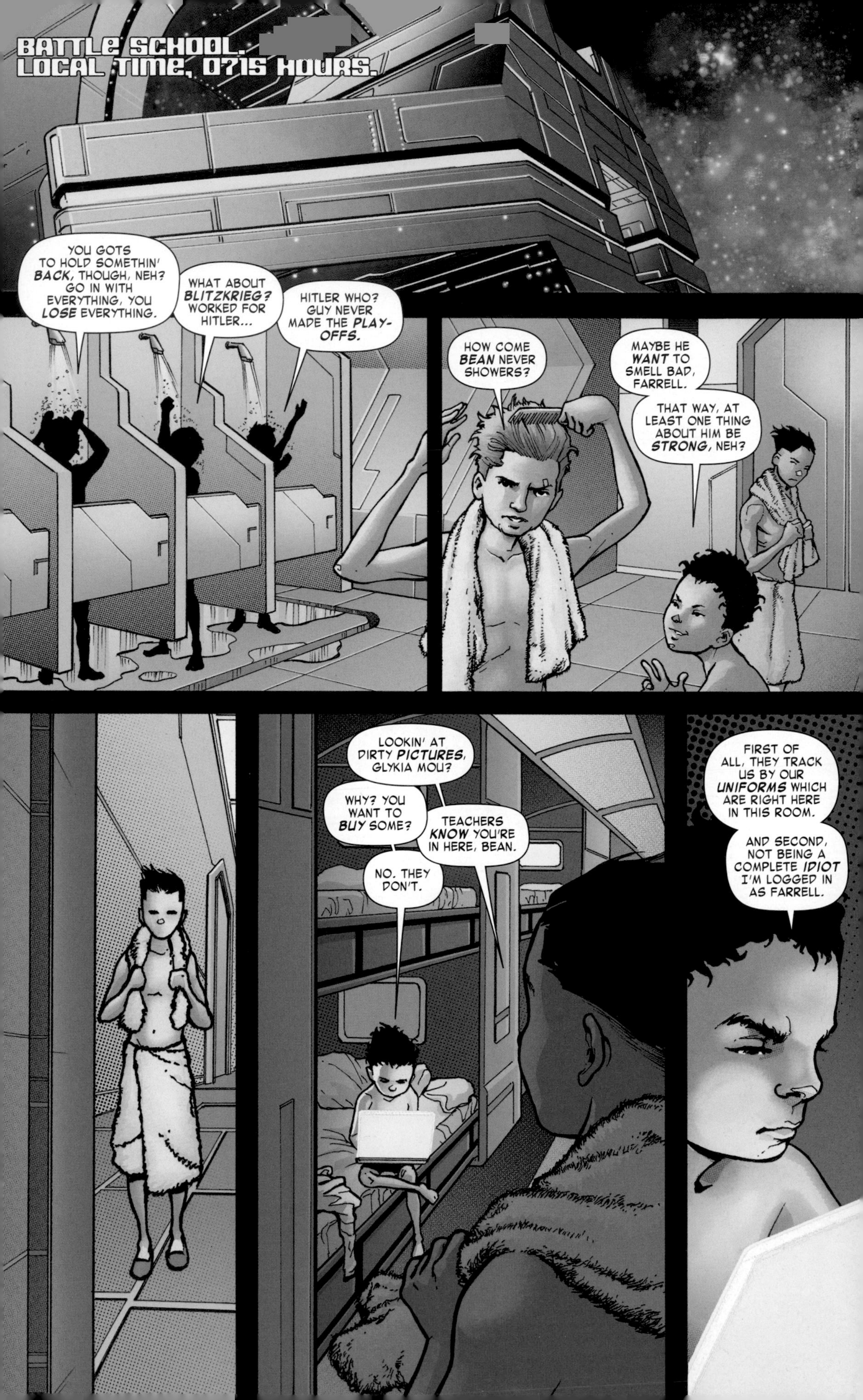
BATTLE SCHOOL.
LOCAL TIME, 0715 HOURS.
YOU GOTS TO HOLD SOMETHIN' BACK, THOUGH, NEH? GO IN WITH EVERYTHING, YOU LOSE EVERYTHING.
WHAT ABOUT BLITZKRIEG? WORKED FOR HITLER...
HITLER WHO? GUY NEVER MADE THE PLAY-OFFS.
HOW COME BEAN NEVER SHOWERS?
MAYBE HE WANT TO SMELL BAD, FARRELL.
THAT WAY, AT LEAST ONE THING ABOUT HIM BE STRONG, NEH?
LOOKIN' AT DIRTY PICTURES, GLYKIA MOU?
WHY? YOU WANT TO BUY SOME?
TEACHERS KNOW YOU'RE IN HERE, BEAN.
NO. THEY DON'T.
FIRST OF ALL, THEY TRACK US BY OUR UNIFORMS WHICH ARE RIGHT HERE IN THIS ROOM.
AND SECOND, NOT BEING A COMPLETE IDIOT I'M LOGGED IN AS FARRELL.

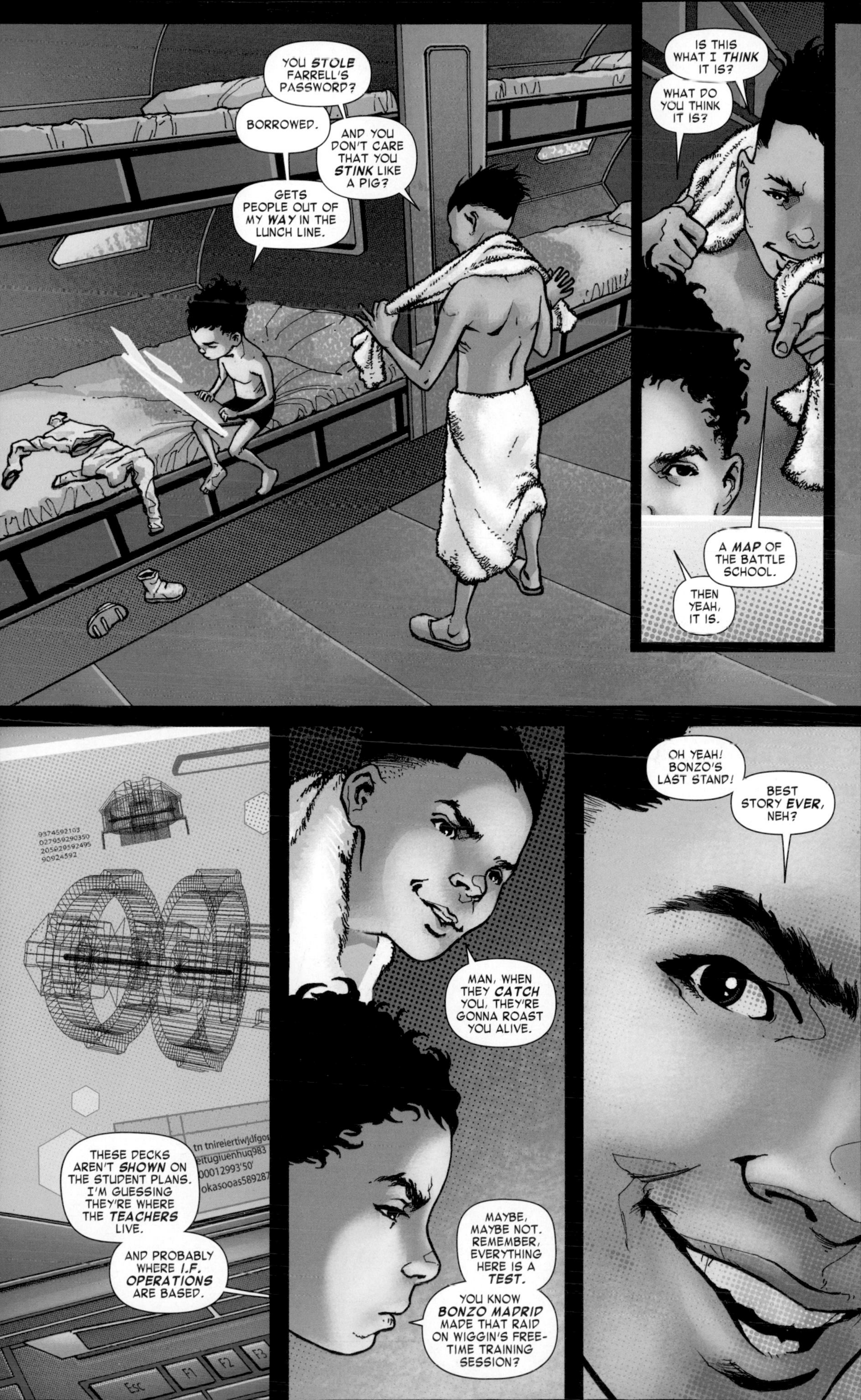

YOU STOLE FARRELL'S PASSWORD?
BORROWED.
AND YOU DON'T CARE THAT YOU STINK LIKE A PIG?
GETS PEOPLE OUT OF MY WAY IN THE LUNCH LINE.
IS THIS WHAT I THINK IT IS?
WHAT DO YOU THINK IT IS?
A MAP OF THE BATTLE SCHOOL.
THEN YEAH, IT IS.
THESE DECKS AREN'T SHOWN ON THE STUDENT PLANS. I'M GUESSING THEY'RE WHERE THE TEACHERS LIVE.
AND PROBABLY WHERE I.F. OPERATIONS ARE BASED.
MAN, WHEN THEY CATCH YOU, THEY'RE GONNA ROAST YOU ALIVE.
MAYBE, MAYBE NOT. REMEMBER, EVERYTHING HERE IS A TEST.
YOU KNOW BONZO MADRID MADE THAT RAID ON WIGGIN'S FREE-TIME TRAINING SESSION?
OH YEAH! BONZO'S LAST STAND!
BEST STORY EVER, NEH?

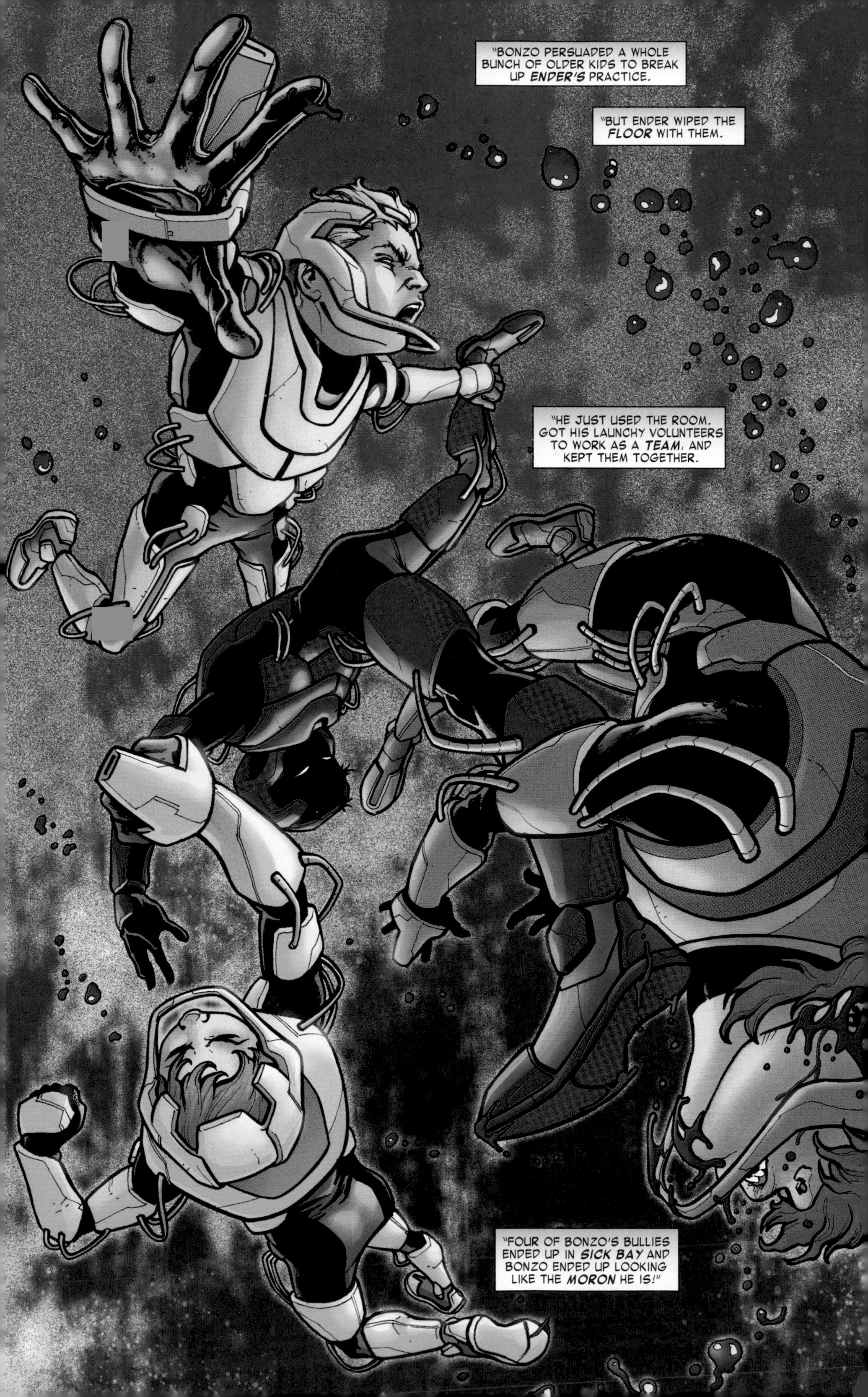
"BONZO PERSUADED A WHOLE BUNCH OF OLDER KIDS TO BREAK UP ENDER'S PRACTICE.
"BUT ENDER WIPED THE FLOOR WITH THEM.
"HE JUST USED THE ROOM. GOT HIS LAUNCHY VOLUNTEERS TO WORK AS A TEAM, AND KEPT THEM TOGETHER.
"FOUR OF BONZO'S BULLIES ENDED UP IN SICK BAY AND BONZO ENDED UP LOOKING LIKE THE MORON HE IS!"

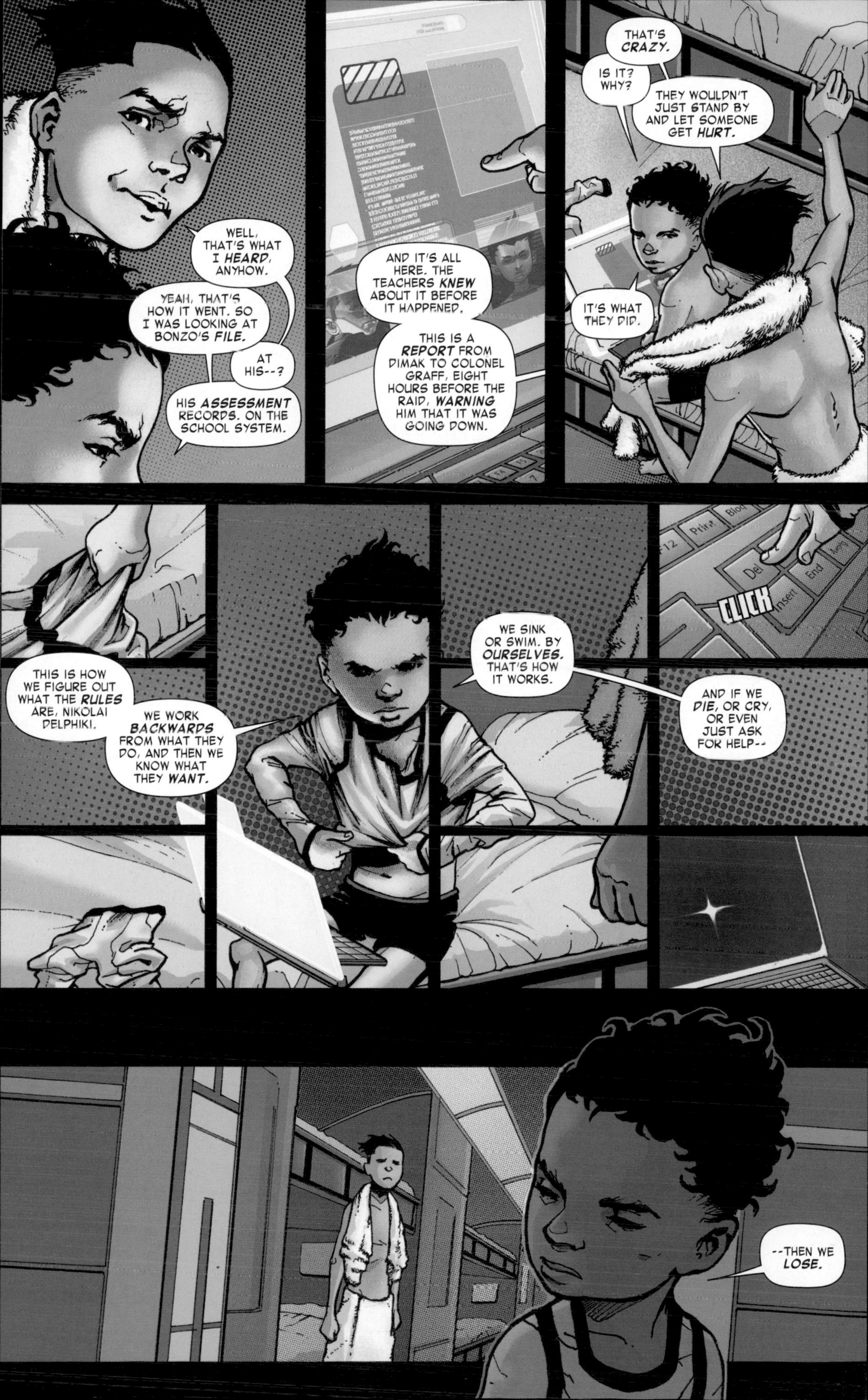
WELL, THAT'S WHAT I HEARD, ANYHOW.
YEAH, THAT'S HOW IT WENT. SO I WAS LOOKING AT BONZO'S FILE.
AT HIS--?
HIS ASSESSMENT RECORDS. ON THE SCHOOL SYSTEM.
AND IT'S ALL HERE. THE TEACHERS KNEW ABOUT IT BEFORE IT HAPPENED.
THIS IS A REPORT FROM DIMAK TO COLONEL GRAFF, EIGHT HOURS BEFORE THE RAID, WARNING HIM THAT IT WAS GOING DOWN.
THAT'S CRAZY.
IS IT? WHY?
THEY WOULDN'T JUST STAND BY AND LET SOMEONE GET HURT.
IT'S WHAT THEY DID.
CLICK
THIS IS HOW WE FIGURE OUT WHAT THE RULES ARE, NIKOLAI DELPHIKI.
WE WORK BACKWARDS FROM WHAT THEY DO, AND THEN WE KNOW WHAT THEY WANT.
WE SINK OR SWIM. BY OURSELVES. THAT'S HOW IT WORKS.
AND IF WE DIE, OR CRY, OR EVEN JUST ASK FOR HELP--
--THEN WE LOSE.

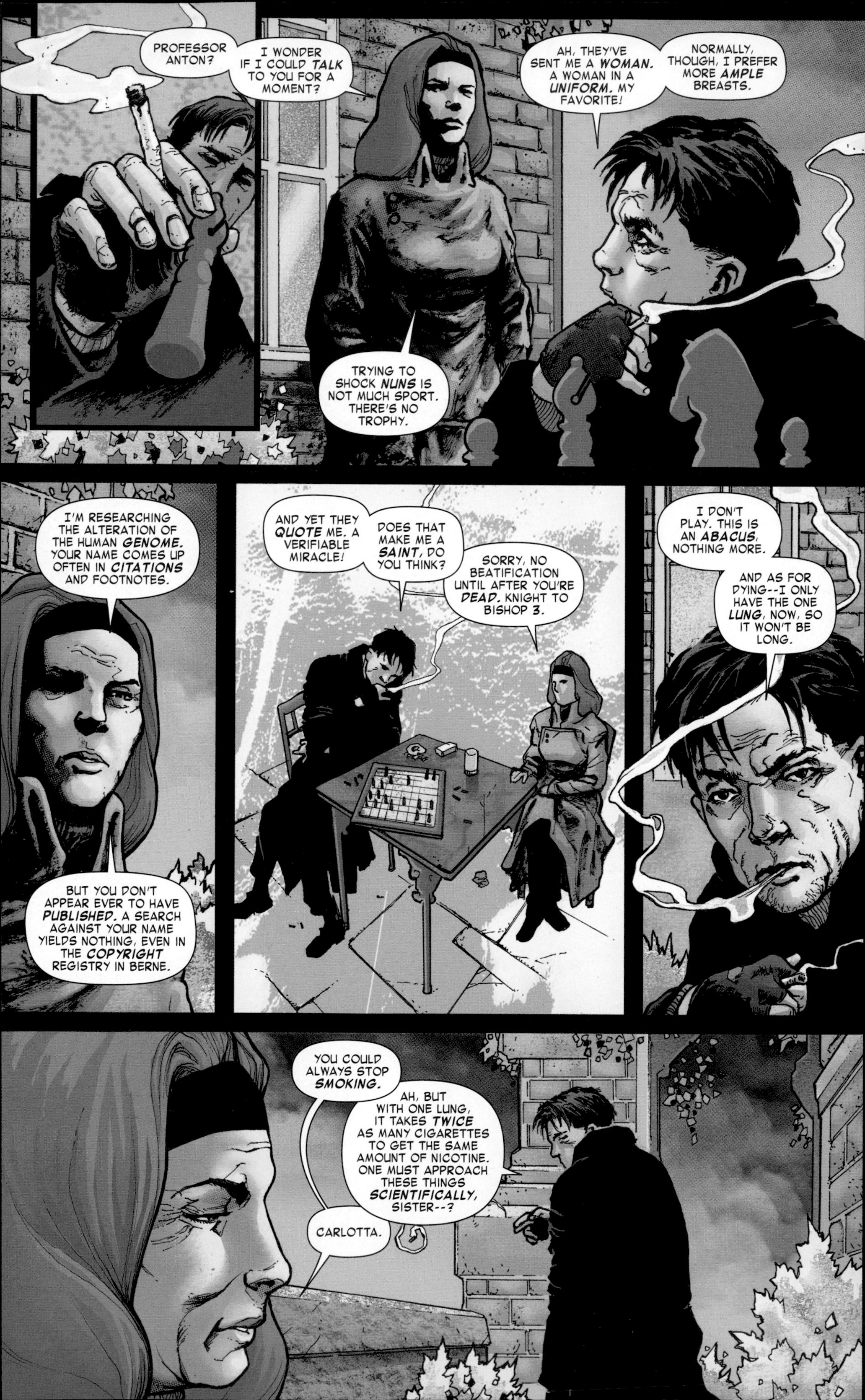
PROFESSOR ANTON?
I WONDER IF I COULD TALK TO YOU FOR A MOMENT?
AH, THEY'VE SENT ME A WOMAN. A WOMAN IN A UNIFORM. MY FAVORITE!
NORMALLY, THOUGH, I PREFER MORE AMPLE BREASTS.
TRYING TO SHOCK NUNS IS NOT MUCH SPORT. THERE'S NO TROPHY.
I'M RESEARCHING THE ALTERATION OF THE HUMAN GENOME. YOUR NAME COMES UP OFTEN IN CITATIONS AND FOOTNOTES.
BUT YOU DON'T APPEAR EVER TO HAVE PUBLISHED. A SEARCH AGAINST YOUR NAME YIELDS NOTHING, EVEN IN THE COPYRIGHT REGISTRY IN BERNE.
AND YET THEY QUOTE ME. A VERIFIABLE MIRACLE!
DOES THAT MAKE ME A SAINT, DO YOU THINK?
SORRY, NO BEATIFICATION UNTIL AFTER YOU'RE DEAD. KNIGHT TO BISHOP 3.
I DON'T PLAY. THIS IS AN ABACUS, NOTHING MORE.
AND AS FOR DYING--I ONLY HAVE THE ONE LUNG, NOW, SO IT WON'T BE LONG.
YOU COULD ALWAYS STOP SMOKING.
AH, BUT WITH ONE LUNG, IT TAKES TWICE AS MANY CIGARETTES TO GET THE SAME AMOUNT OF NICOTINE. ONE MUST APPROACH THESE THINGS SCIENTIFICALLY, SISTER--?
CARLOTTA.

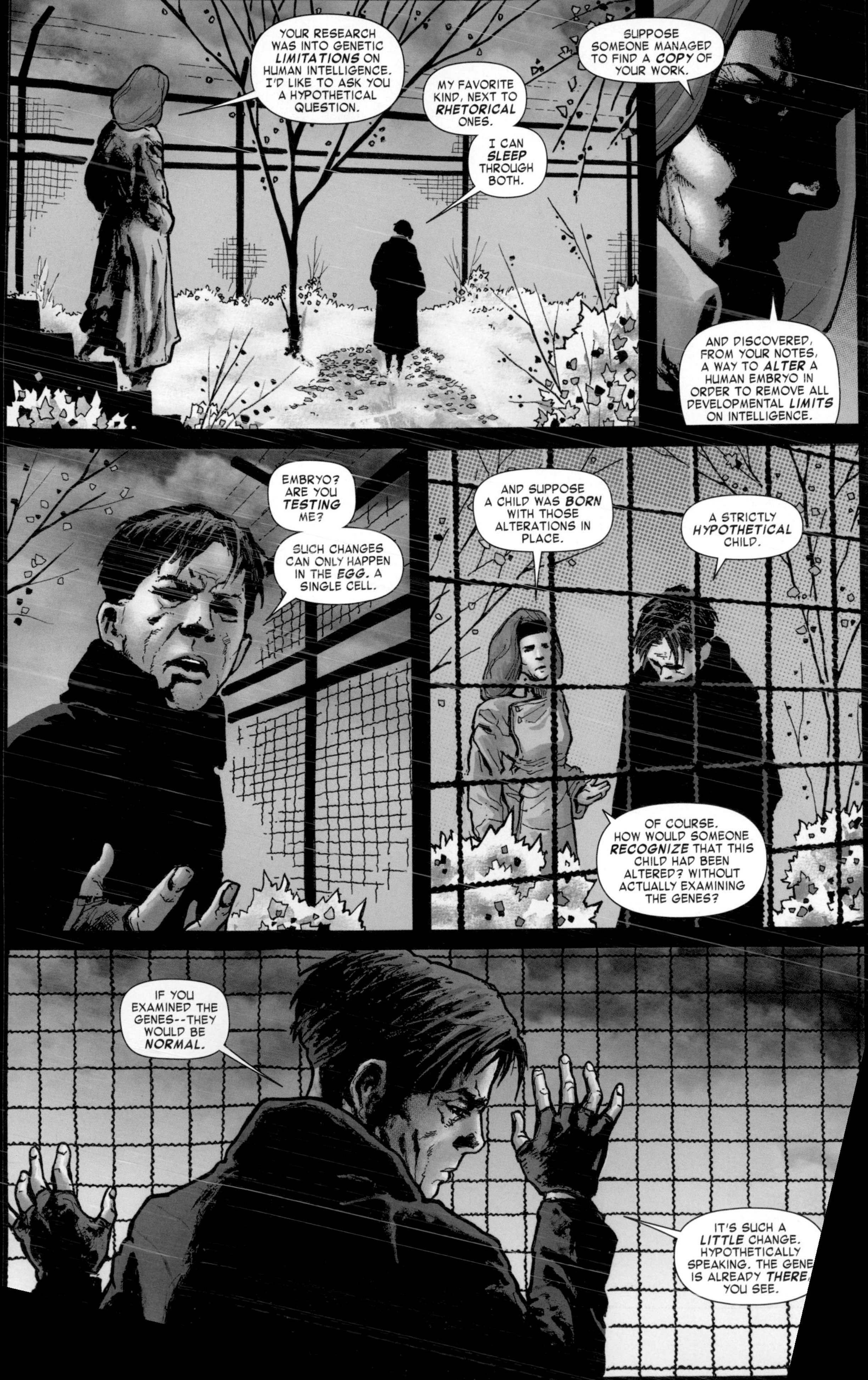
YOUR RESEARCH WAS INTO GENETIC LIMITATIONS ON HUMAN INTELLIGENCE. I'D LIKE TO ASK YOU A HYPOTHETICAL QUESTION.
MY FAVORITE KIND, NEXT TO RHETORICAL ONES.
I CAN SLEEP THROUGH BOTH.
SUPPOSE SOMEONE MANAGED TO FIND A COPY OF YOUR WORK.
AND DISCOVERED, FROM YOUR NOTES, A WAY TO ALTER A HUMAN EMBRYO IN ORDER TO REMOVE ALL DEVELOPMENTAL LIMITS ON INTELLIGENCE.
EMBRYO? ARE YOU TESTING ME?
SUCH CHANGES CAN ONLY HAPPEN IN THE EGG. A SINGLE CELL.
AND SUPPOSE A CHILD WAS BORN WITH THOSE ALTERATIONS IN PLACE.
A STRICTLY HYPOTHETICAL CHILD.
OF COURSE. HOW WOULD SOMEONE RECOGNIZE THAT THIS CHILD HAD BEEN ALTERED? WITHOUT ACTUALLY EXAMINING THE GENES?
IF YOU EXAMINED THE GENES--THEY WOULD BE NORMAL.
IT'S SUCH A LITTLE CHANGE. HYPOTHETICALLY SPEAKING. THE GENE IS ALREADY THERE, YOU SEE.

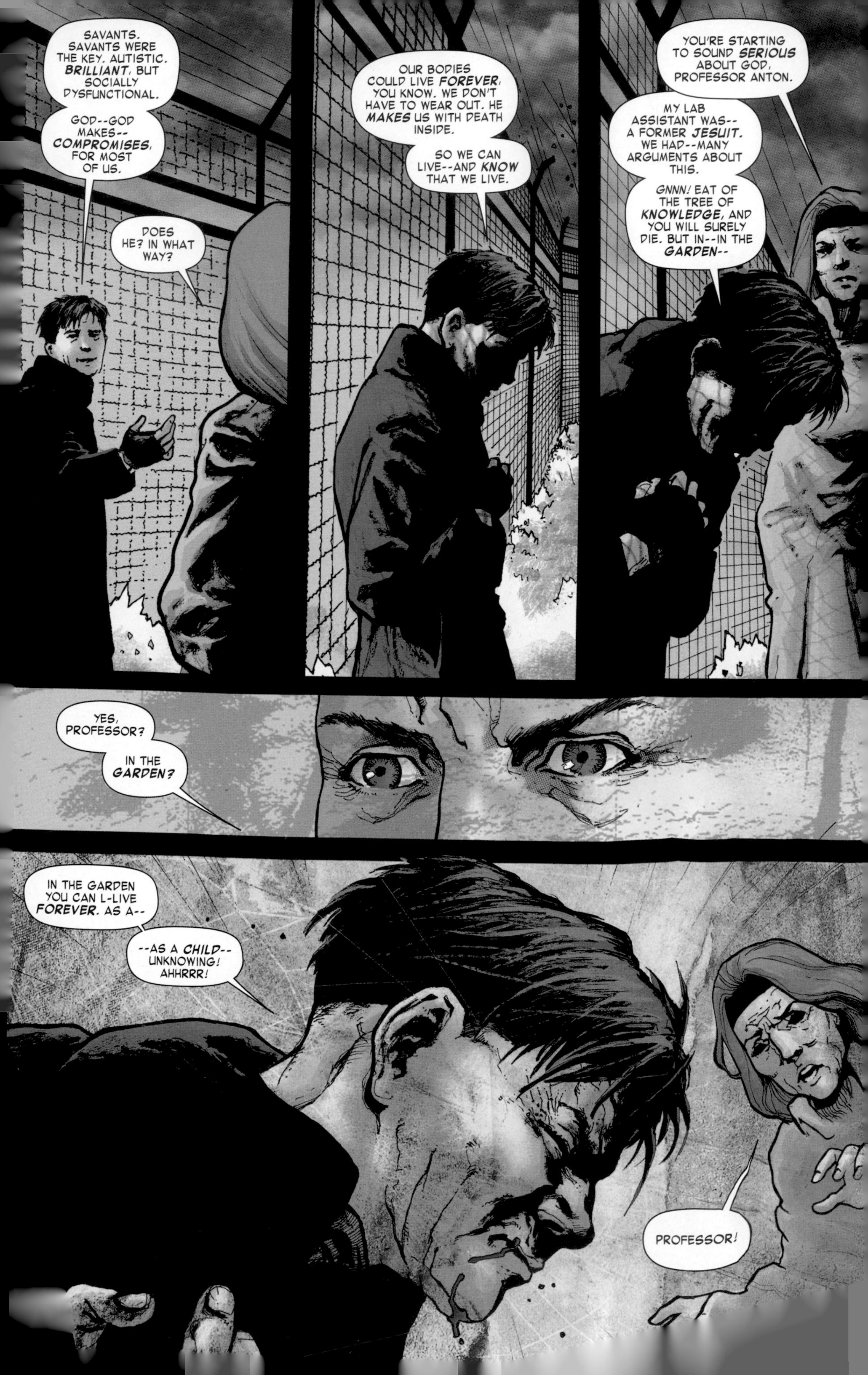
SAVANTS. SAVANTS WERE THE KEY. AUTISTIC. BRILLIANT, BUT SOCIALLY DYSFUNCTIONAL.
GOD--GOD MAKES-- COMPROMISES, FOR MOST OF US.
DOES HE? IN WHAT WAY?
OUR BODIES COULD LIVE FOREVER, YOU KNOW. WE DON'T HAVE TO WEAR OUT. HE MAKES US WITH DEATH INSIDE.
SO WE CAN LIVE--AND KNOW THAT WE LIVE.
YOU'RE STARTING TO SOUND SERIOUS ABOUT GOD, PROFESSOR ANTON.
MY LAB ASSISTANT WAS-- A FORMER JESUIT. WE HAD--MANY ARGUMENTS ABOUT THIS.
GNNN! EAT OF THE TREE OF KNOWLEDGE, AND YOU WILL SURELY DIE. BUT IN--IN THE GARDEN--
YES, PROFESSOR?
IN THE GARDEN?
IN THE GARDEN YOU CAN L-LIVE FOREVER. AS A--
--AS A CHILD-- UNKNOWING! AHHRRR!
PROFESSOR!

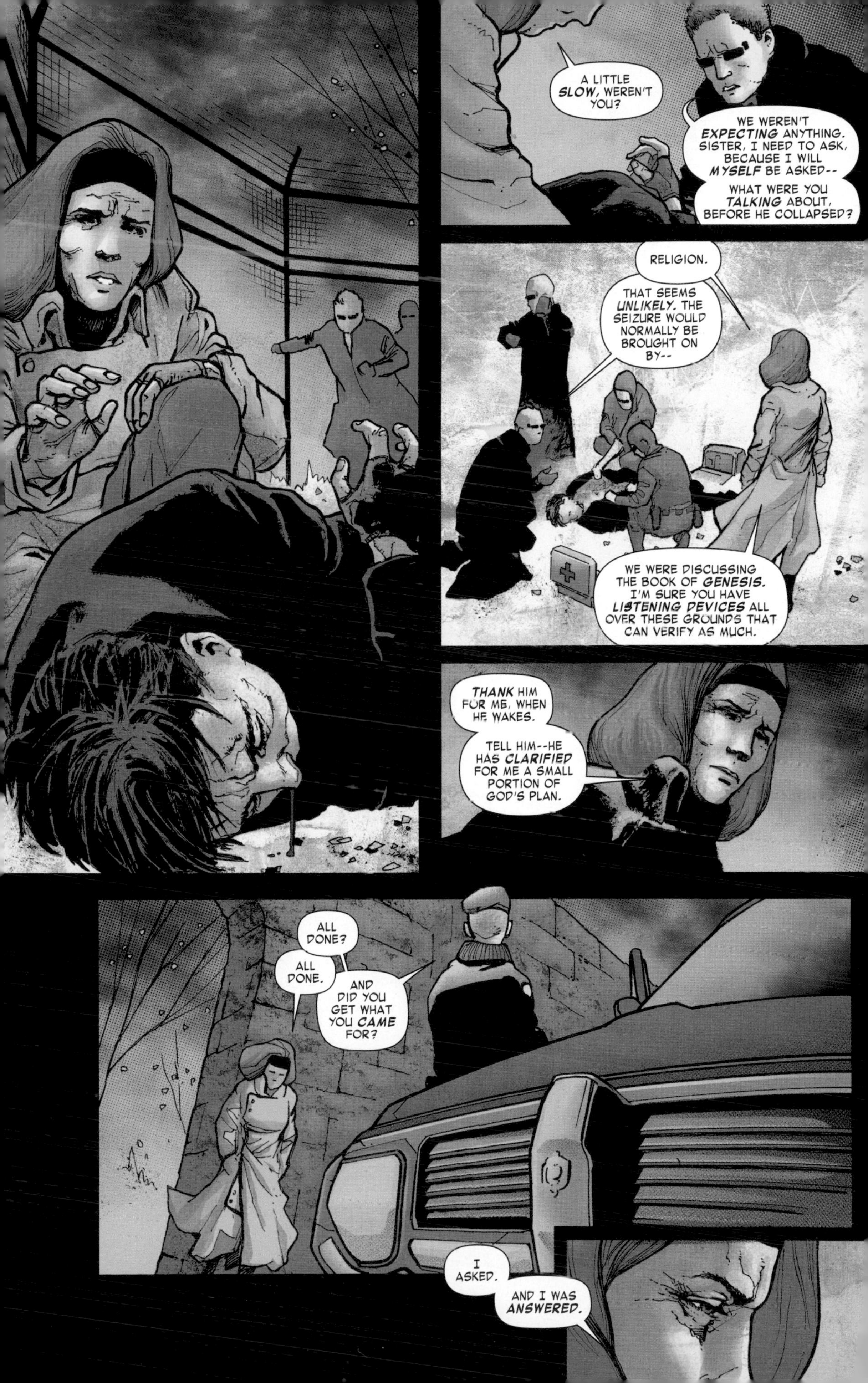

A LITTLE SLOW, WEREN'T YOU?
WE WEREN'T EXPECTING ANYTHING. SISTER, I NEED TO ASK, BECAUSE I WILL MYSELF BE ASKED--
WHAT WERE YOU TALKING ABOUT, BEFORE HE COLLAPSED?
RELIGION.
THAT SEEMS UNLIKELY. THE SEIZURE WOULD NORMALLY BE BROUGHT ON BY--
WE WERE DISCUSSING THE BOOK OF GENESIS. I'M SURE YOU HAVE LISTENING DEVICES ALL OVER THESE GROUNDS THAT CAN VERIFY AS MUCH.
THANK HIM FOR ME, WHEN HE WAKES.
TELL HIM--HE HAS CLARIFIED FOR ME A SMALL PORTION OF GOD'S PLAN.
ALL DONE?
ALL DONE.
AND DID YOU GET WHAT YOU CAME FOR?
I ASKED.
AND I WAS ANSWERED.

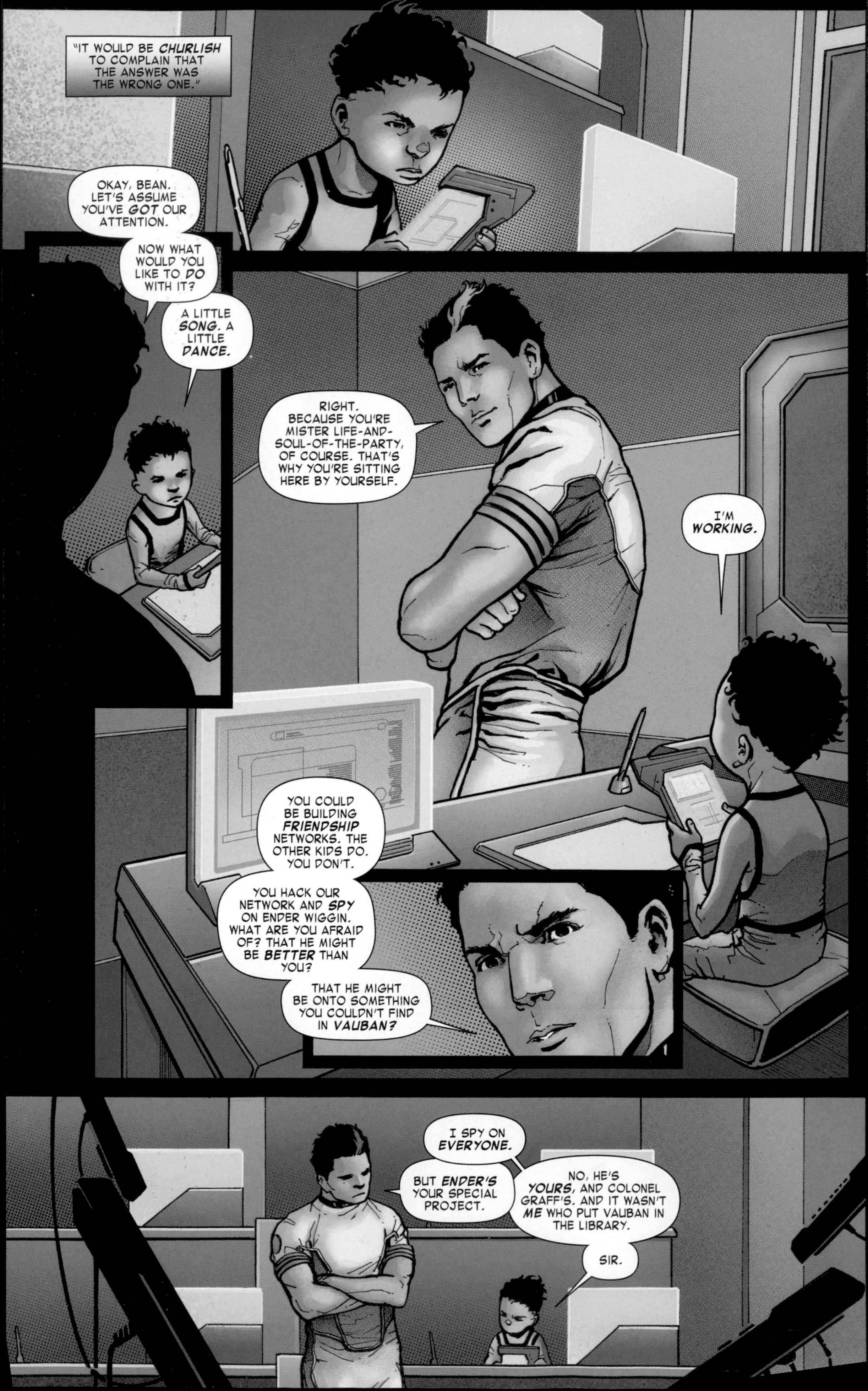
"IT WOULD BE CHURLISH TO COMPLAIN THAT THE ANSWER WAS THE WRONG ONE."
OKAY, BEAN. LET'S ASSUME YOU'VE GOT OUR ATTENTION.
NOW WHAT WOULD YOU LIKE TO DO WITH IT?
A LITTLE SONG. A LITTLE DANCE.
RIGHT. BECAUSE YOU'RE MISTER LIFE-AND-SOUL-OF-THE-PARTY, OF COURSE. THAT'S WHY YOU'RE SITTING HERE BY YOURSELF.
I'M WORKING.
YOU COULD BE BUILDING FRIENDSHIP NETWORKS. THE OTHER KIDS DO. YOU DON'T.
YOU HACK OUR NETWORK AND SPY ON ENDER WIGGIN. WHAT ARE YOU AFRAID OF? THAT HE MIGHT BE BETTER THAN YOU?
THAT HE MIGHT BE ONTO SOMETHING YOU COULDN'T FIND IN VAUBAN?
I SPY ON EVERYONE.
BUT ENDER'S YOUR SPECIAL PROJECT.
NO, HE'S YOURS, AND COLONEL GRAFF'S. AND IT WASN'T ME WHO PUT VAUBAN IN THE LIBRARY.
SIR.

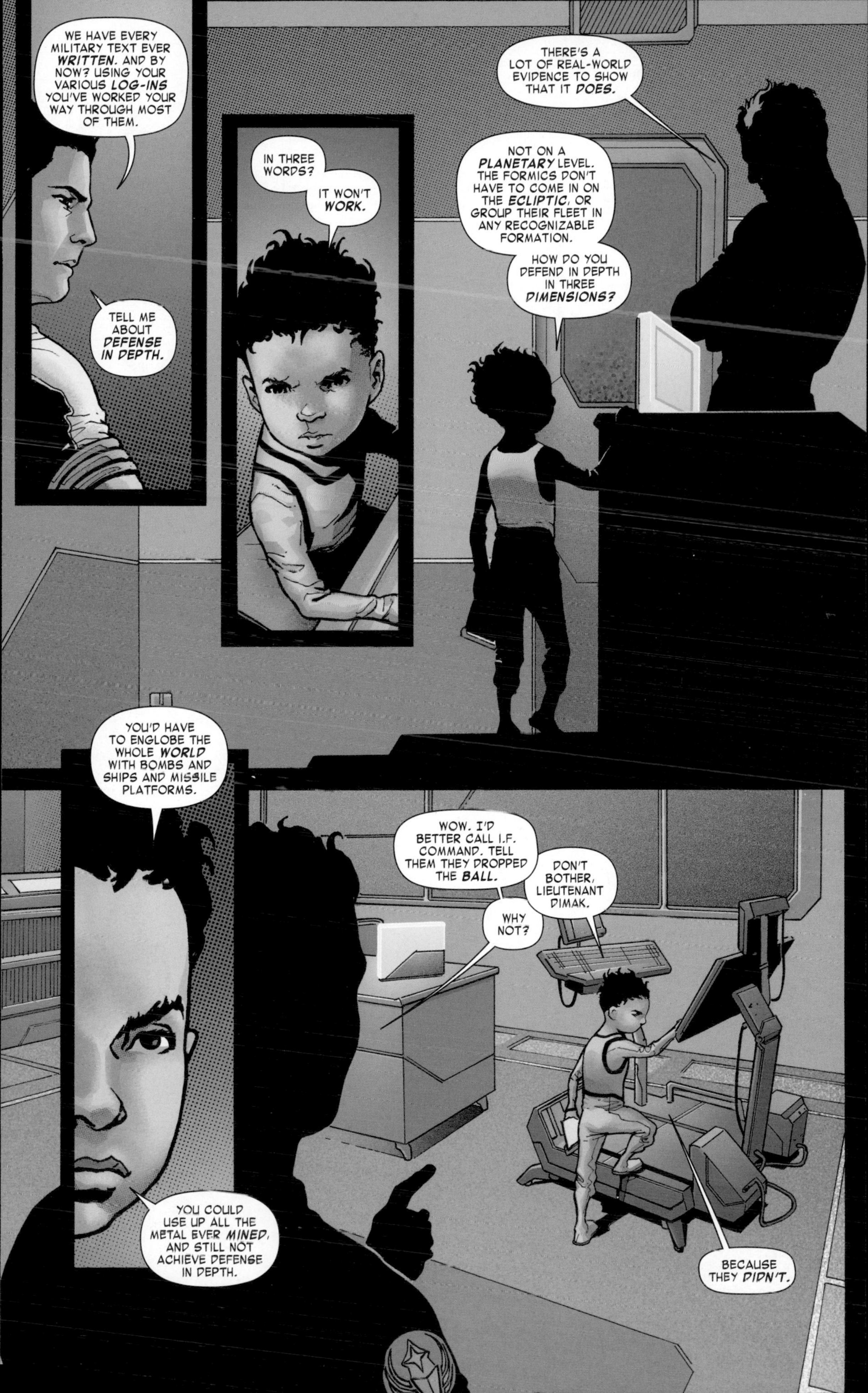
WE HAVE EVERY MILITARY TEXT EVER WRITTEN. AND BY NOW? USING YOUR VARIOUS LOG-INS YOU'VE WORKED YOUR WAY THROUGH MOST OF THEM.
TELL ME ABOUT DEFENSE IN DEPTH.
IN THREE WORDS?
IT WON'T WORK.
THERE'S A LOT OF REAL-WORLD EVIDENCE TO SHOW THAT IT DOES.
NOT ON A PLANETARY LEVEL. THE FORMICS DON'T HAVE TO COME IN ON THE ECLIPTIC, OR GROUP THEIR FLEET IN ANY RECOGNIZABLE FORMATION.
HOW DO YOU DEFEND IN DEPTH IN THREE DIMENSIONS?
YOU'D HAVE TO ENGLOBE THE WHOLE WORLD WITH BOMBS AND SHIPS AND MISSILE PLATFORMS.
YOU COULD USE UP ALL THE METAL EVER MINED, AND STILL NOT ACHIEVE DEFENSE IN DEPTH.
WOW. I'D BETTER CALL I.F. COMMAND. TELL THEM THEY DROPPED THE BALL.
DON'T BOTHER, LIEUTENANT DIMAK.
WHY NOT?
BECAUSE THEY DIDN'T.

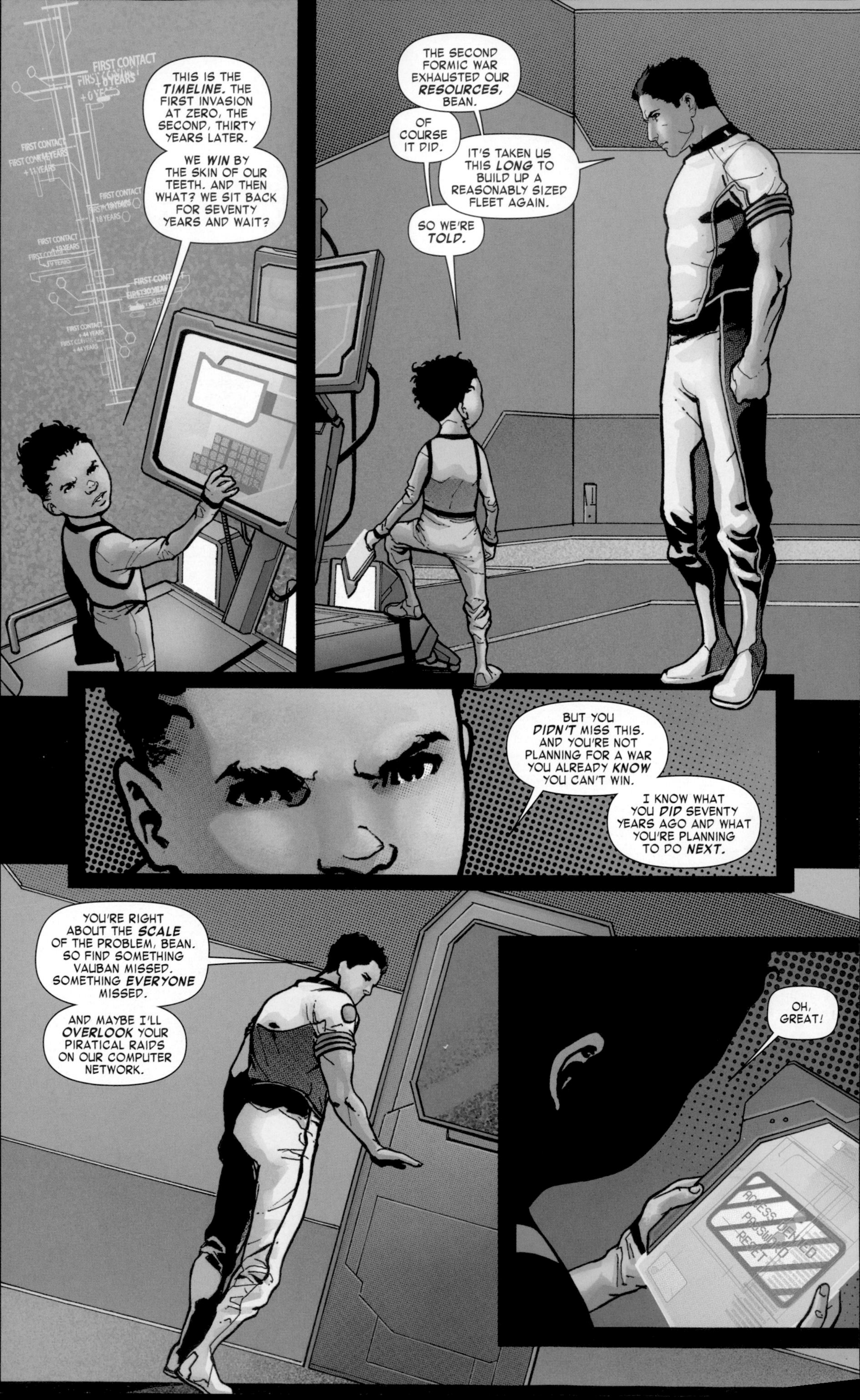
FIRST CONTACT
THIS IS THE TIMELINE. THE FIRST INVASION AT ZERO, THE SECOND, THIRTY YEARS LATER.
WE WIN BY THE SKIN OF OUR TEETH. AND THEN WHAT? WE SIT BACK FOR SEVENTY YEARS AND WAIT?
THE SECOND FORMIC WAR EXHAUSTED OUR RESOURCES, BEAN.
OF COURSE IT DID.
IT'S TAKEN US THIS LONG TO BUILD UP A REASONABLY SIZED FLEET AGAIN.
SO WE'RE TOLD.
BUT YOU DIDN'T MISS THIS. AND YOU'RE NOT PLANNING FOR A WAR YOU ALREADY KNOW YOU CAN'T WIN.
I KNOW WHAT YOU DID SEVENTY YEARS AGO AND WHAT YOU'RE PLANNING TO DO NEXT.
YOU'RE RIGHT ABOUT THE SCALE OF THE PROBLEM, BEAN. SO FIND SOMETHING VAUBAN MISSED. SOMETHING EVERYONE MISSED.
AND MAYBE I'LL OVERLOOK YOUR PIRATICAL RAIDS ON OUR COMPUTER NETWORK.
OH, GREAT!

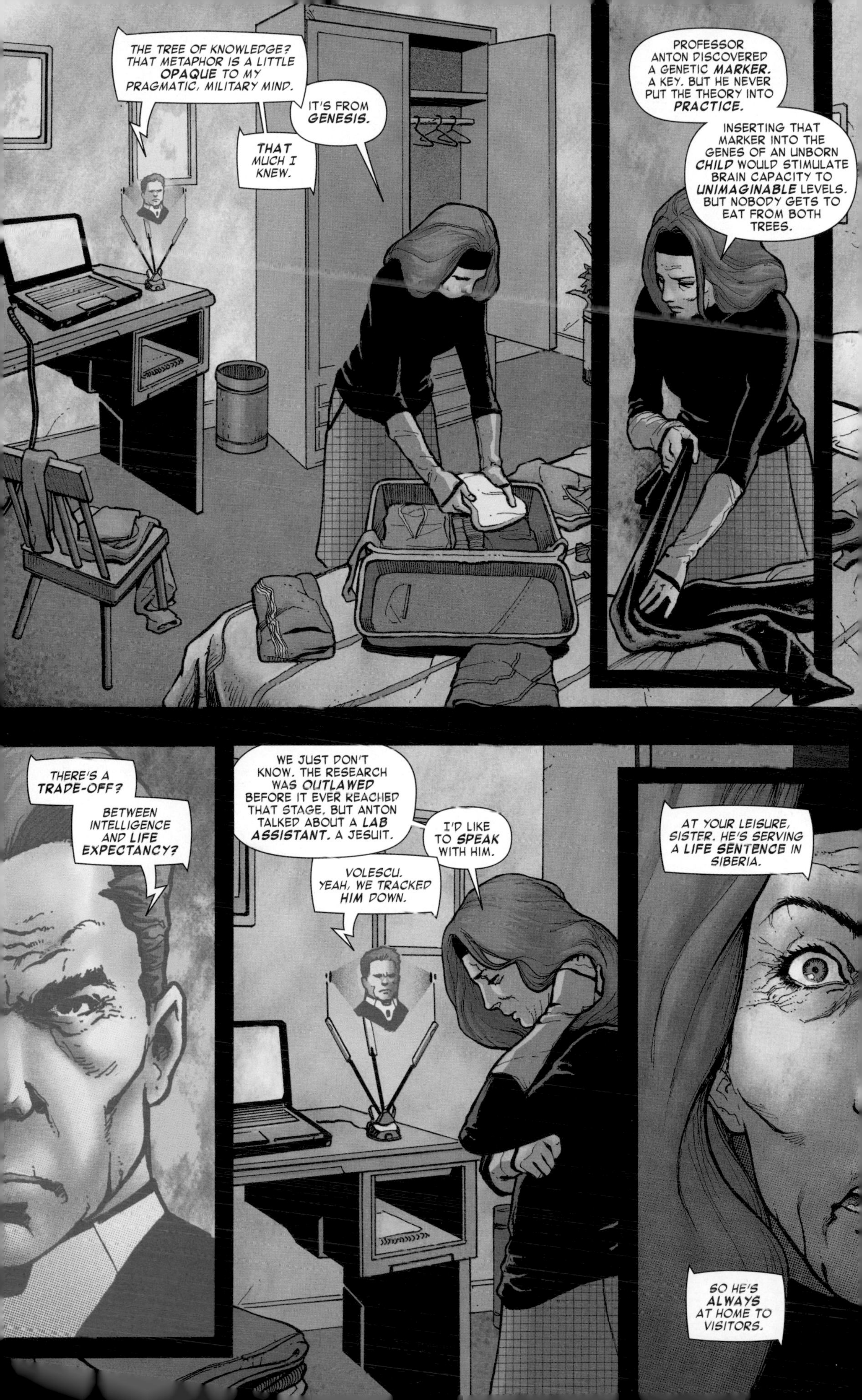
THE TREE OF KNOWLEDGE? THAT METAPHOR IS A LITTLE OPAQUE TO MY PRAGMATIC, MILITARY MIND.
IT'S FROM GENESIS.
THAT MUCH I KNEW.
PROFESSOR ANTON DISCOVERED A GENETIC MARKER. A KEY. BUT HE NEVER PUT THE THEORY INTO PRACTICE.
INSERTING THAT MARKER INTO THE GENES OF AN UNBORN CHILD WOULD STIMULATE BRAIN CAPACITY TO UNIMAGINABLE LEVELS. BUT NOBODY GETS TO EAT FROM BOTH TREES.
THERE'S A TRADE-OFF?
BETWEEN INTELLIGENCE AND LIFE EXPECTANCY?
WE JUST DON'T KNOW. THE RESEARCH WAS OUTLAWED BEFORE IT EVER REACHED THAT STAGE. BUT ANTON TALKED ABOUT A LAB ASSISTANT. A JESUIT.
I'D LIKE TO SPEAK WITH HIM.
VOLESCU. YEAH, WE TRACKED HIM DOWN.
AT YOUR LEISURE, SISTER. HE'S SERVING A LIFE SENTENCE IN SIBERIA.
SO HE'S ALWAYS AT HOME TO VISITORS.

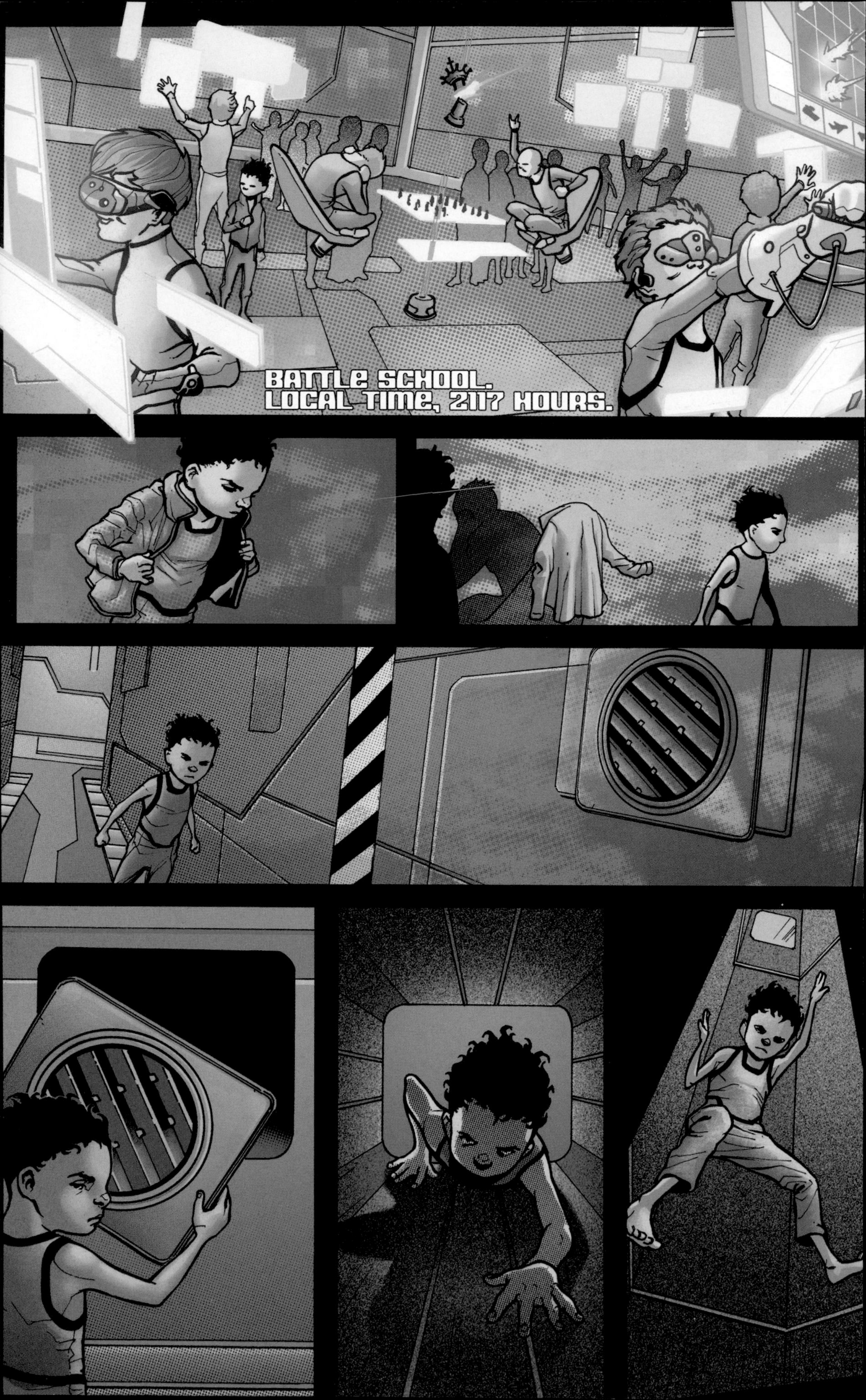
BATTLE SCHOOL.
LOCAL TIME, 2117 HOURS.

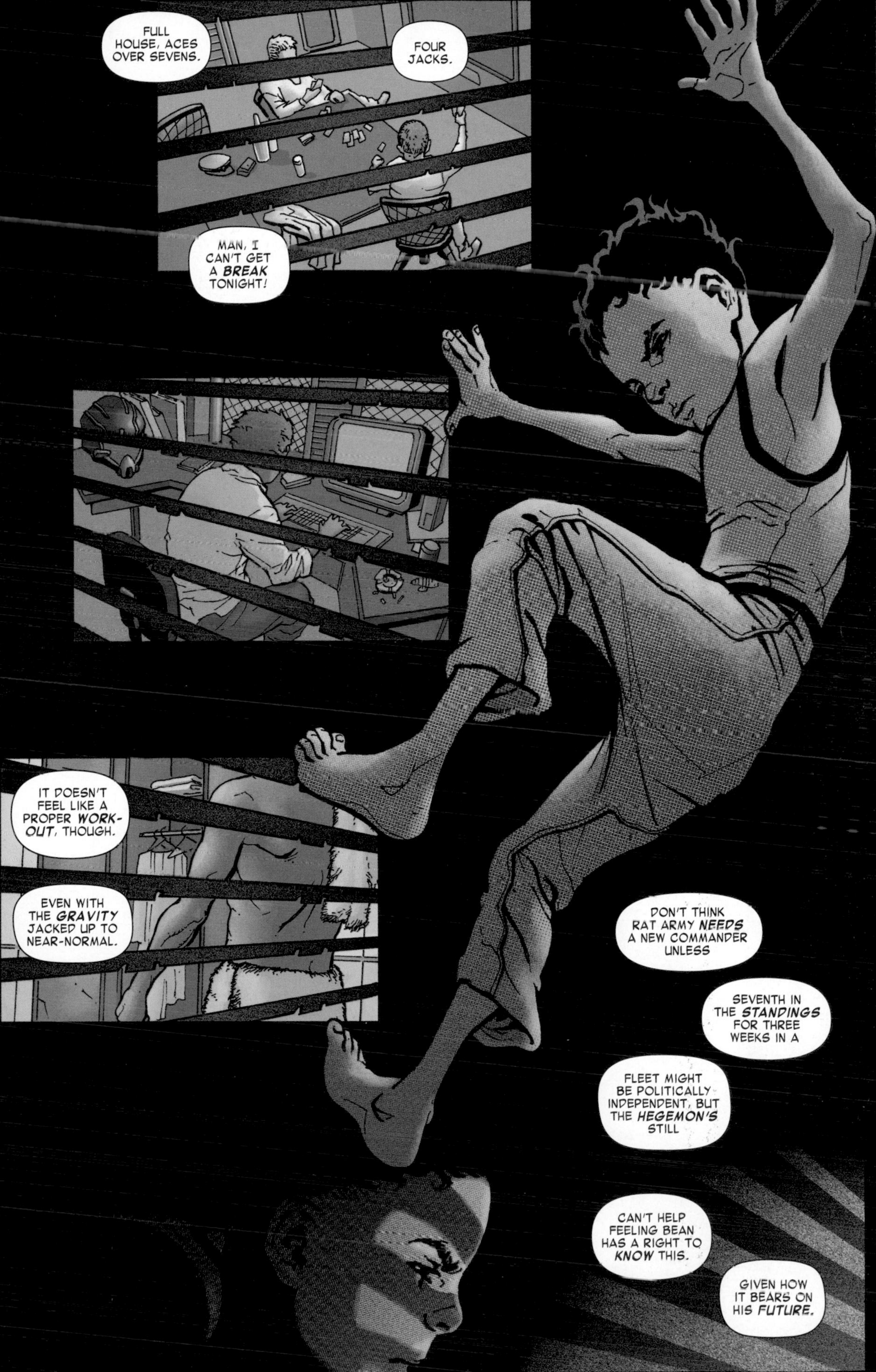
FULL HOUSE, ACES OVER SEVENS.
FOUR JACKS.
MAN, I CAN'T GET A BREAK TONIGHT!
IT DOESN'T FEEL LIKE A PROPER WORK-OUT, THOUGH.
EVEN WITH THE GRAVITY JACKED UP TO NEAR-NORMAL.
DON'T THINK RAT ARMY NEEDS A NEW COMMANDER UNLESS
SEVENTH IN THE STANDINGS FOR THREE WEEKS IN A
FLEET MIGHT BE POLITICALLY INDEPENDENT, BUT THE HEGEMON'S STILL
CAN'T HELP FEELING BEAN HAS A RIGHT TO KNOW THIS.
GIVEN HOW IT BEARS ON HIS FUTURE.

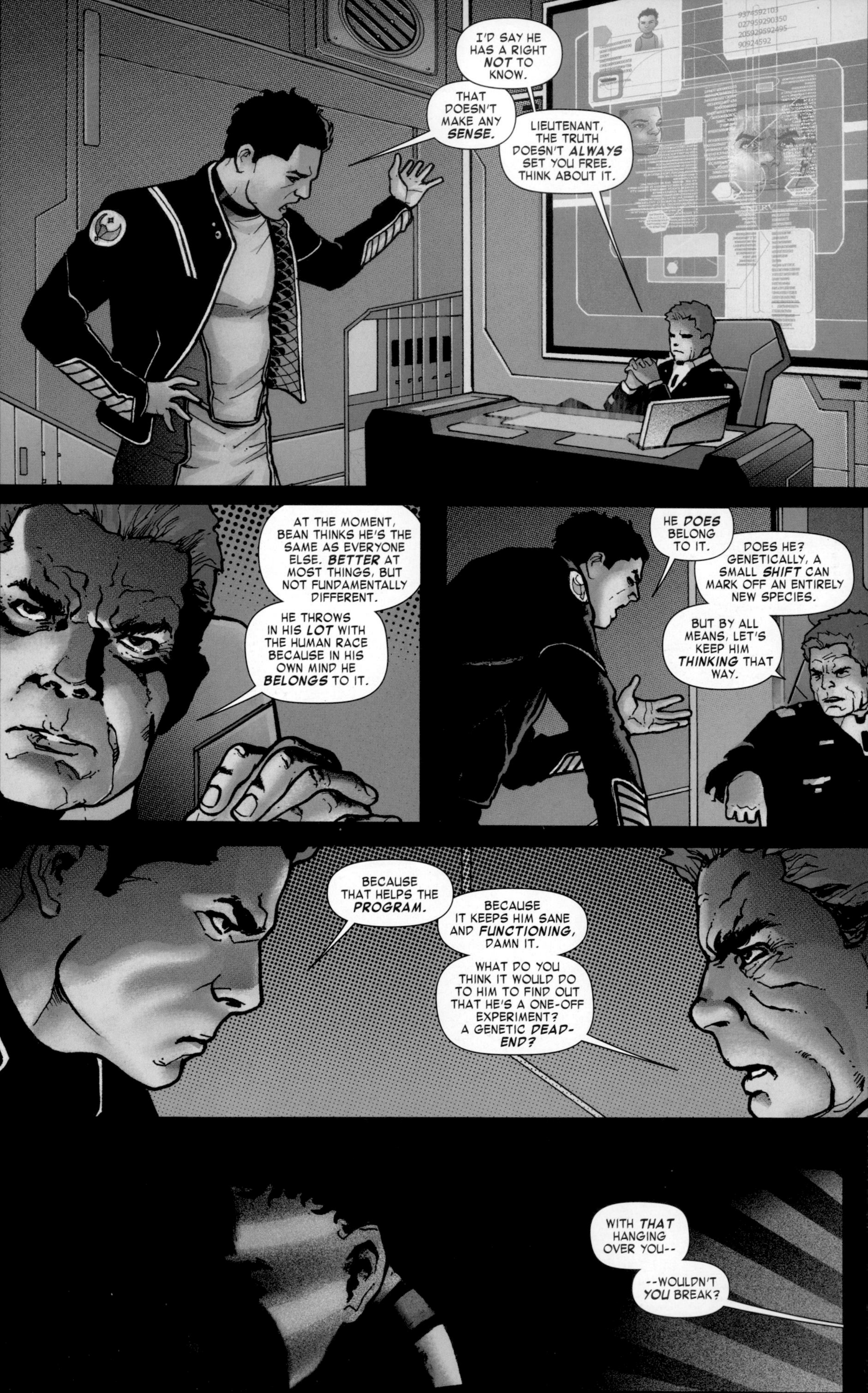
I'D SAY HE HAS A RIGHT NOT TO KNOW.
THAT DOESN'T MAKE ANY SENSE.
LIEUTENANT, THE TRUTH DOESN'T ALWAYS SET YOU FREE. THINK ABOUT IT.
AT THE MOMENT, BEAN THINKS HE'S THE SAME AS EVERYONE ELSE. BETTER AT MOST THINGS, BUT NOT FUNDAMENTALLY DIFFERENT.
HE THROWS IN HIS LOT WITH THE HUMAN RACE BECAUSE IN HIS OWN MIND HE BELONGS TO IT.
HE DOES BELONG TO IT.
DOES HE? GENETICALLY, A SMALL SHIFT CAN MARK OFF AN ENTIRELY NEW SPECIES.
BUT BY ALL MEANS, LET'S KEEP HIM THINKING THAT WAY.
BECAUSE THAT HELPS THE PROGRAM.
BECAUSE IT KEEPS HIM SANE AND FUNCTIONING, DAMN IT.
WHAT DO YOU THINK IT WOULD DO TO HIM TO FIND OUT THAT HE'S A ONE-OFF EXPERIMENT? A GENETIC DEAD-END?
WITH THAT HANGING OVER YOU--
--WOULDN'T YOU BREAK?

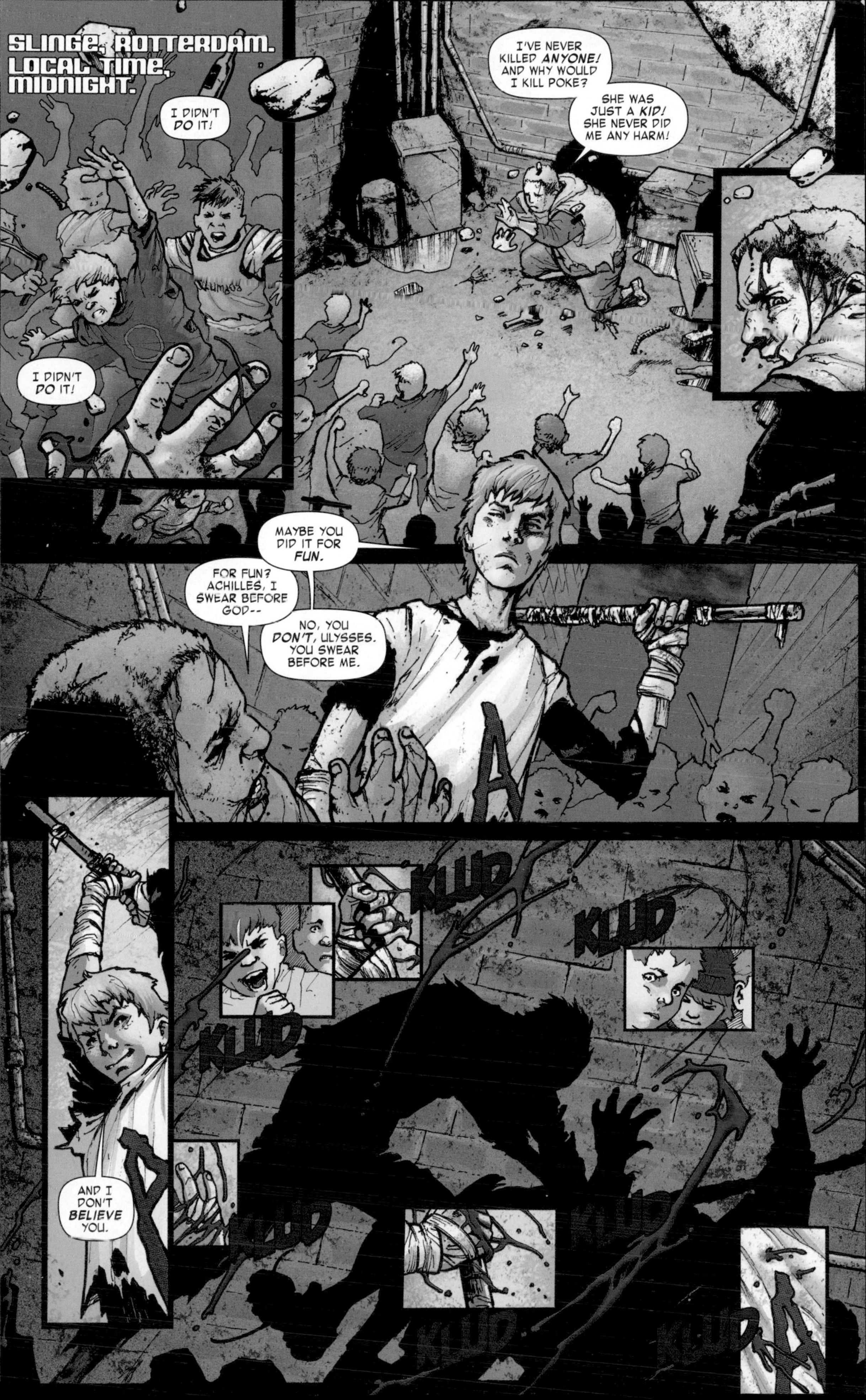
SLINGE, ROTTERDAM. LOCAL TIME, MIDNIGHT.
I DIDN'T DO IT!
I DIDN'T DO IT!
I'VE NEVER KILLED ANYONE! AND WHY WOULD I KILL POKE?
SHE WAS JUST A KID! SHE NEVER DID ME ANY HARM!
MAYBE YOU DID IT FOR FUN.
FOR FUN? ACHILLES, I SWEAR BEFORE GOD--
NO, YOU DON'T, ULYSSES. YOU SWEAR BEFORE ME.
KLUD
KLUD
KLUD
AND I DON'T BELIEVE YOU.
KLUD
KLUD
KLUD
KLUD

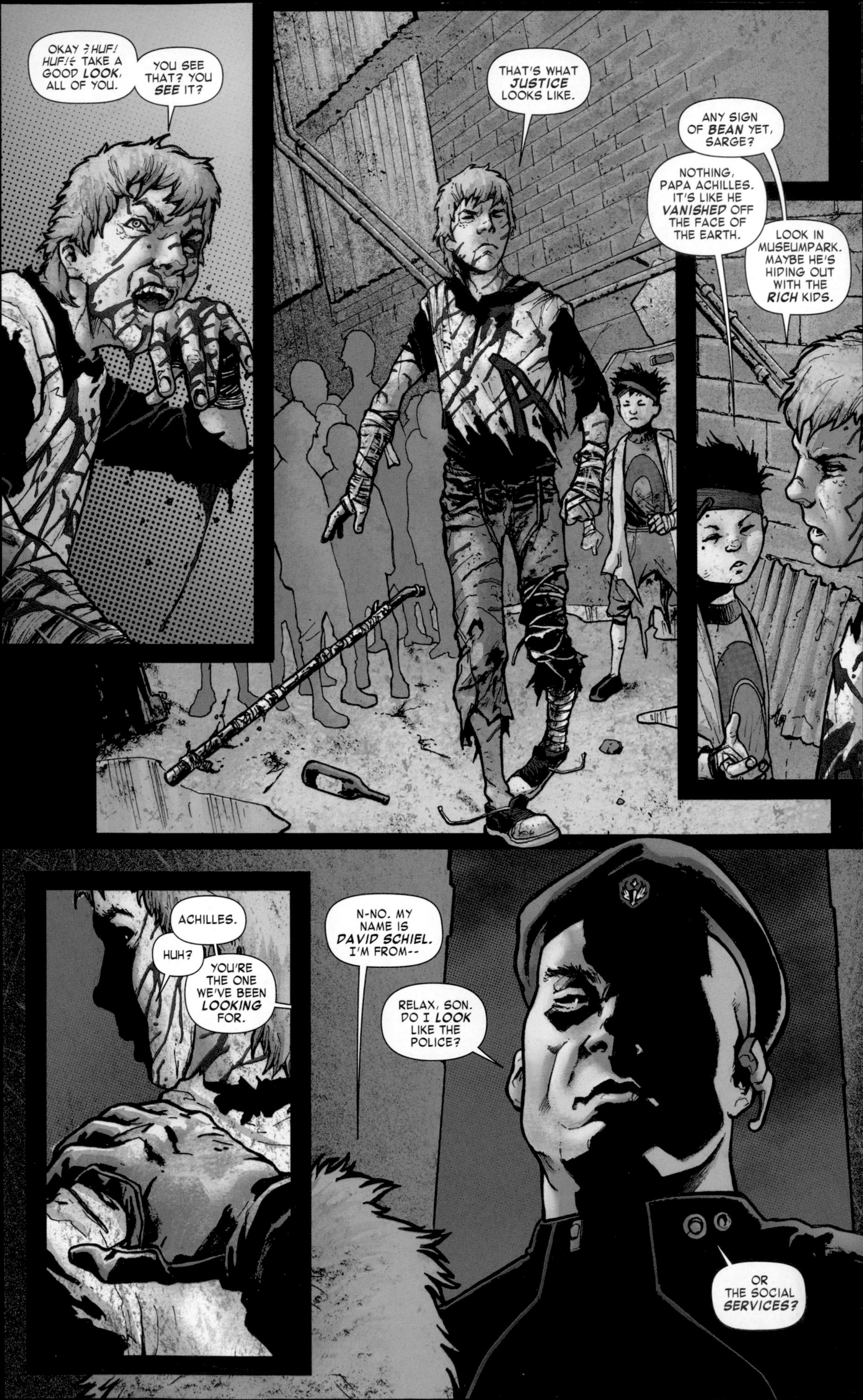
OKAY ;HUF! HUF!; TAKE A GOOD LOOK, ALL OF YOU.
YOU SEE THAT? YOU SEE IT?
THAT'S WHAT JUSTICE LOOKS LIKE.
ANY SIGN OF BEAN YET, SARGE?
NOTHING, PAPA ACHILLES. IT'S LIKE HE VANISHED OFF THE FACE OF THE EARTH.
LOOK IN MUSEUMPARK. MAYBE HE'S HIDING OUT WITH THE RICH KIDS.
ACHILLES.
HUH?
YOU'RE THE ONE WE'VE BEEN LOOKING FOR.
N-NO. MY NAME IS DAVID SCHIEL. I'M FROM--
RELAX, SON. DO I LOOK LIKE THE POLICE?
OR THE SOCIAL SERVICES?

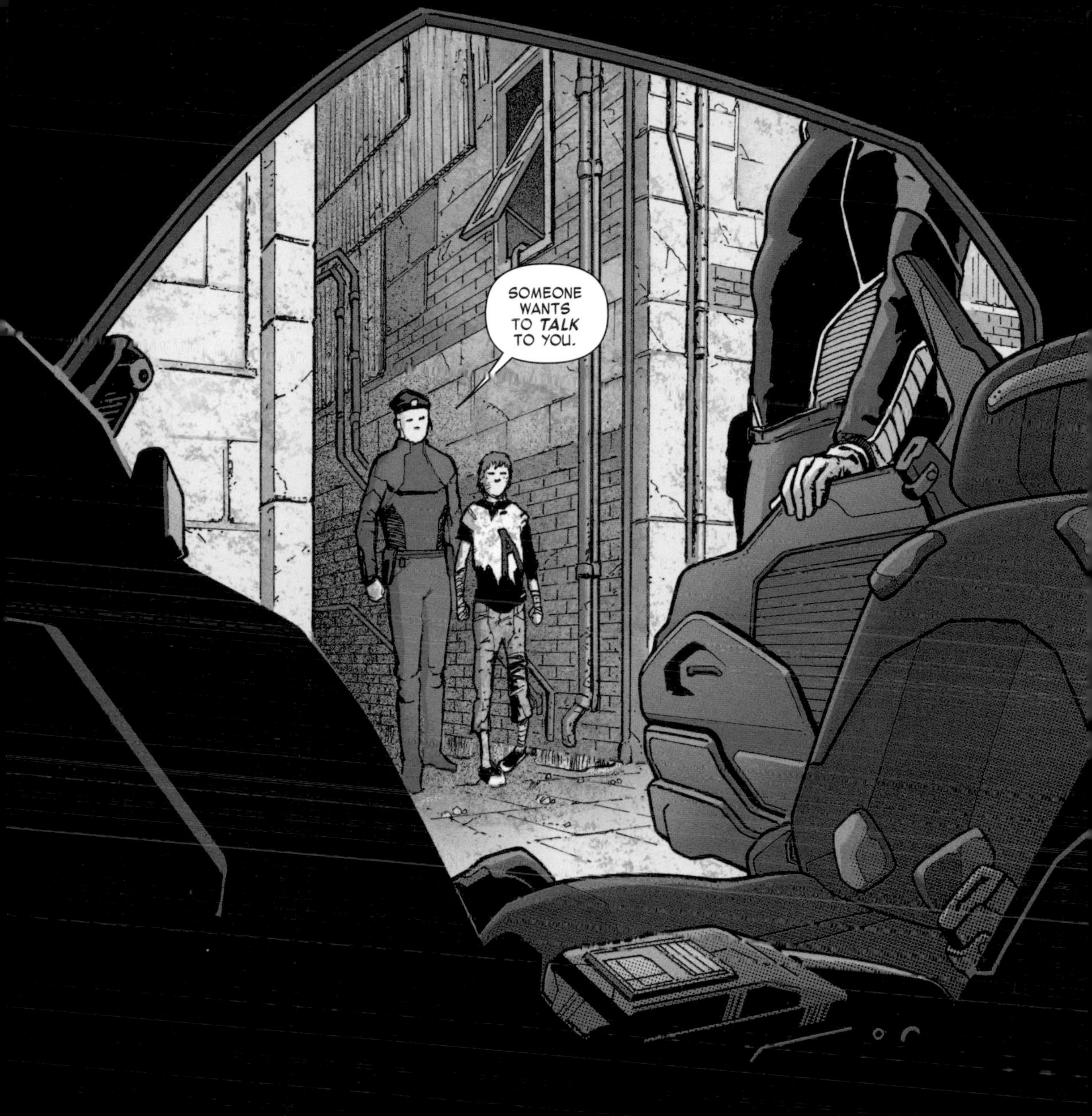
SOMEONE WANTS TO TALK TO YOU.

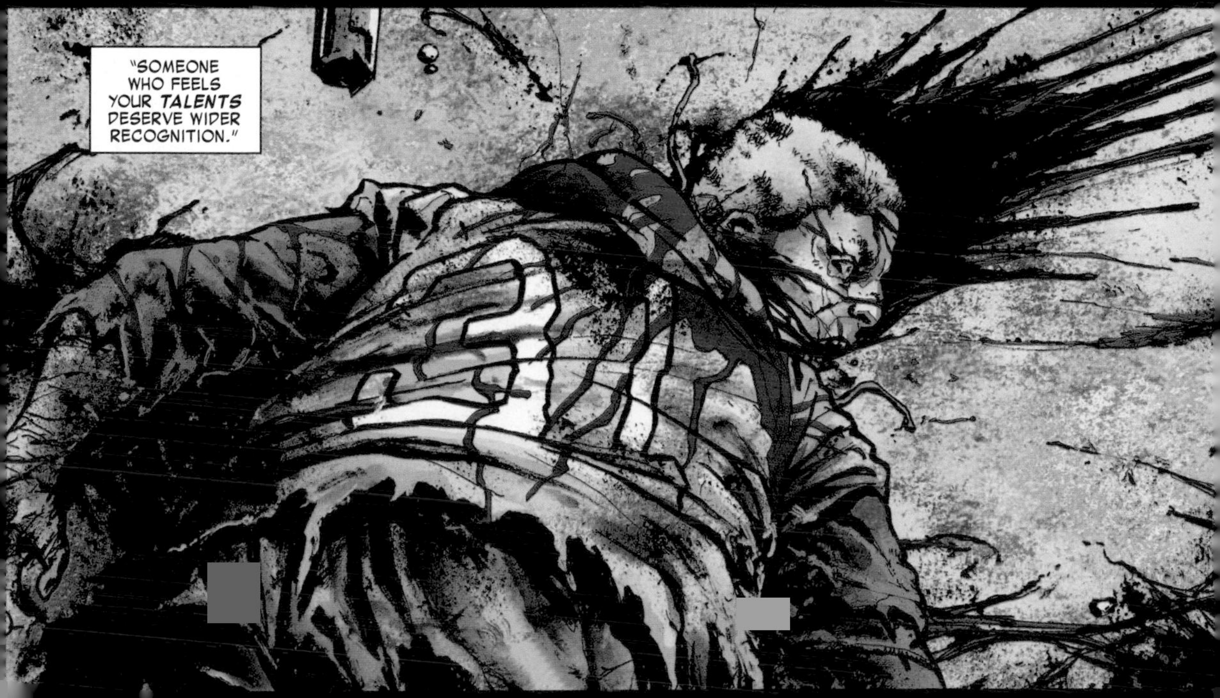
"SOMEONE WHO FEELS YOUR TALENTS DESERVE WIDER RECOGNITION."

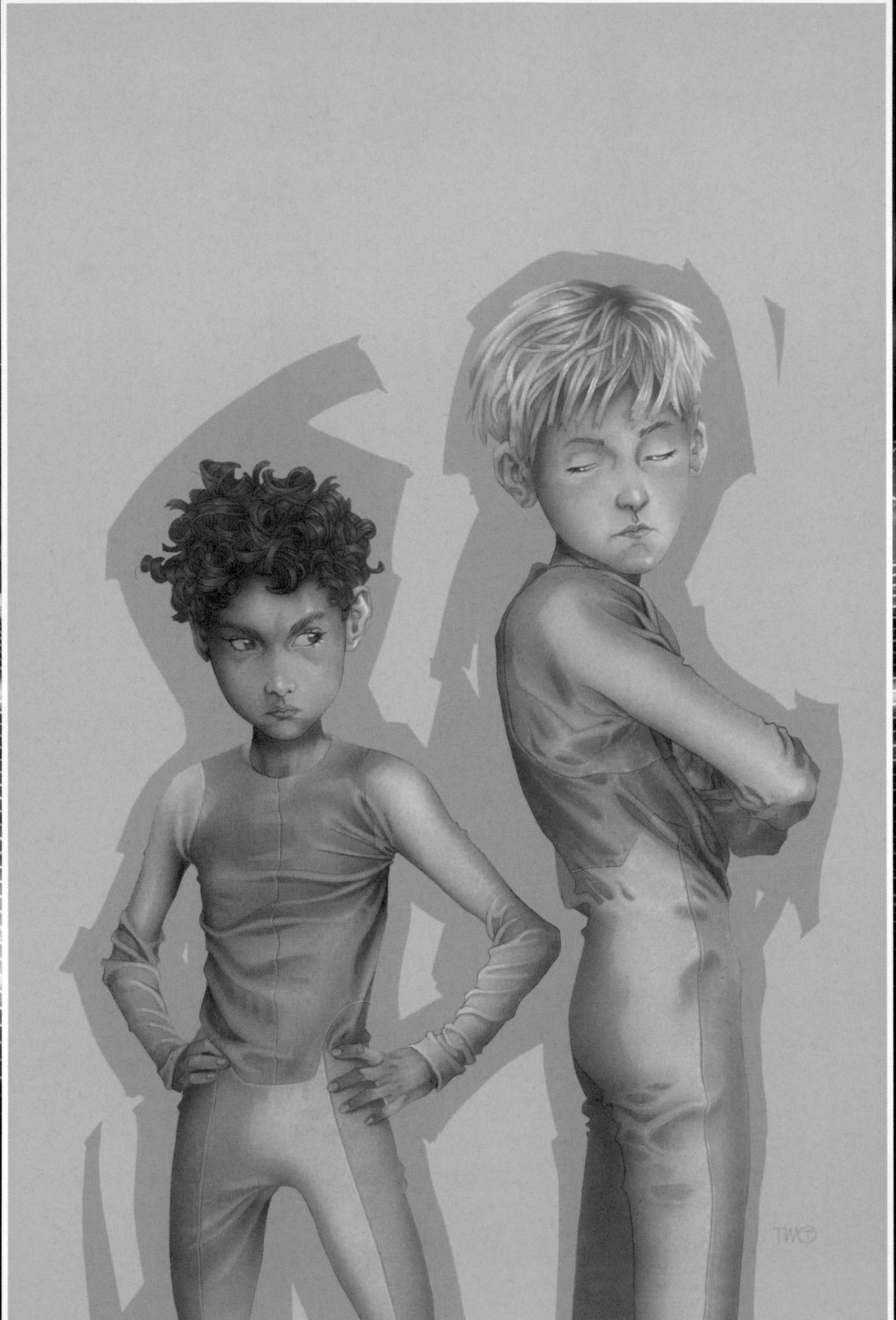
TMD

F I V E

"I can't help you. You didn't give me the information I asked for."

"We gave you the summaries."

"You gave me nothing, and you know it. And now you come to me asking me to evaluate Bean for you – but you don't tell me why, and you give me no context. You expect an answer but you deprive me of the means of providing it."

"Frustrating, isn't it?"

"Not for me. I simply won't give you any answer."

"Perhaps you haven't heard, sister, but there's a war on."

"I could say the same thing to you. We're fighting a war, and yet you fence me around with foolish secrecy."

"This information is secret in order to prevent some terrible experiments from being performed."

"Only a fool closes the door when the wolf is already inside the barn."

"Do you have proof that Bean is the result of a genetic experiment?"

"How can I prove it, when you've cut me off from all the evidence? Besides, what matters is not whether he has altered genes, but what those genes might lead him to do. Your tests were all designed to predict the behaviour of normal human beings. They may not apply to Bean."

"If he's that unpredictable, then we can't rely on him at all. We should drop him from the program."

"Do that, Colonel, and your war may be lost before it even starts."

"Very well. You can visit Volescu. But don't come crying to me afterwards about what you find out..."

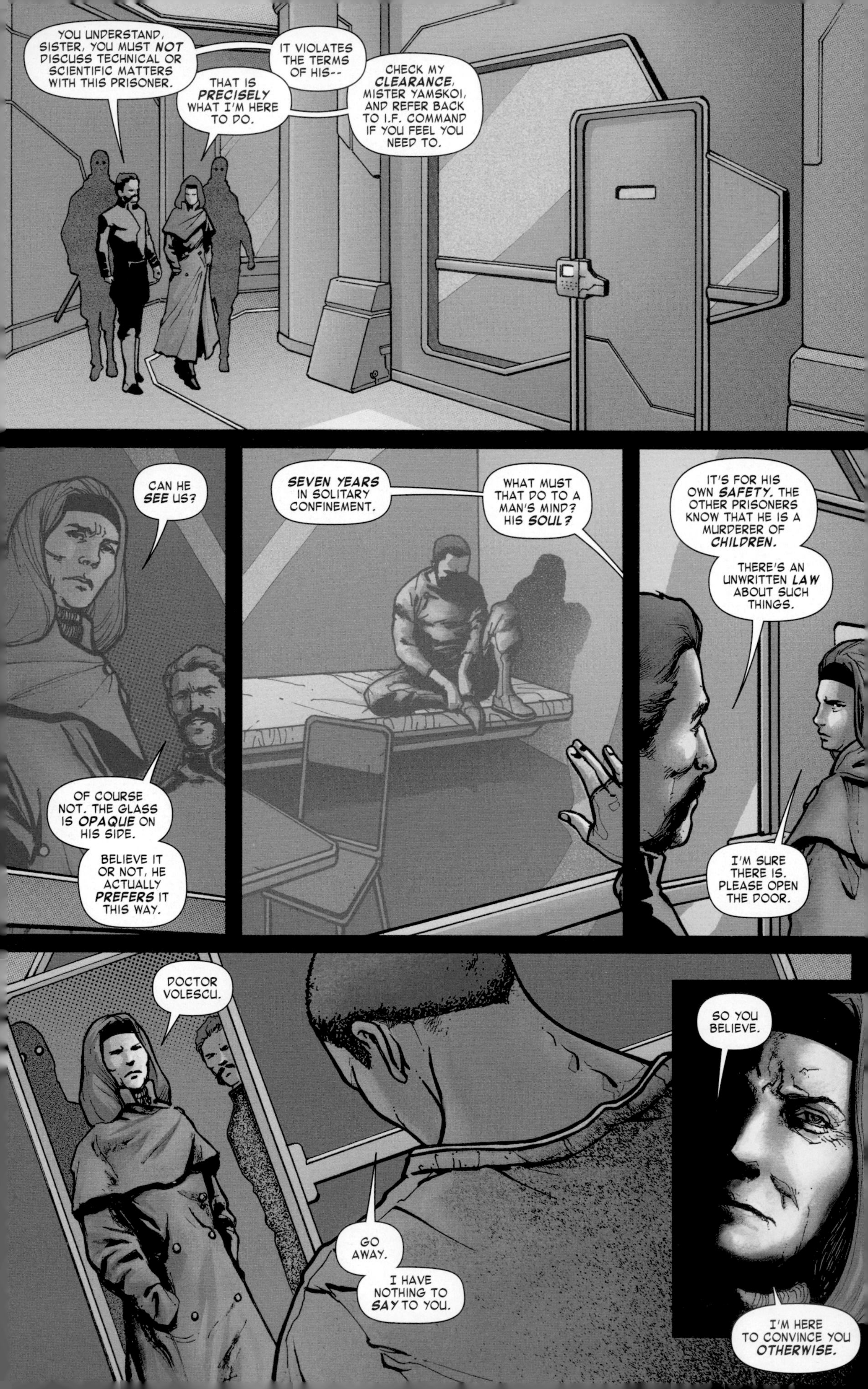

YOU UNDERSTAND, SISTER, YOU MUST NOT DISCUSS TECHNICAL OR SCIENTIFIC MATTERS WITH THIS PRISONER.
IT VIOLATES THE TERMS OF HIS--
THAT IS PRECISELY WHAT I'M HERE TO DO.
CHECK MY CLEARANCE, MISTER YAMSKOI, AND REFER BACK TO I.F. COMMAND IF YOU FEEL YOU NEED TO.
CAN HE SEE US?
OF COURSE NOT. THE GLASS IS OPAQUE ON HIS SIDE.
BELIEVE IT OR NOT, HE ACTUALLY PREFERS IT THIS WAY.
SEVEN YEARS IN SOLITARY CONFINEMENT.
WHAT MUST THAT DO TO A MAN'S MIND? HIS SOUL?
IT'S FOR HIS OWN SAFETY. THE OTHER PRISONERS KNOW THAT HE IS A MURDERER OF CHILDREN.
THERE'S AN UNWRITTEN LAW ABOUT SUCH THINGS.
I'M SURE THERE IS. PLEASE OPEN THE DOOR.
DOCTOR VOLESCU.
GO AWAY.
I HAVE NOTHING TO SAY TO YOU.
SO YOU BELIEVE.
I'M HERE TO CONVINCE YOU OTHERWISE.

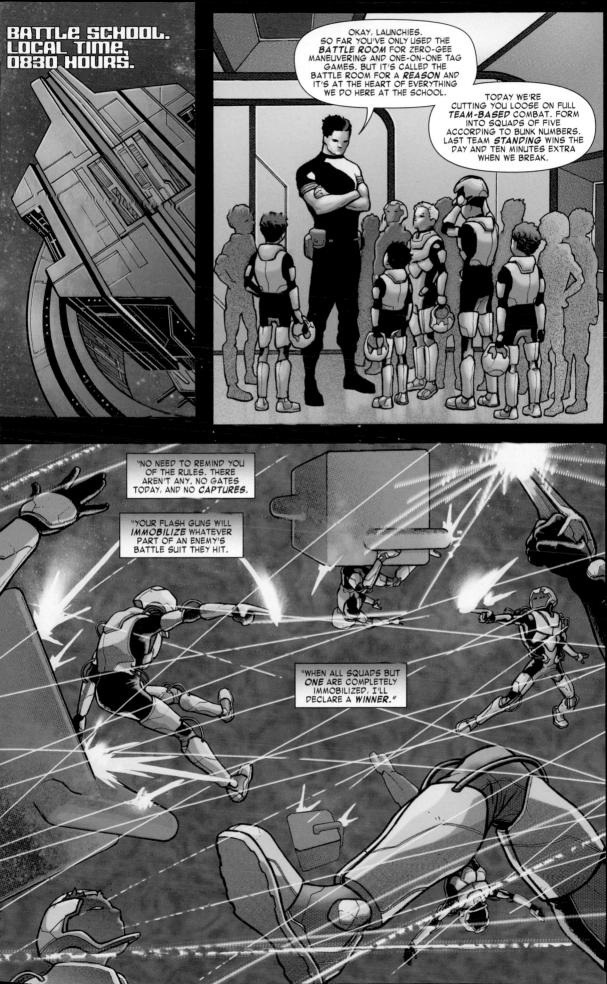

BATTLE SCHOOL. LOCAL TIME, 0830 HOURS.

OKAY, LAUNCHIES. SO FAR YOU'VE ONLY USED THE *BATTLE ROOM* FOR ZERO-GEE MANEUVERING AND ONE-ON-ONE TAG GAMES. BUT IT'S CALLED THE BATTLE ROOM FOR A *REASON* AND IT'S AT THE HEART OF EVERYTHING WE DO HERE AT THE SCHOOL.

TODAY WE'RE CUTTING YOU LOOSE ON FULL *TEAM-BASED* COMBAT. FORM INTO SQUADS OF FIVE ACCORDING TO BUNK NUMBERS. LAST TEAM *STANDING* WINS THE DAY AND TEN MINUTES EXTRA WHEN WE BREAK.

"NO NEED TO REMIND YOU OF THE RULES. THERE AREN'T ANY. NO GATES TODAY, AND NO *CAPTURES*.

"YOUR FLASH GUNS WILL *IMMOBILIZE* WHATEVER PART OF AN ENEMY'S BATTLE SUIT THEY HIT.

"WHEN ALL SQUADS BUT *ONE* ARE COMPLETELY IMMOBILIZED, I'LL DECLARE A *WINNER*."

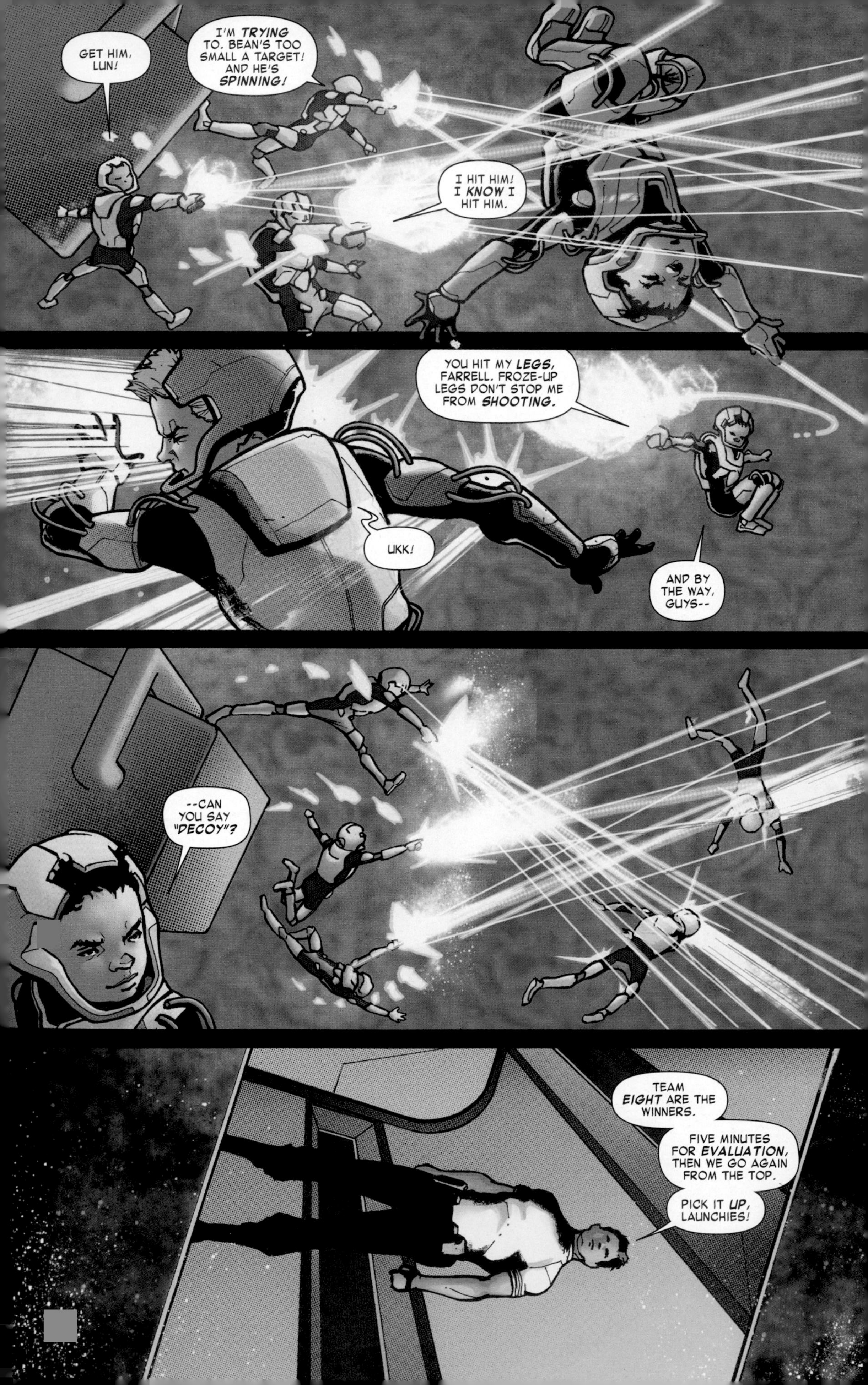
GET HIM, LUN!
I'M TRYING TO. BEAN'S TOO SMALL A TARGET! AND HE'S SPINNING!
I HIT HIM! I KNOW I HIT HIM.
YOU HIT MY LEGS, FARRELL. FROZE-UP LEGS DON'T STOP ME FROM SHOOTING.
UKK!
AND BY THE WAY, GUYS--
--CAN YOU SAY "DECOY"?
TEAM EIGHT ARE THE WINNERS.
FIVE MINUTES FOR EVALUATION, THEN WE GO AGAIN FROM THE TOP.
PICK IT UP, LAUNCHIES!

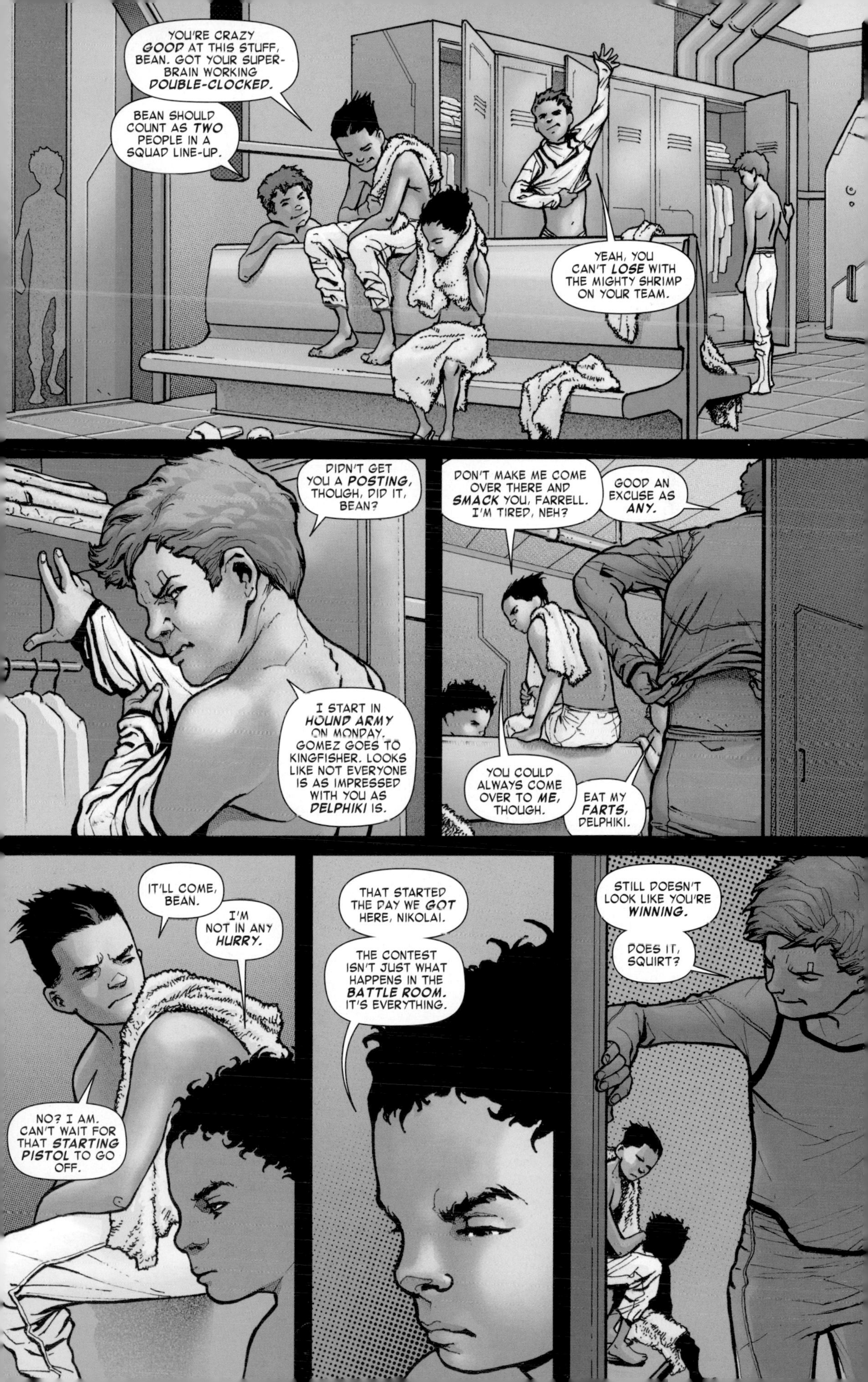
YOU'RE CRAZY GOOD AT THIS STUFF, BEAN. GOT YOUR SUPER-BRAIN WORKING DOUBLE-CLOCKED.
BEAN SHOULD COUNT AS TWO PEOPLE IN A SQUAD LINE-UP.
YEAH, YOU CAN'T LOSE WITH THE MIGHTY SHRIMP ON YOUR TEAM.
DIDN'T GET YOU A POSTING, THOUGH, DID IT, BEAN?
I START IN HOUND ARMY ON MONDAY. GOMEZ GOES TO KINGFISHER. LOOKS LIKE NOT EVERYONE IS AS IMPRESSED WITH YOU AS DELPHIKI IS.
DON'T MAKE ME COME OVER THERE AND SMACK YOU, FARRELL. I'M TIRED, NEH?
GOOD AN EXCUSE AS ANY.
YOU COULD ALWAYS COME OVER TO ME, THOUGH.
EAT MY FARTS, DELPHIKI.
IT'LL COME, BEAN.
I'M NOT IN ANY HURRY.
NO? I AM. CAN'T WAIT FOR THAT STARTING PISTOL TO GO OFF.
THAT STARTED THE DAY WE GOT HERE, NIKOLAI.
THE CONTEST ISN'T JUST WHAT HAPPENS IN THE BATTLE ROOM. IT'S EVERYTHING.
STILL DOESN'T LOOK LIKE YOU'RE WINNING.
DOES IT, SQUIRT?

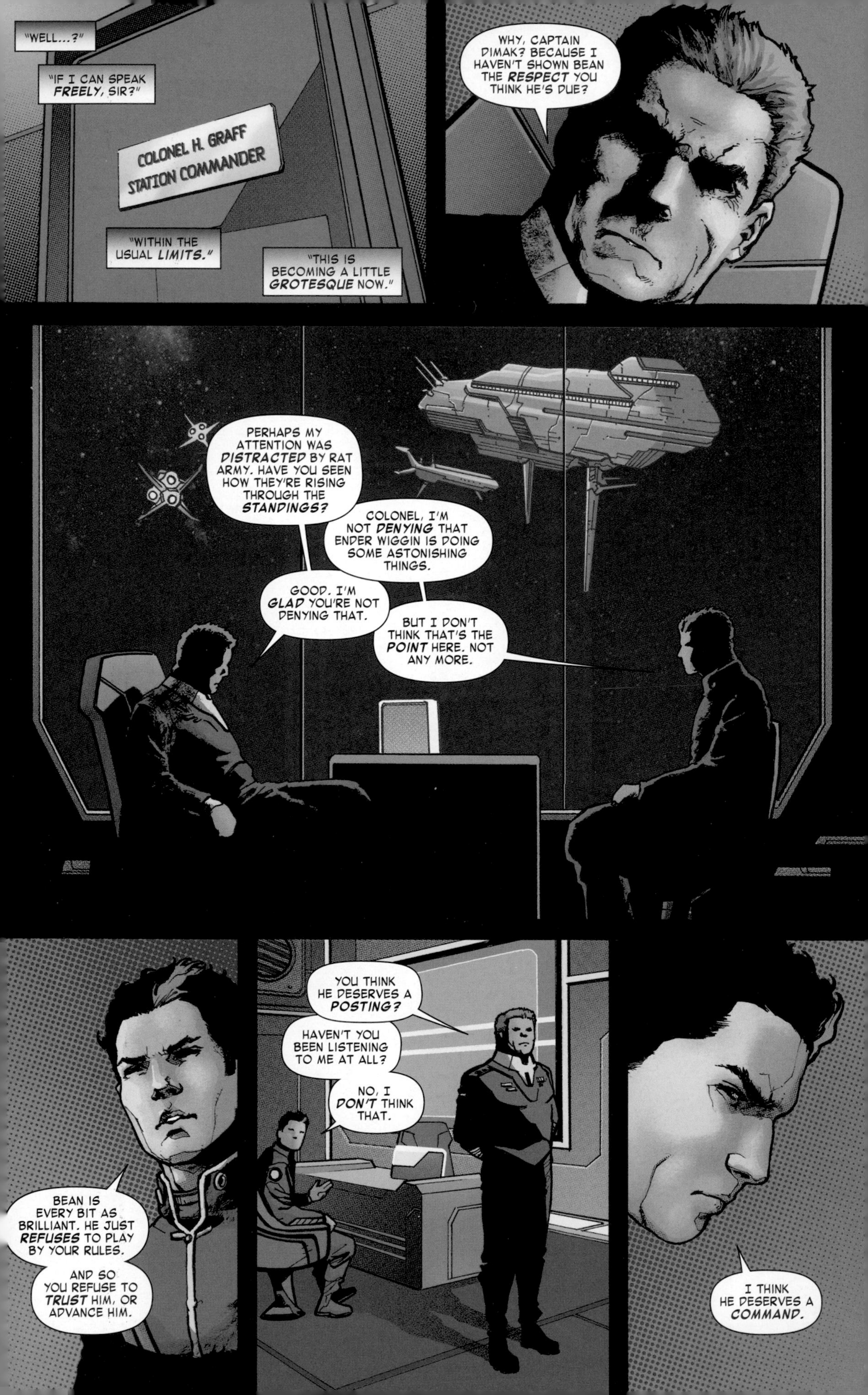
"WELL...?"
"IF I CAN SPEAK FREELY, SIR?"
COLONEL H. GRAFF STATION COMMANDER
"WITHIN THE USUAL LIMITS."
"THIS IS BECOMING A LITTLE GROTESQUE NOW."
WHY, CAPTAIN DIMAK? BECAUSE I HAVEN'T SHOWN BEAN THE RESPECT YOU THINK HE'S DUE?
PERHAPS MY ATTENTION WAS DISTRACTED BY RAT ARMY. HAVE YOU SEEN HOW THEY'RE RISING THROUGH THE STANDINGS?
COLONEL, I'M NOT DENYING THAT ENDER WIGGIN IS DOING SOME ASTONISHING THINGS.
GOOD. I'M GLAD YOU'RE NOT DENYING THAT.
BUT I DON'T THINK THAT'S THE POINT HERE. NOT ANY MORE.
BEAN IS EVERY BIT AS BRILLIANT. HE JUST REFUSES TO PLAY BY YOUR RULES.
AND SO YOU REFUSE TO TRUST HIM, OR ADVANCE HIM.
YOU THINK HE DESERVES A POSTING?
HAVEN'T YOU BEEN LISTENING TO ME AT ALL?
NO, I DON'T THINK THAT.
I THINK HE DESERVES A COMMAND.

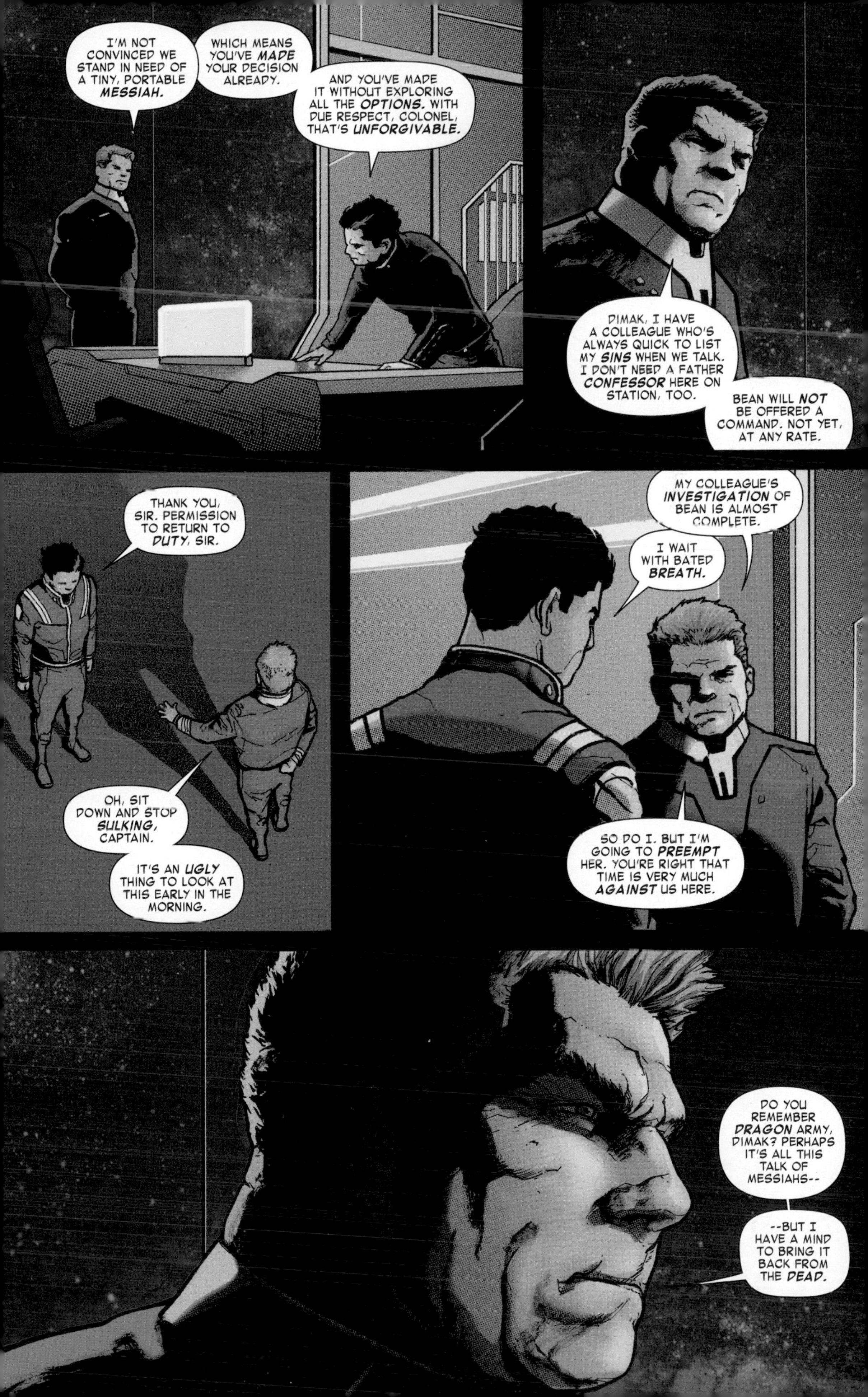
I'M NOT CONVINCED WE STAND IN NEED OF A TINY, PORTABLE MESSIAH.
WHICH MEANS YOU'VE MADE YOUR DECISION ALREADY.
AND YOU'VE MADE IT WITHOUT EXPLORING ALL THE OPTIONS. WITH DUE RESPECT, COLONEL, THAT'S UNFORGIVABLE.
DIMAK, I HAVE A COLLEAGUE WHO'S ALWAYS QUICK TO LIST MY SINS WHEN WE TALK. I DON'T NEED A FATHER CONFESSOR HERE ON STATION, TOO.
BEAN WILL NOT BE OFFERED A COMMAND. NOT YET, AT ANY RATE.
THANK YOU, SIR. PERMISSION TO RETURN TO DUTY, SIR.
OH, SIT DOWN AND STOP SULKING, CAPTAIN.
IT'S AN UGLY THING TO LOOK AT THIS EARLY IN THE MORNING.
MY COLLEAGUE'S INVESTIGATION OF BEAN IS ALMOST COMPLETE.
I WAIT WITH BATED BREATH.
SO DO I. BUT I'M GOING TO PREEMPT HER. YOU'RE RIGHT THAT TIME IS VERY MUCH AGAINST US HERE.
DO YOU REMEMBER DRAGON ARMY, DIMAK? PERHAPS IT'S ALL THIS TALK OF MESSIAHS--
--BUT I HAVE A MIND TO BRING IT BACK FROM THE DEAD.

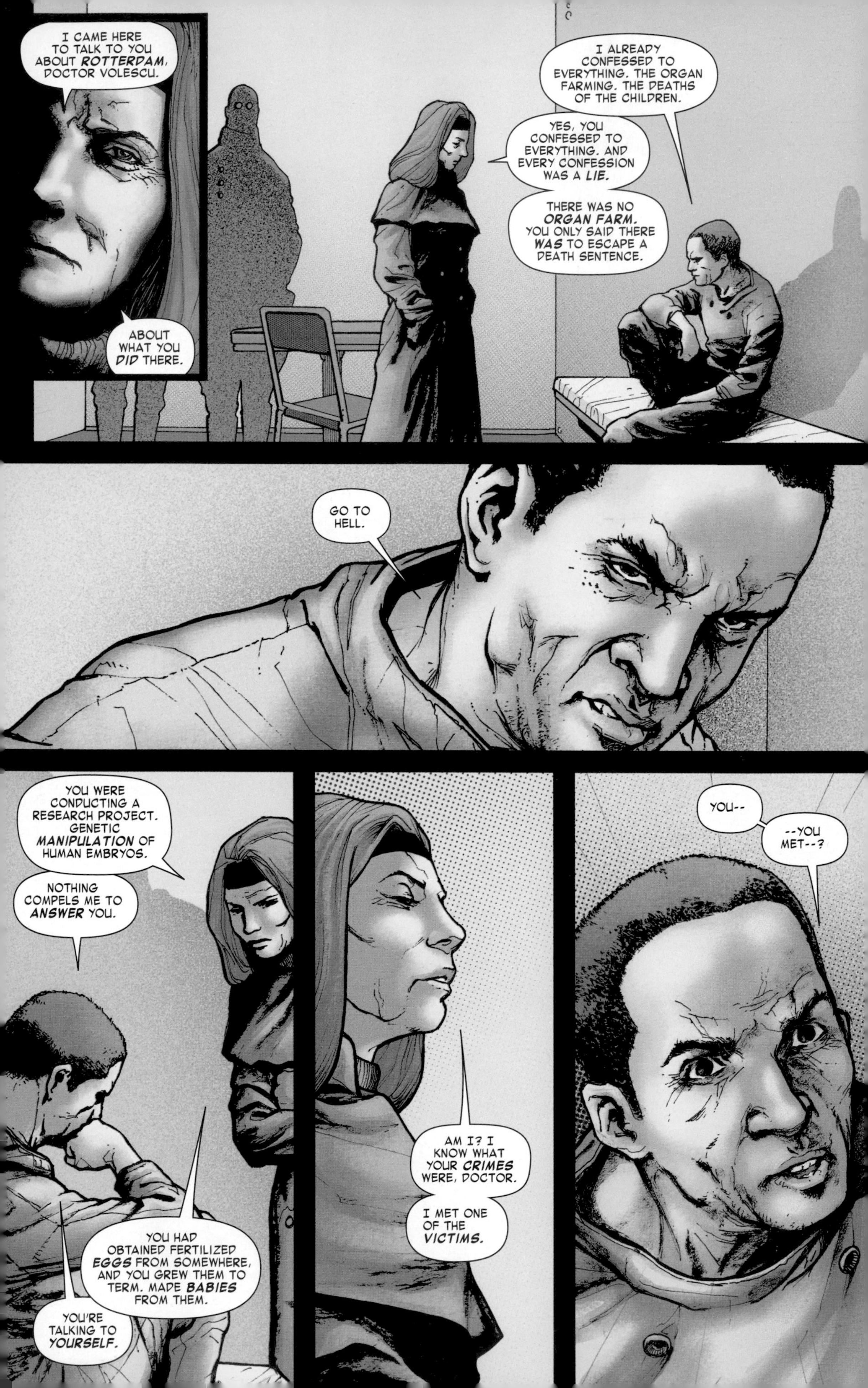
I CAME HERE TO TALK TO YOU ABOUT *ROTTERDAM*, DOCTOR VOLESCU.
ABOUT WHAT YOU *DID* THERE.
I ALREADY CONFESSED TO EVERYTHING. THE ORGAN FARMING. THE DEATHS OF THE CHILDREN.
YES, YOU CONFESSED TO EVERYTHING. AND EVERY CONFESSION WAS A *LIE.*
THERE WAS NO *ORGAN FARM.* YOU ONLY SAID THERE *WAS* TO ESCAPE A DEATH SENTENCE.
GO TO HELL.
YOU WERE CONDUCTING A RESEARCH PROJECT. GENETIC *MANIPULATION* OF HUMAN EMBRYOS.
NOTHING COMPELS ME TO *ANSWER* YOU.
YOU HAD OBTAINED FERTILIZED *EGGS* FROM SOMEWHERE, AND YOU GREW THEM TO TERM. MADE *BABIES* FROM THEM.
YOU'RE TALKING TO *YOURSELF.*
AM I? I KNOW WHAT YOUR *CRIMES* WERE, DOCTOR.
I MET ONE OF THE *VICTIMS.*
YOU--
--YOU MET--?

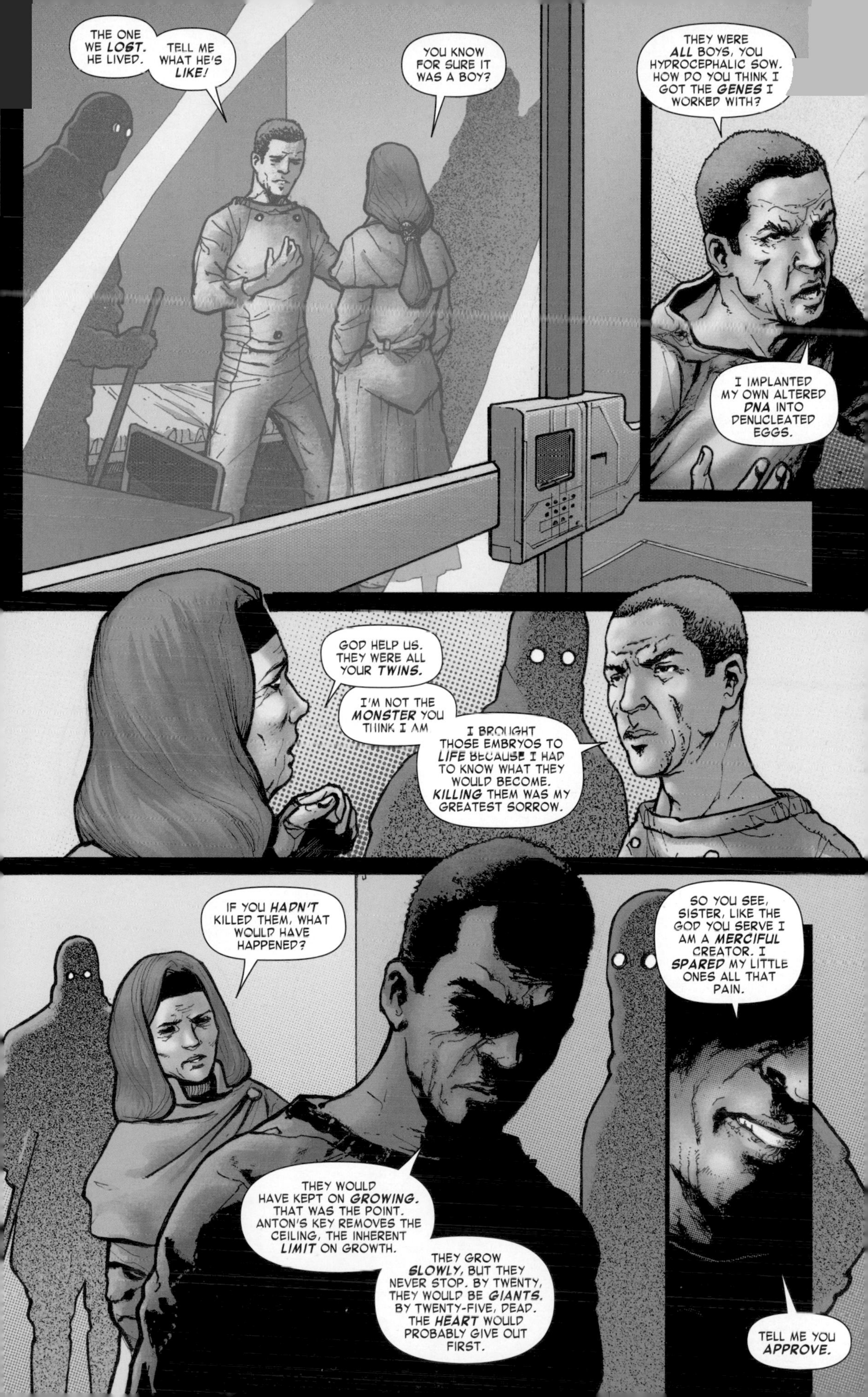
THE ONE WE LOST. HE LIVED.
TELL ME WHAT HE'S LIKE!
YOU KNOW FOR SURE IT WAS A BOY?
THEY WERE ALL BOYS, YOU HYDROCEPHALIC SOW. HOW DO YOU THINK I GOT THE GENES I WORKED WITH?
I IMPLANTED MY OWN ALTERED DNA INTO DENUCLEATED EGGS.
GOD HELP US. THEY WERE ALL YOUR TWINS.
I'M NOT THE MONSTER YOU THINK I AM.
I BROUGHT THOSE EMBRYOS TO LIFE BECAUSE I HAD TO KNOW WHAT THEY WOULD BECOME. KILLING THEM WAS MY GREATEST SORROW.
IF YOU HADN'T KILLED THEM, WHAT WOULD HAVE HAPPENED?
THEY WOULD HAVE KEPT ON GROWING. THAT WAS THE POINT. ANTON'S KEY REMOVES THE CEILING, THE INHERENT LIMIT ON GROWTH.
THEY GROW SLOWLY, BUT THEY NEVER STOP. BY TWENTY, THEY WOULD BE GIANTS. BY TWENTY-FIVE, DEAD. THE HEART WOULD PROBABLY GIVE OUT FIRST.
SO YOU SEE, SISTER, LIKE THE GOD YOU SERVE I AM A MERCIFUL CREATOR. I SPARED MY LITTLE ONES ALL THAT PAIN.
TELL ME YOU APPROVE.

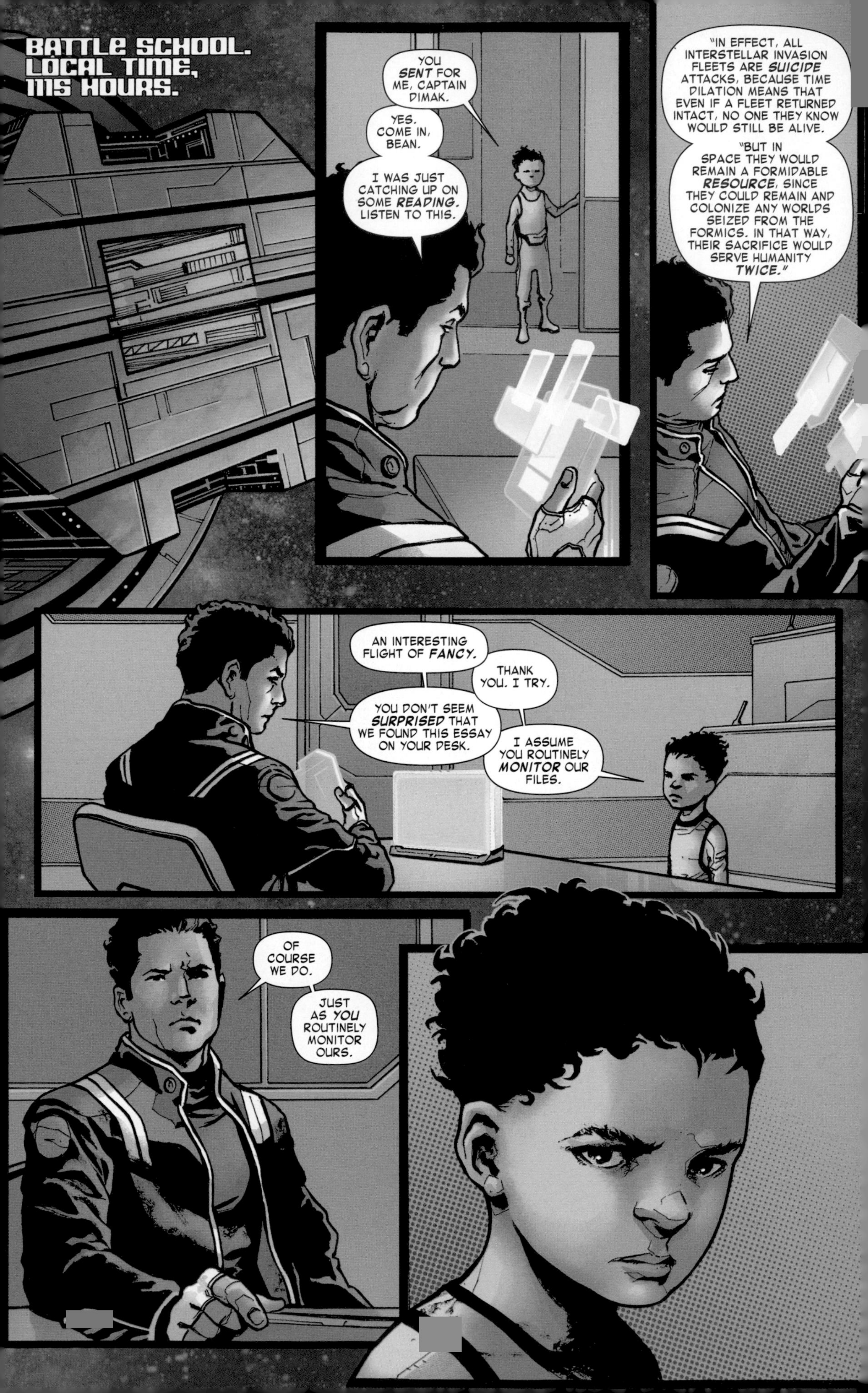

BATTLE SCHOOL. LOCAL TIME, 1115 HOURS.
YOU SENT FOR ME, CAPTAIN DIMAK.
YES. COME IN, BEAN.
I WAS JUST CATCHING UP ON SOME READING. LISTEN TO THIS.
"IN EFFECT, ALL INTERSTELLAR INVASION FLEETS ARE SUICIDE ATTACKS, BECAUSE TIME DILATION MEANS THAT EVEN IF A FLEET RETURNED INTACT, NO ONE THEY KNOW WOULD STILL BE ALIVE.
"BUT IN SPACE THEY WOULD REMAIN A FORMIDABLE RESOURCE, SINCE THEY COULD REMAIN AND COLONIZE ANY WORLDS SEIZED FROM THE FORMICS. IN THAT WAY, THEIR SACRIFICE WOULD SERVE HUMANITY TWICE."
AN INTERESTING FLIGHT OF FANCY.
THANK YOU. I TRY.
YOU DON'T SEEM SURPRISED THAT WE FOUND THIS ESSAY ON YOUR DESK.
I ASSUME YOU ROUTINELY MONITOR OUR FILES.
OF COURSE WE DO.
JUST AS YOU ROUTINELY MONITOR OURS.

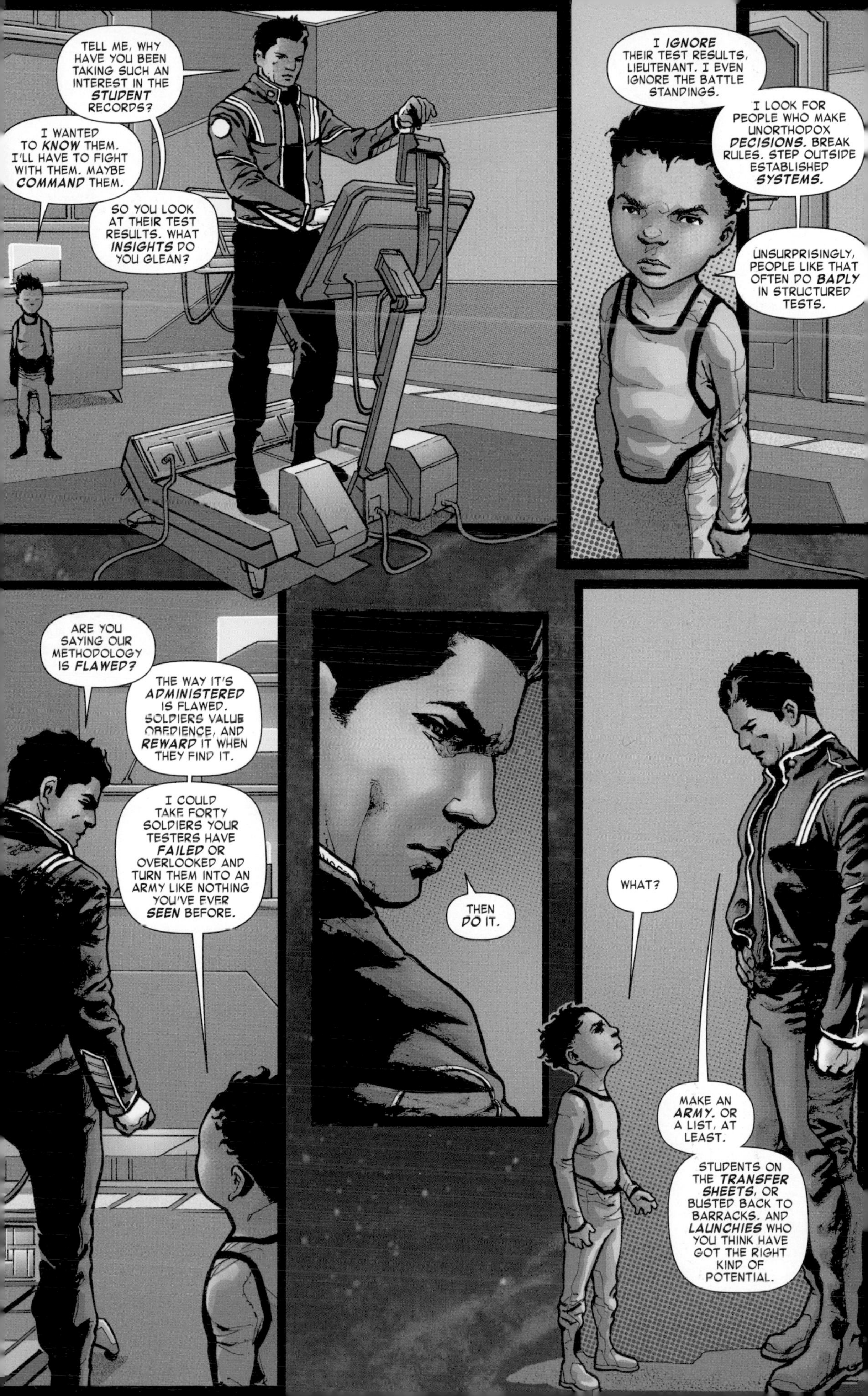
TELL ME, WHY HAVE YOU BEEN TAKING SUCH AN INTEREST IN THE STUDENT RECORDS?
I WANTED TO KNOW THEM. I'LL HAVE TO FIGHT WITH THEM. MAYBE COMMAND THEM.
SO YOU LOOK AT THEIR TEST RESULTS. WHAT INSIGHTS DO YOU GLEAN?
I IGNORE THEIR TEST RESULTS, LIEUTENANT. I EVEN IGNORE THE BATTLE STANDINGS.
I LOOK FOR PEOPLE WHO MAKE UNORTHODOX DECISIONS. BREAK RULES. STEP OUTSIDE ESTABLISHED SYSTEMS.
UNSURPRISINGLY, PEOPLE LIKE THAT OFTEN DO BADLY IN STRUCTURED TESTS.
ARE YOU SAYING OUR METHODOLOGY IS FLAWED?
THE WAY IT'S ADMINISTERED IS FLAWED. SOLDIERS VALUE OBEDIENCE, AND REWARD IT WHEN THEY FIND IT.
I COULD TAKE FORTY SOLDIERS YOUR TESTERS HAVE FAILED OR OVERLOOKED AND TURN THEM INTO AN ARMY LIKE NOTHING YOU'VE EVER SEEN BEFORE.
THEN DO IT.
WHAT?
MAKE AN ARMY. OR A LIST, AT LEAST.
STUDENTS ON THE TRANSFER SHEETS, OR BUSTED BACK TO BARRACKS. AND LAUNCHIES WHO YOU THINK HAVE GOT THE RIGHT KIND OF POTENTIAL.

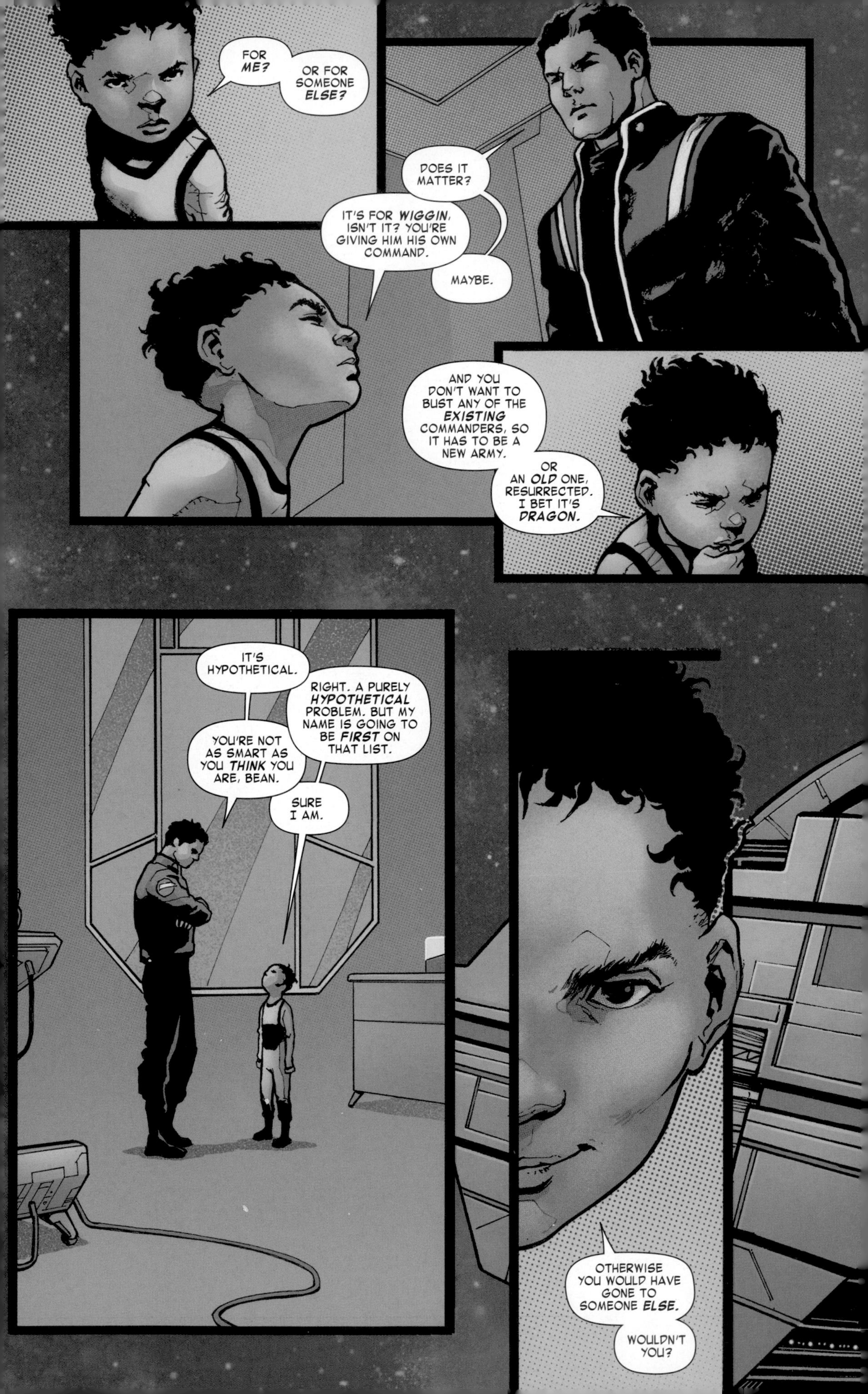
FOR ME?
OR FOR SOMEONE ELSE?
DOES IT MATTER?
IT'S FOR WIGGIN, ISN'T IT? YOU'RE GIVING HIM HIS OWN COMMAND.
MAYBE.
AND YOU DON'T WANT TO BUST ANY OF THE EXISTING COMMANDERS, SO IT HAS TO BE A NEW ARMY.
OR AN OLD ONE, RESURRECTED. I BET IT'S DRAGON.
IT'S HYPOTHETICAL.
RIGHT. A PURELY HYPOTHETICAL PROBLEM. BUT MY NAME IS GOING TO BE FIRST ON THAT LIST.
YOU'RE NOT AS SMART AS YOU THINK YOU ARE, BEAN.
SURE I AM.
OTHERWISE YOU WOULD HAVE GONE TO SOMEONE ELSE.
WOULDN'T YOU?

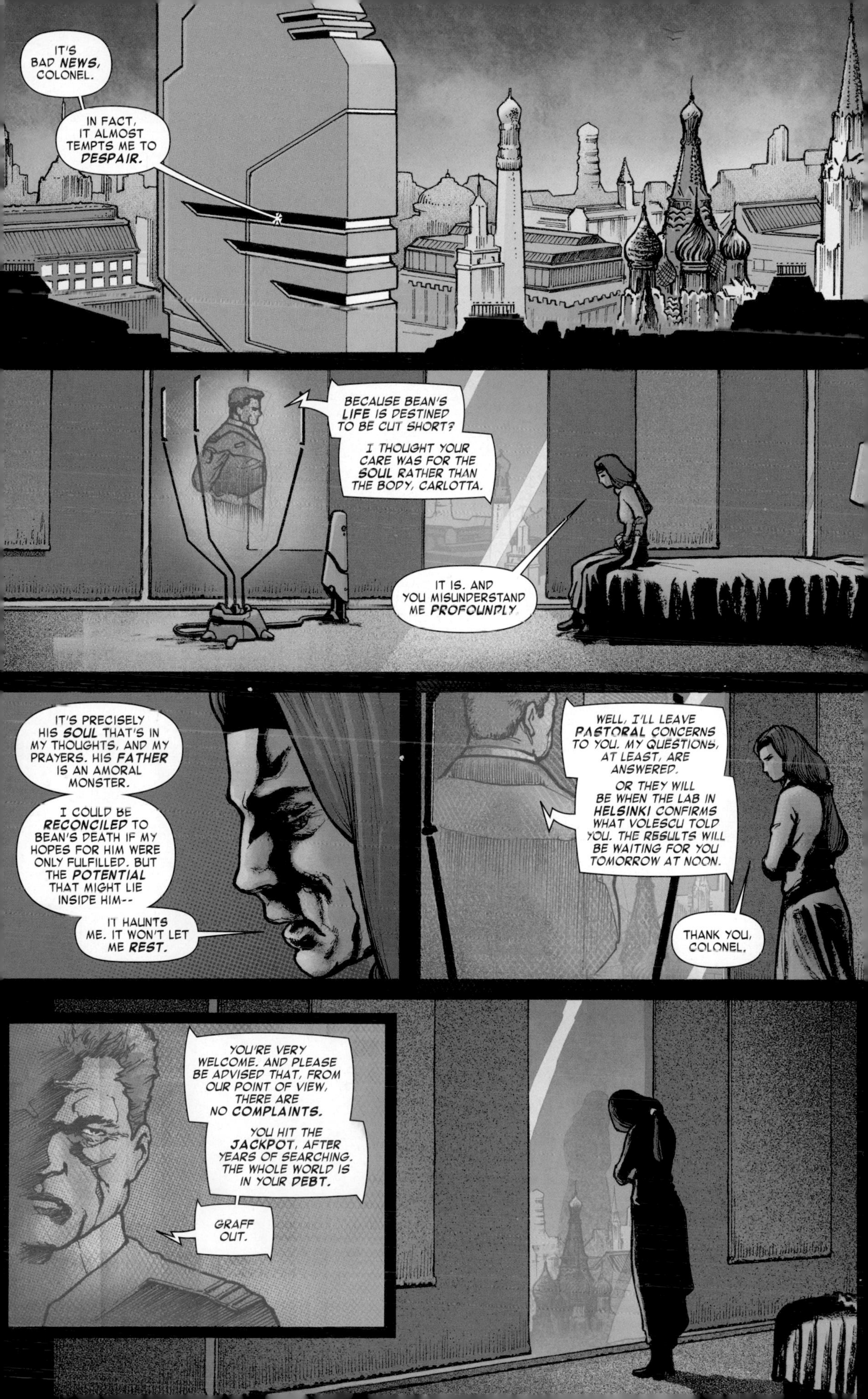
IT'S BAD NEWS, COLONEL.
IN FACT, IT ALMOST TEMPTS ME TO DESPAIR.
BECAUSE BEAN'S LIFE IS DESTINED TO BE CUT SHORT?
I THOUGHT YOUR CARE WAS FOR THE SOUL RATHER THAN THE BODY, CARLOTTA.
IT IS. AND YOU MISUNDERSTAND ME PROFOUNDLY.
IT'S PRECISELY HIS SOUL THAT'S IN MY THOUGHTS, AND MY PRAYERS. HIS FATHER IS AN AMORAL MONSTER.
I COULD BE RECONCILED TO BEAN'S DEATH IF MY HOPES FOR HIM WERE ONLY FULFILLED. BUT THE POTENTIAL THAT MIGHT LIE INSIDE HIM--
IT HAUNTS ME. IT WON'T LET ME REST.
WELL, I'LL LEAVE PASTORAL CONCERNS TO YOU. MY QUESTIONS, AT LEAST, ARE ANSWERED.
OR THEY WILL BE WHEN THE LAB IN HELSINKI CONFIRMS WHAT VOLESCU TOLD YOU. THE RESULTS WILL BE WAITING FOR YOU TOMORROW AT NOON.
THANK YOU, COLONEL.
YOU'RE VERY WELCOME. AND PLEASE BE ADVISED THAT, FROM OUR POINT OF VIEW, THERE ARE NO COMPLAINTS.
YOU HIT THE JACKPOT, AFTER YEARS OF SEARCHING. THE WHOLE WORLD IS IN YOUR DEBT.
GRAFF OUT.

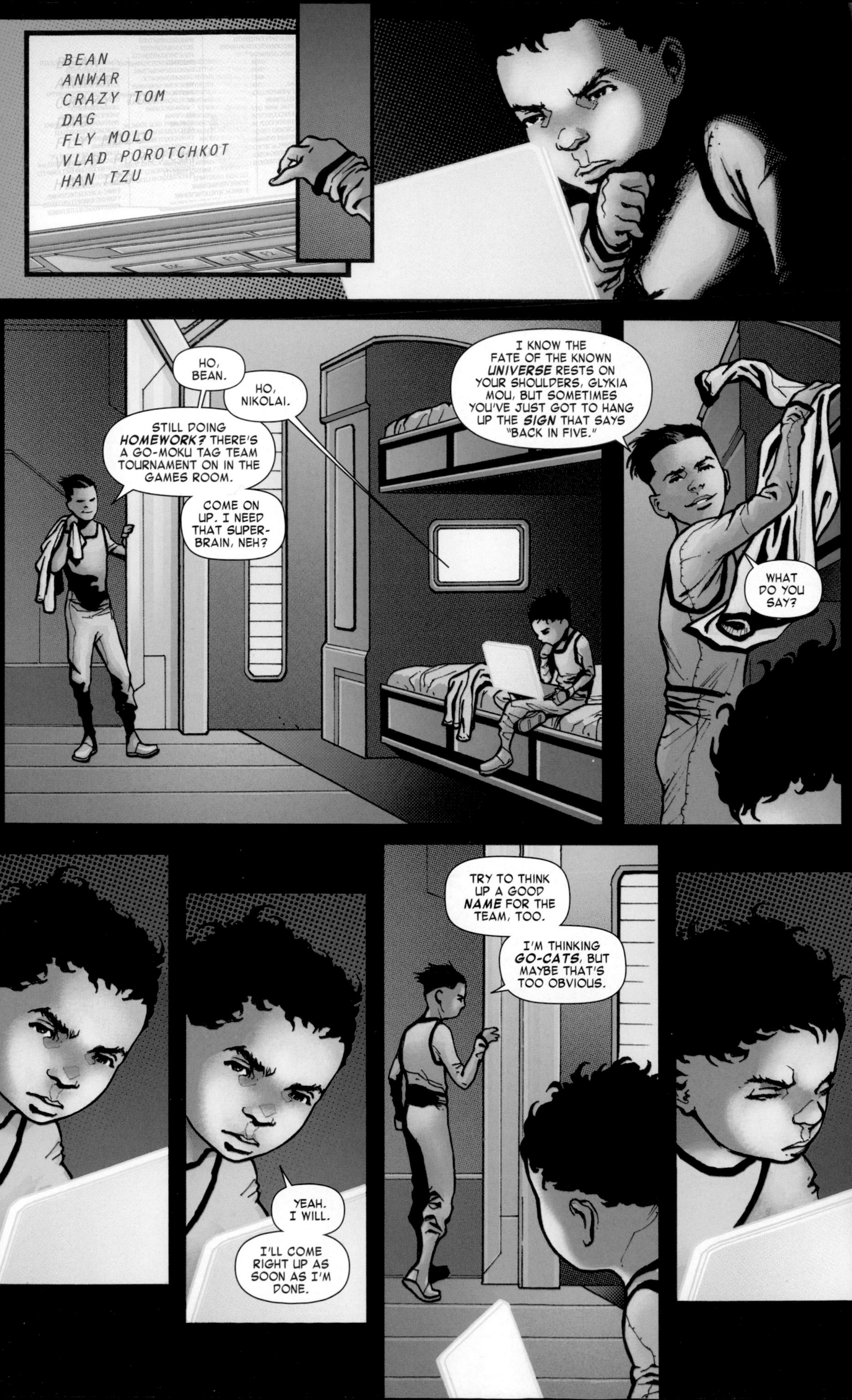
BEAN
ANWAR
CRAZY TOM
DAG
FLY MOLO
VLAD POROTCHKOT
HAN TZU
HO, BEAN.
HO, NIKOLAI.
STILL DOING HOMEWORK? THERE'S A GO-MOKU TAG TEAM TOURNAMENT ON IN THE GAMES ROOM.
COME ON UP. I NEED THAT SUPER-BRAIN, NEH?
I KNOW THE FATE OF THE KNOWN UNIVERSE RESTS ON YOUR SHOULDERS, GLYKIA MOU, BUT SOMETIMES YOU'VE JUST GOT TO HANG UP THE SIGN THAT SAYS "BACK IN FIVE."
WHAT DO YOU SAY?
YEAH. I WILL.
I'LL COME RIGHT UP AS SOON AS I'M DONE.
TRY TO THINK UP A GOOD NAME FOR THE TEAM, TOO.
I'M THINKING GO-CATS, BUT MAYBE THAT'S TOO OBVIOUS.

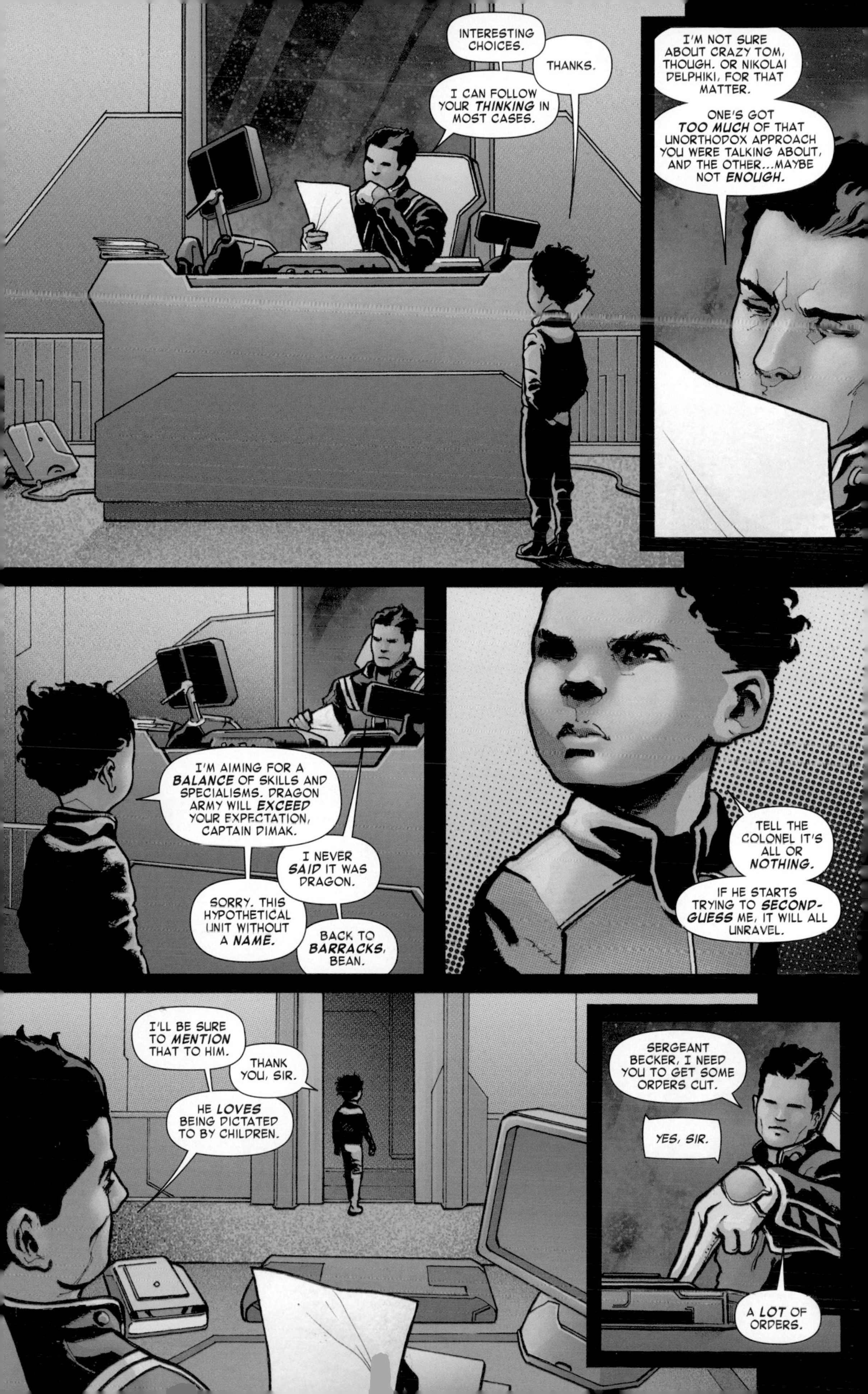
INTERESTING CHOICES.
THANKS.
I CAN FOLLOW YOUR THINKING IN MOST CASES.
I'M NOT SURE ABOUT CRAZY TOM, THOUGH. OR NIKOLAI DELPHIKI, FOR THAT MATTER.
ONE'S GOT TOO MUCH OF THAT UNORTHODOX APPROACH YOU WERE TALKING ABOUT, AND THE OTHER...MAYBE NOT ENOUGH.
I'M AIMING FOR A BALANCE OF SKILLS AND SPECIALISMS. DRAGON ARMY WILL EXCEED YOUR EXPECTATION, CAPTAIN DIMAK.
I NEVER SAID IT WAS DRAGON.
SORRY. THIS HYPOTHETICAL UNIT WITHOUT A NAME.
BACK TO BARRACKS, BEAN.
TELL THE COLONEL IT'S ALL OR NOTHING.
IF HE STARTS TRYING TO SECOND-GUESS ME, IT WILL ALL UNRAVEL.
I'LL BE SURE TO MENTION THAT TO HIM.
THANK YOU, SIR.
HE LOVES BEING DICTATED TO BY CHILDREN.
SERGEANT BECKER, I NEED YOU TO GET SOME ORDERS CUT.
YES, SIR.
A LOT OF ORDERS.

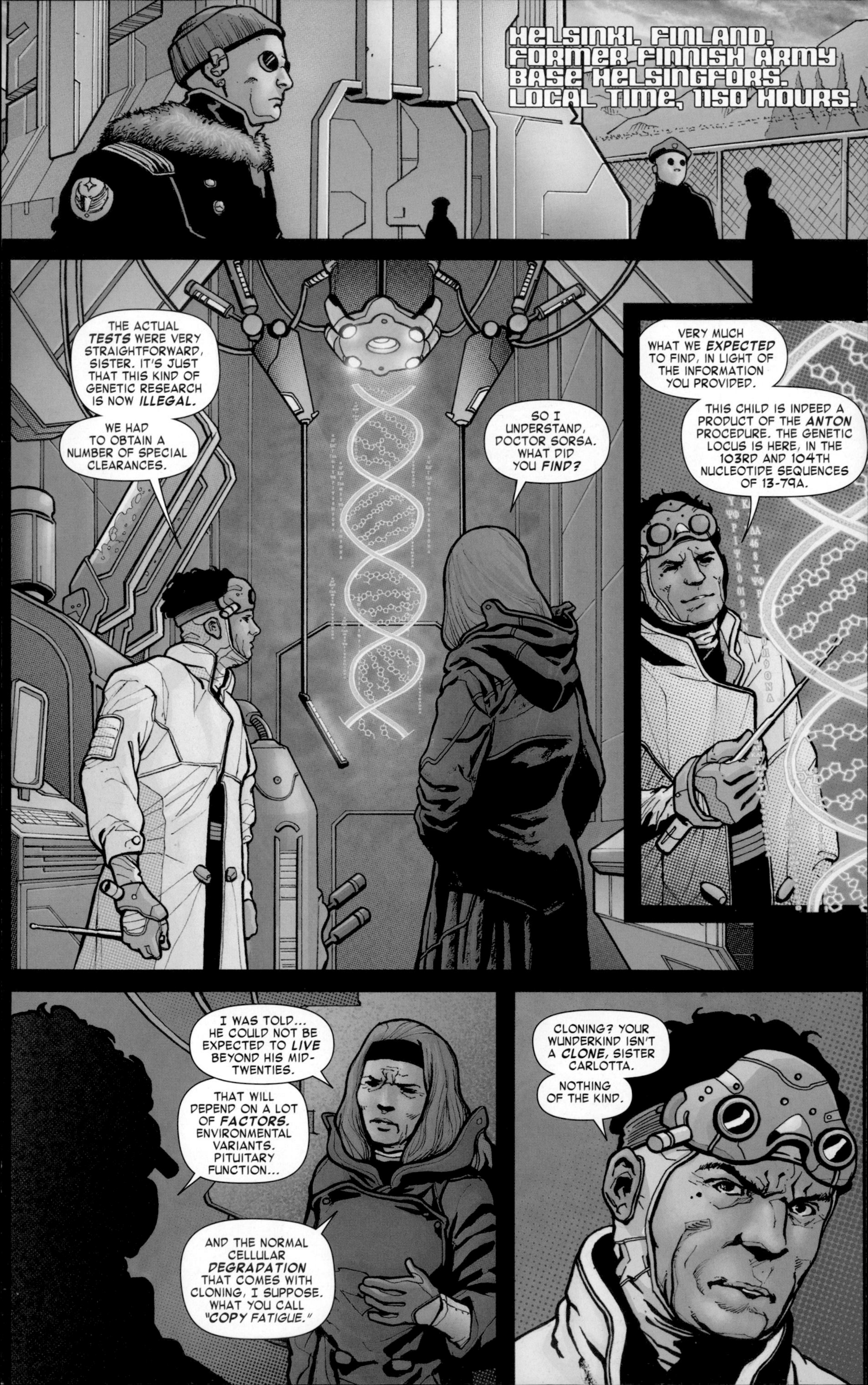
HELSINKI, FINLAND. FORMER FINNISH ARMY BASE HELSINGFORS. LOCAL TIME, 1150 HOURS.
THE ACTUAL TESTS WERE VERY STRAIGHTFORWARD, SISTER. IT'S JUST THAT THIS KIND OF GENETIC RESEARCH IS NOW ILLEGAL.
WE HAD TO OBTAIN A NUMBER OF SPECIAL CLEARANCES.
SO I UNDERSTAND, DOCTOR SORSA. WHAT DID YOU FIND?
VERY MUCH WHAT WE EXPECTED TO FIND, IN LIGHT OF THE INFORMATION YOU PROVIDED.
THIS CHILD IS INDEED A PRODUCT OF THE ANTON PROCEDURE. THE GENETIC LOCUS IS HERE, IN THE 103RD AND 104TH NUCLEOTIDE SEQUENCES OF 13-79A.
I WAS TOLD... HE COULD NOT BE EXPECTED TO LIVE BEYOND HIS MID-TWENTIES.
THAT WILL DEPEND ON A LOT OF FACTORS. ENVIRONMENTAL VARIANTS. PITUITARY FUNCTION...
AND THE NORMAL CELLULAR DEGRADATION THAT COMES WITH CLONING, I SUPPOSE. WHAT YOU CALL "COPY FATIGUE."
CLONING? YOUR WUNDERKIND ISN'T A CLONE, SISTER CARLOTTA.
NOTHING OF THE KIND.

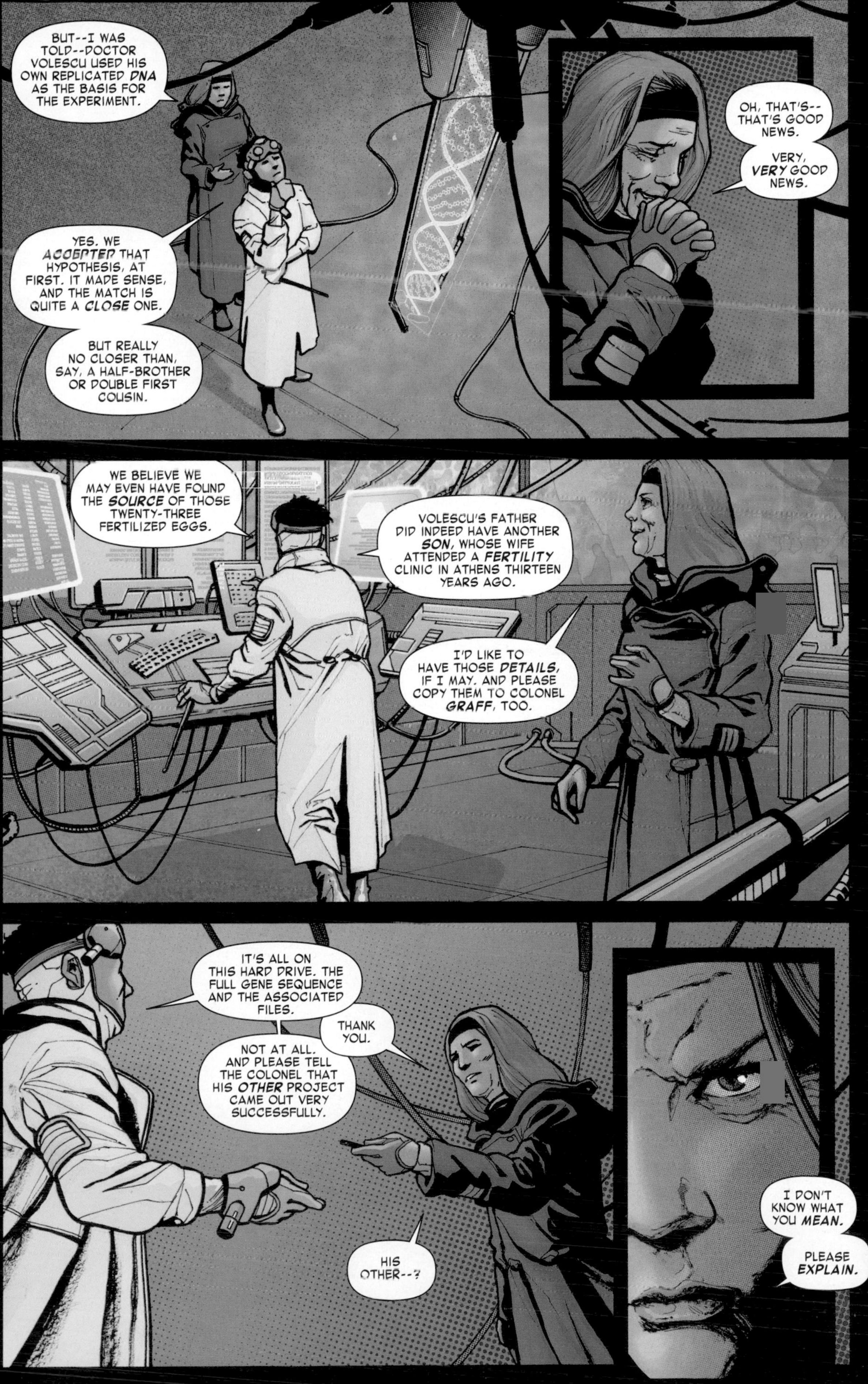
BUT--I WAS TOLD--DOCTOR VOLESCU USED HIS OWN REPLICATED DNA AS THE BASIS FOR THE EXPERIMENT.
YES. WE ACCEPTED THAT HYPOTHESIS, AT FIRST. IT MADE SENSE, AND THE MATCH IS QUITE A CLOSE ONE.
BUT REALLY NO CLOSER THAN, SAY, A HALF-BROTHER OR DOUBLE FIRST COUSIN.
OH, THAT'S--THAT'S GOOD NEWS.
VERY, VERY GOOD NEWS.
WE BELIEVE WE MAY EVEN HAVE FOUND THE SOURCE OF THOSE TWENTY-THREE FERTILIZED EGGS.
VOLESCU'S FATHER DID INDEED HAVE ANOTHER SON, WHOSE WIFE ATTENDED A FERTILITY CLINIC IN ATHENS THIRTEEN YEARS AGO.
I'D LIKE TO HAVE THOSE DETAILS, IF I MAY. AND PLEASE COPY THEM TO COLONEL GRAFF, TOO.
IT'S ALL ON THIS HARD DRIVE. THE FULL GENE SEQUENCE AND THE ASSOCIATED FILES.
THANK YOU.
NOT AT ALL. AND PLEASE TELL THE COLONEL THAT HIS OTHER PROJECT CAME OUT VERY SUCCESSFULLY.
HIS OTHER--?
I DON'T KNOW WHAT YOU MEAN.
PLEASE EXPLAIN.

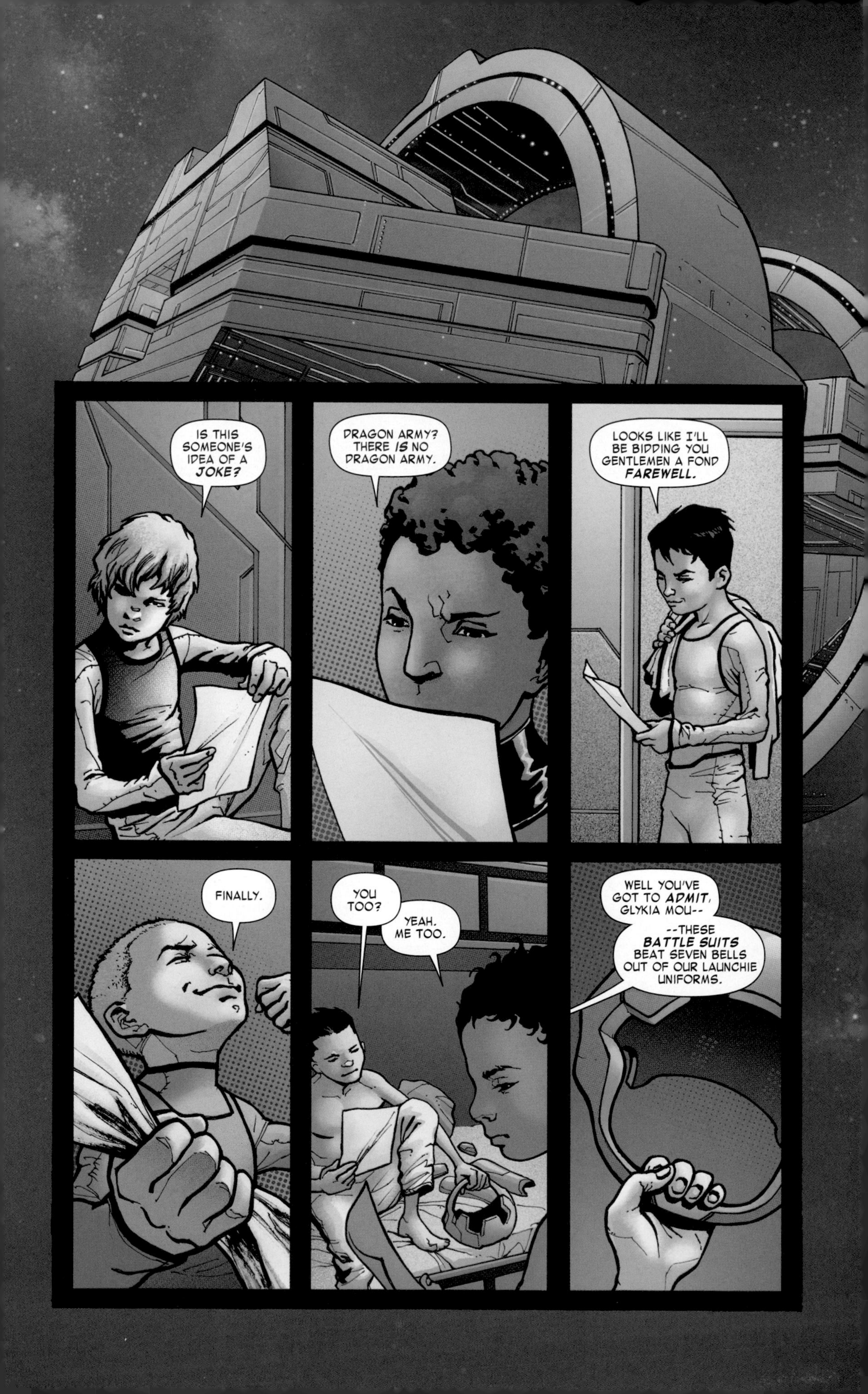

IS THIS SOMEONE'S IDEA OF A JOKE?
DRAGON ARMY? THERE IS NO DRAGON ARMY.
LOOKS LIKE I'LL BE BIDDING YOU GENTLEMEN A FOND FAREWELL.
FINALLY.
YOU TOO?
YEAH. ME TOO.
WELL YOU'VE GOT TO ADMIT, GLYKIA MOU--
--THESE BATTLE SUITS BEAT SEVEN BELLS OUT OF OUR LAUNCHIE UNIFORMS.

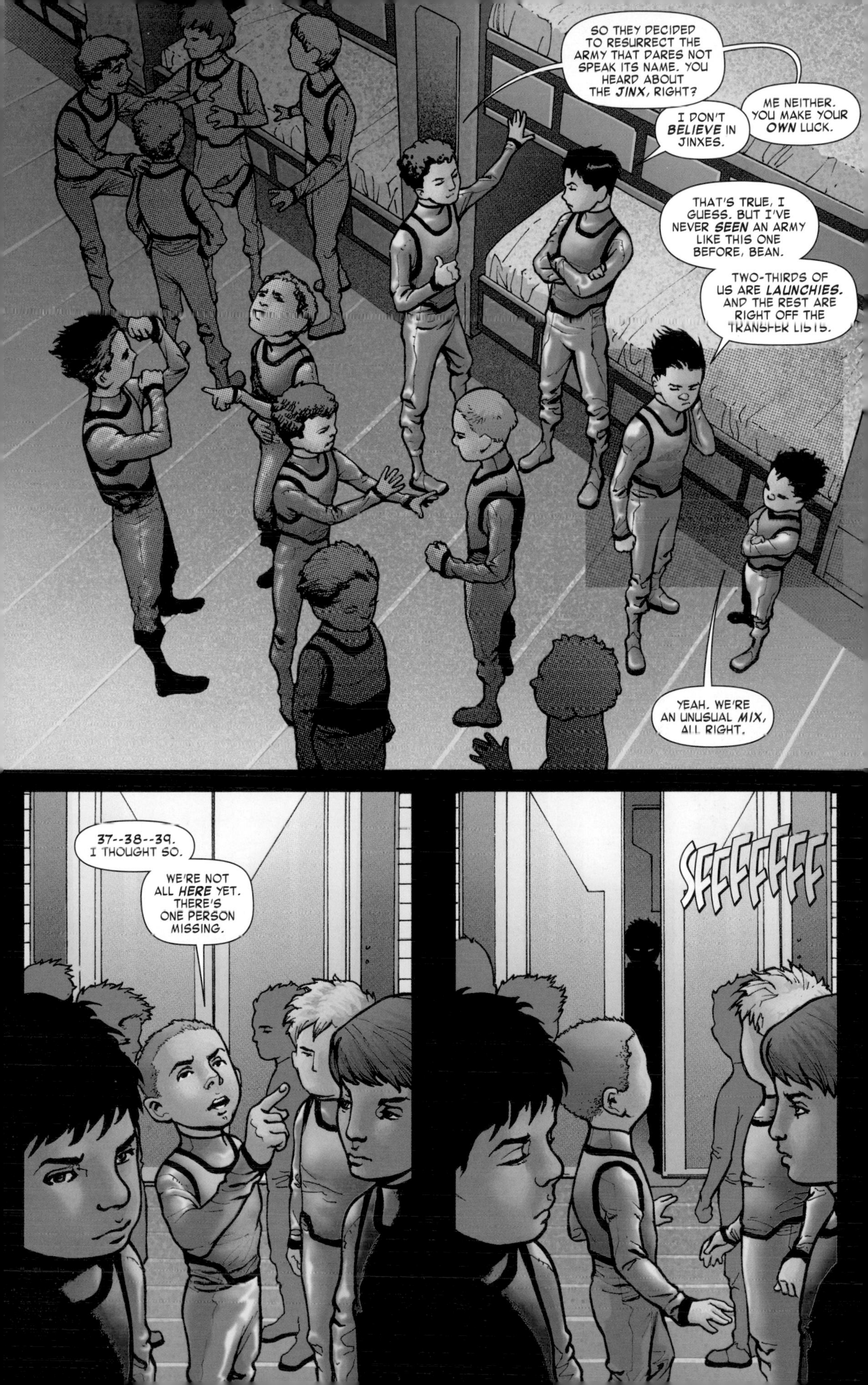
SO THEY DECIDED TO RESURRECT THE ARMY THAT DARES NOT SPEAK ITS NAME. YOU HEARD ABOUT THE JINX, RIGHT?
I DON'T BELIEVE IN JINXES.
ME NEITHER. YOU MAKE YOUR OWN LUCK.
THAT'S TRUE, I GUESS. BUT I'VE NEVER SEEN AN ARMY LIKE THIS ONE BEFORE, BEAN.
TWO-THIRDS OF US ARE LAUNCHIES. AND THE REST ARE RIGHT OFF THE TRANSFER LISTS.
YEAH. WE'RE AN UNUSUAL MIX, ALL RIGHT.
37--38--39. I THOUGHT SO.
WE'RE NOT ALL HERE YET. THERE'S ONE PERSON MISSING.
SFFFFFFF

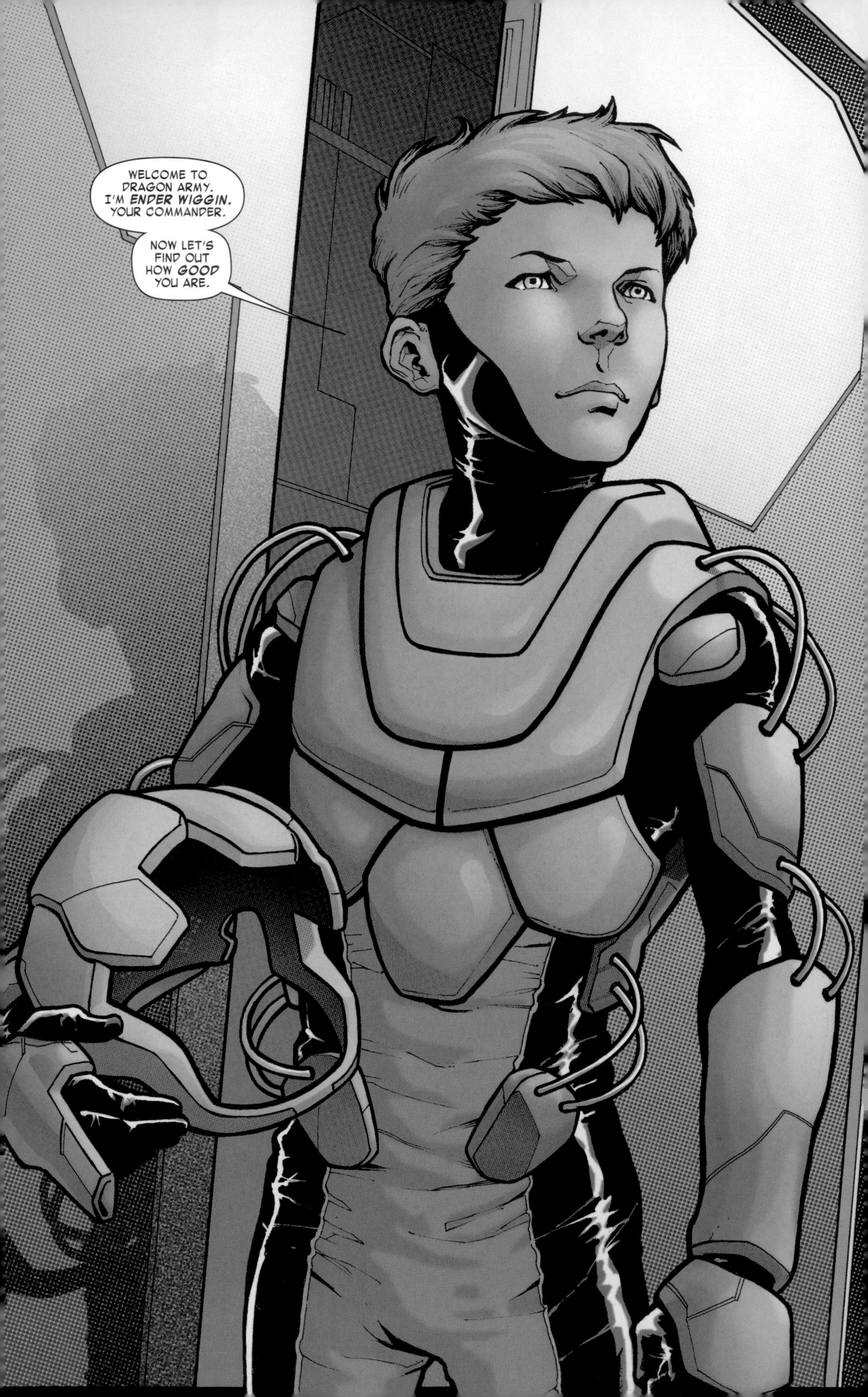
WELCOME TO DRAGON ARMY. I'M ENDER WIGGIN. YOUR COMMANDER.
NOW LET'S FIND OUT HOW GOOD YOU ARE.

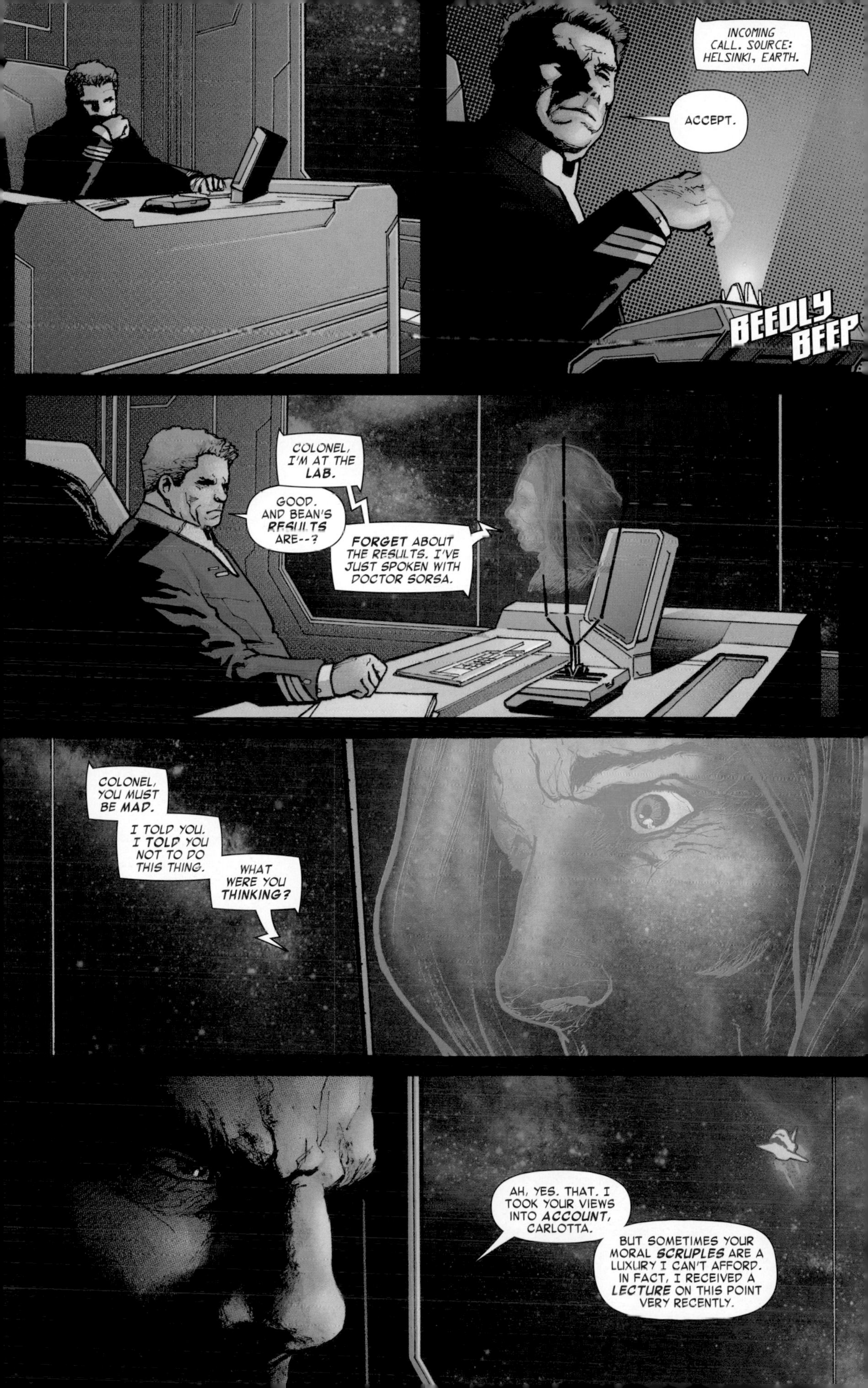
INCOMING CALL. SOURCE: HELSINKI, EARTH.
ACCEPT.
BEEDLY BEEP
COLONEL, I'M AT THE LAB.
GOOD. AND BEAN'S RESULTS ARE--?
FORGET ABOUT THE RESULTS. I'VE JUST SPOKEN WITH DOCTOR SORSA.
COLONEL, YOU MUST BE MAD.
I TOLD YOU. I TOLD YOU NOT TO DO THIS THING.
WHAT WERE YOU THINKING?
AH, YES. THAT. I TOOK YOUR VIEWS INTO ACCOUNT, CARLOTTA.
BUT SOMETIMES YOUR MORAL SCRUPLES ARE A LUXURY I CAN'T AFFORD. IN FACT, I RECEIVED A LECTURE ON THIS POINT VERY RECENTLY.

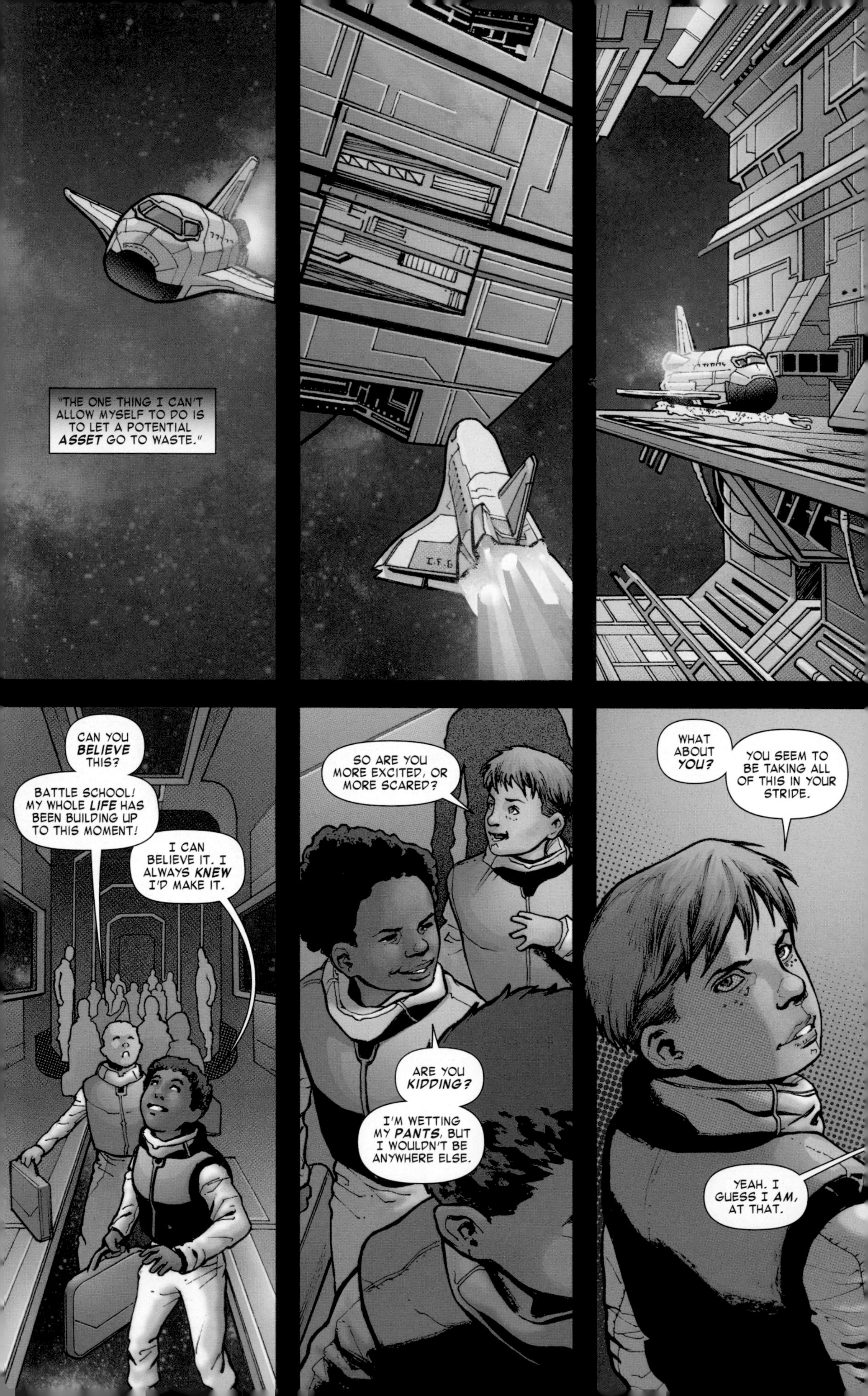
"THE ONE THING I CAN'T ALLOW MYSELF TO DO IS TO LET A POTENTIAL ASSET GO TO WASTE."
I.F.G.
CAN YOU BELIEVE THIS?
BATTLE SCHOOL! MY WHOLE LIFE HAS BEEN BUILDING UP TO THIS MOMENT!
I CAN BELIEVE IT. I ALWAYS KNEW I'D MAKE IT.
SO ARE YOU MORE EXCITED, OR MORE SCARED?
ARE YOU KIDDING?
I'M WETTING MY PANTS, BUT I WOULDN'T BE ANYWHERE ELSE.
WHAT ABOUT YOU?
YOU SEEM TO BE TAKING ALL OF THIS IN YOUR STRIDE.
YEAH. I GUESS I AM, AT THAT.

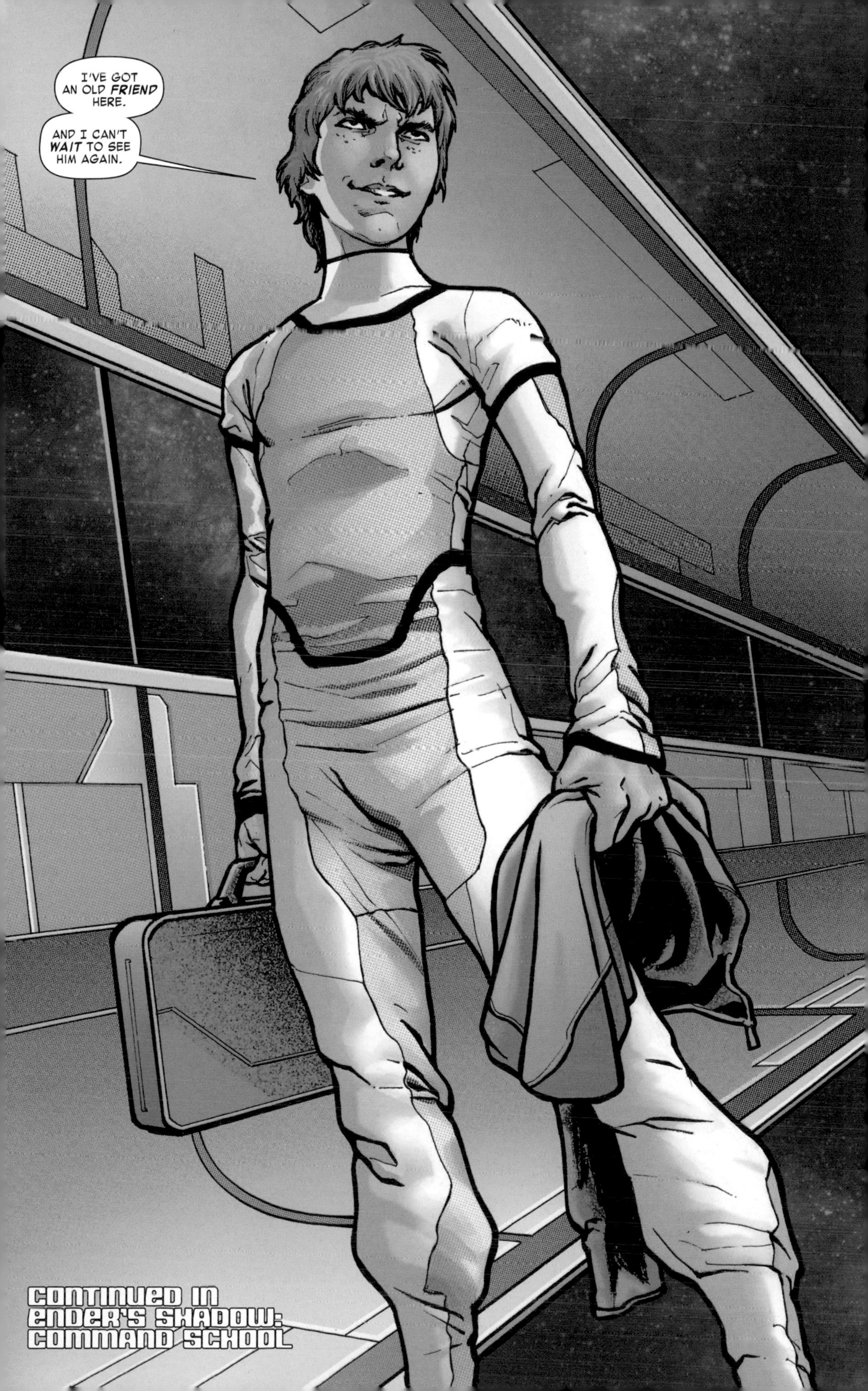
I'VE GOT AN OLD *FRIEND* HERE.
AND I CAN'T *WAIT* TO SEE HIM AGAIN.
CONTINUED IN ENDER'S SHADOW: COMMAND SCHOOL

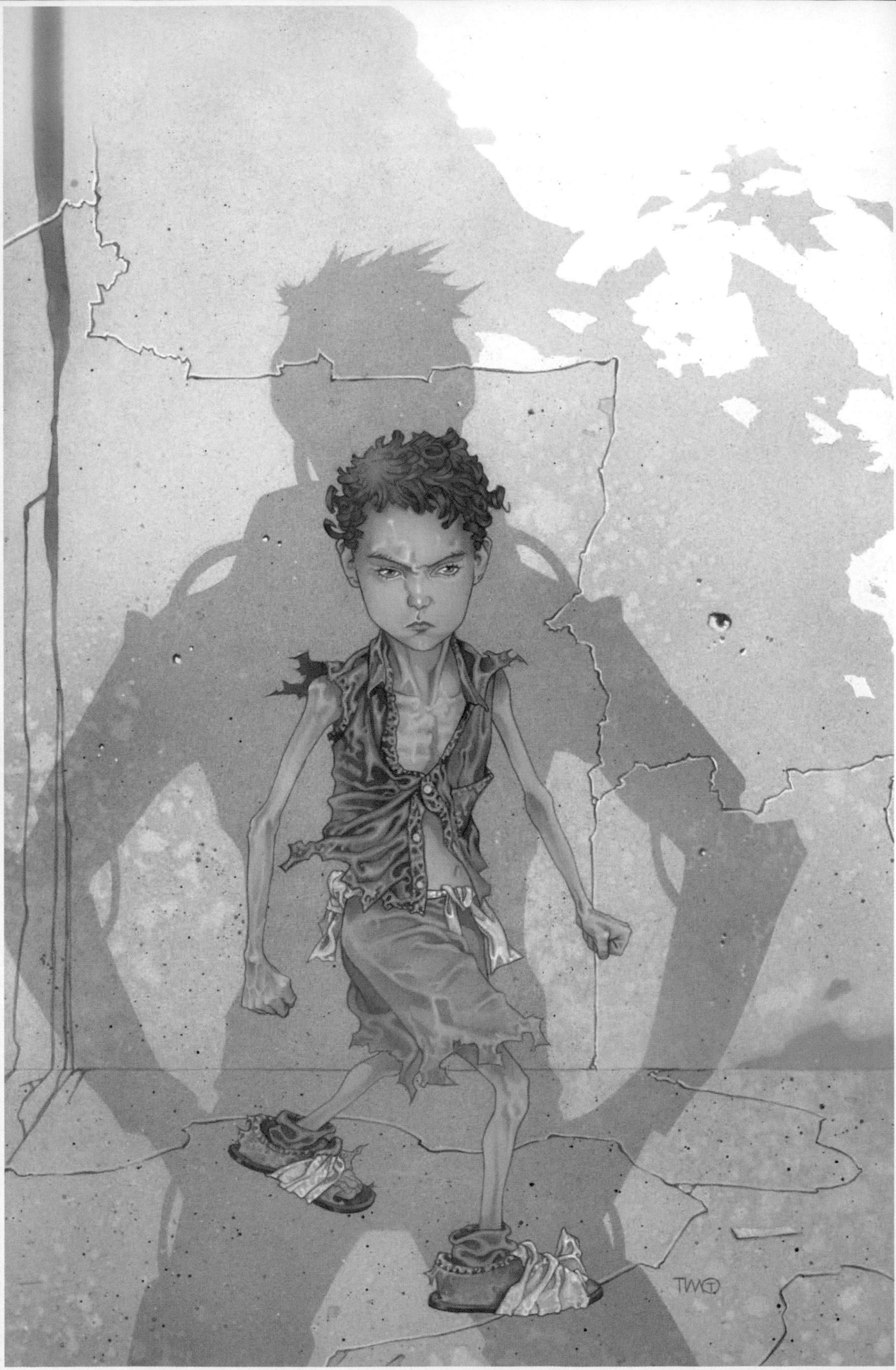
TWG

#1 VARIANT BY TIMOTHY GREEN II

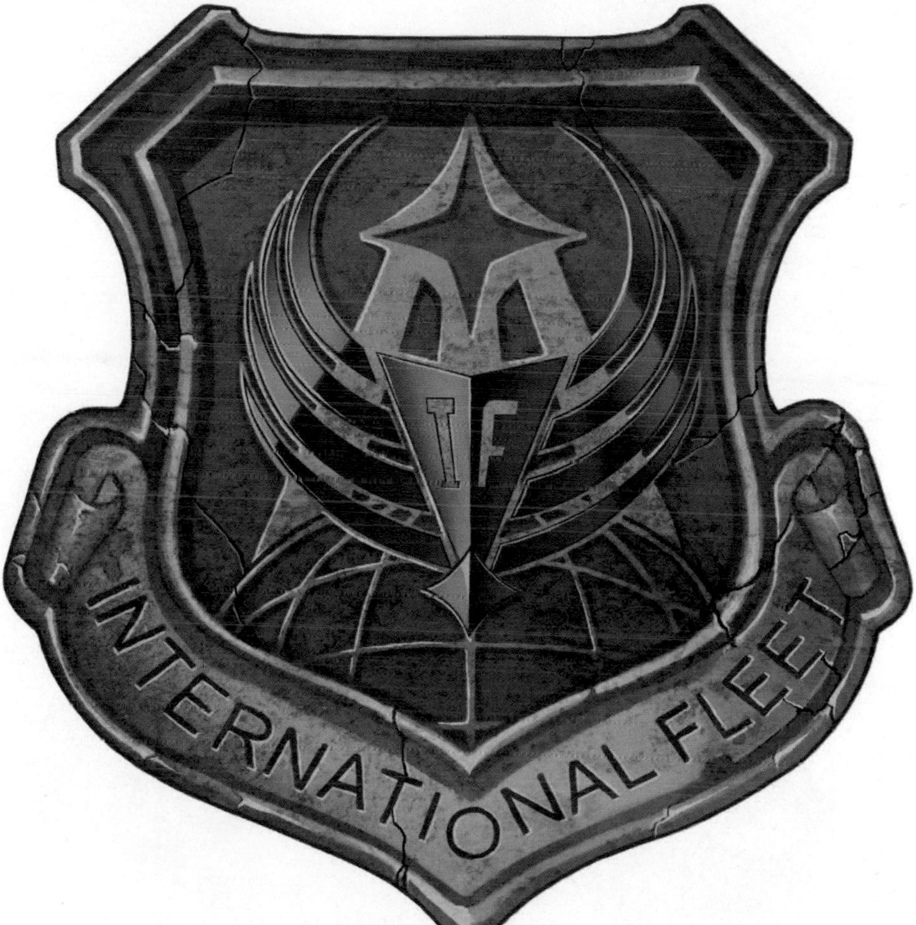
IF
INTERNATIONAL FLEET

#1 SYMBOL VARIANT

CHARACTER SKETCHES
BY SEBASTIAN FIUMARA

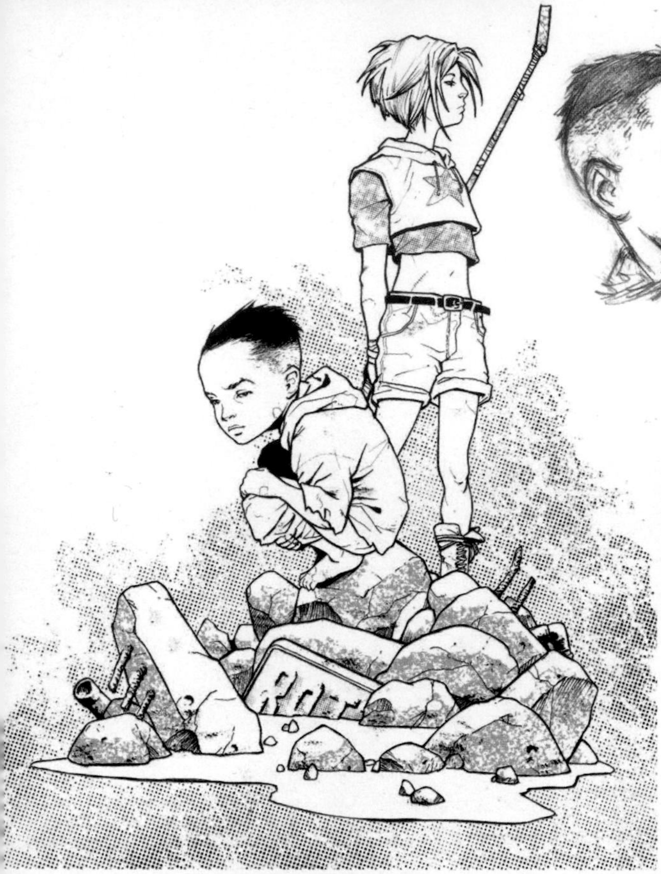

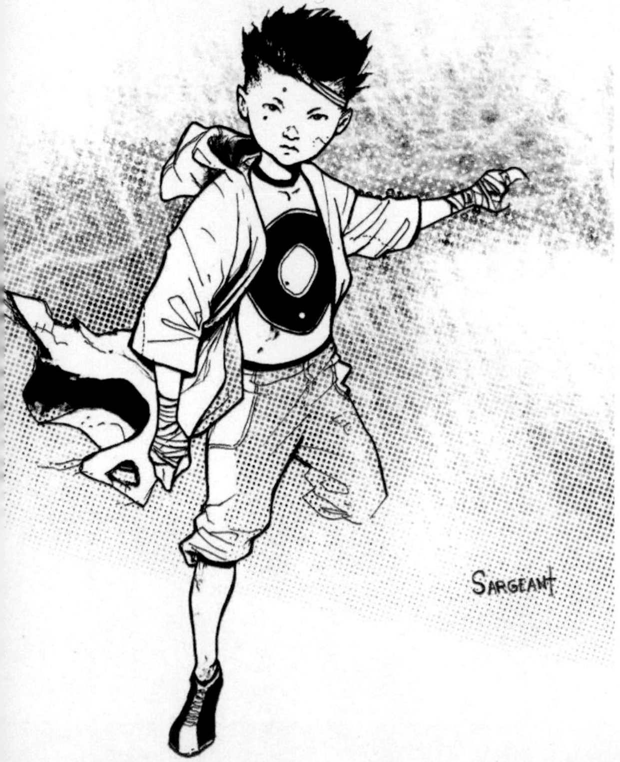
SARGEANT

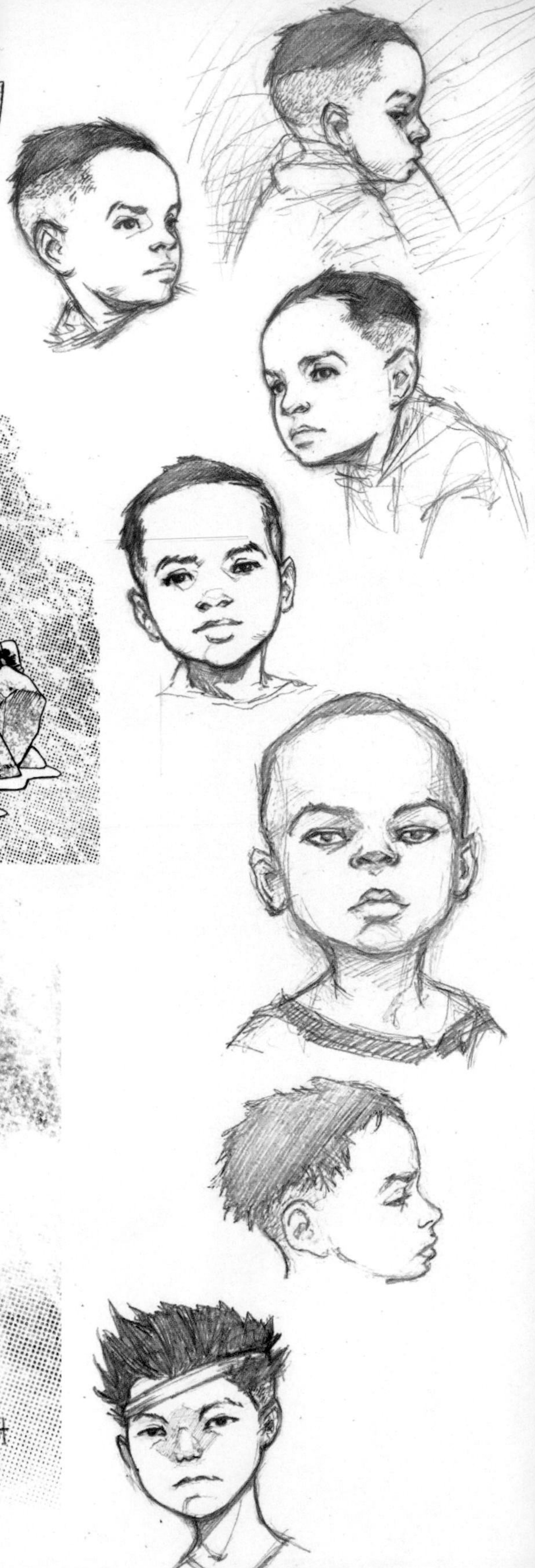
SERGEANT

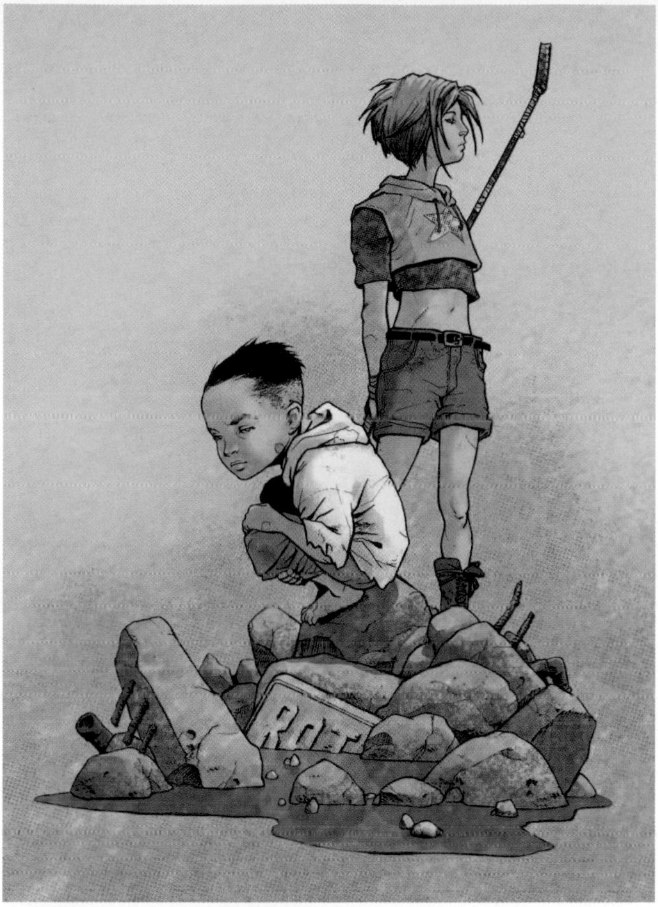

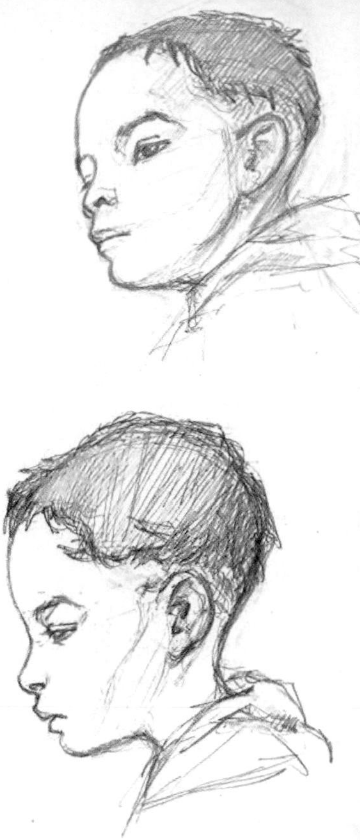

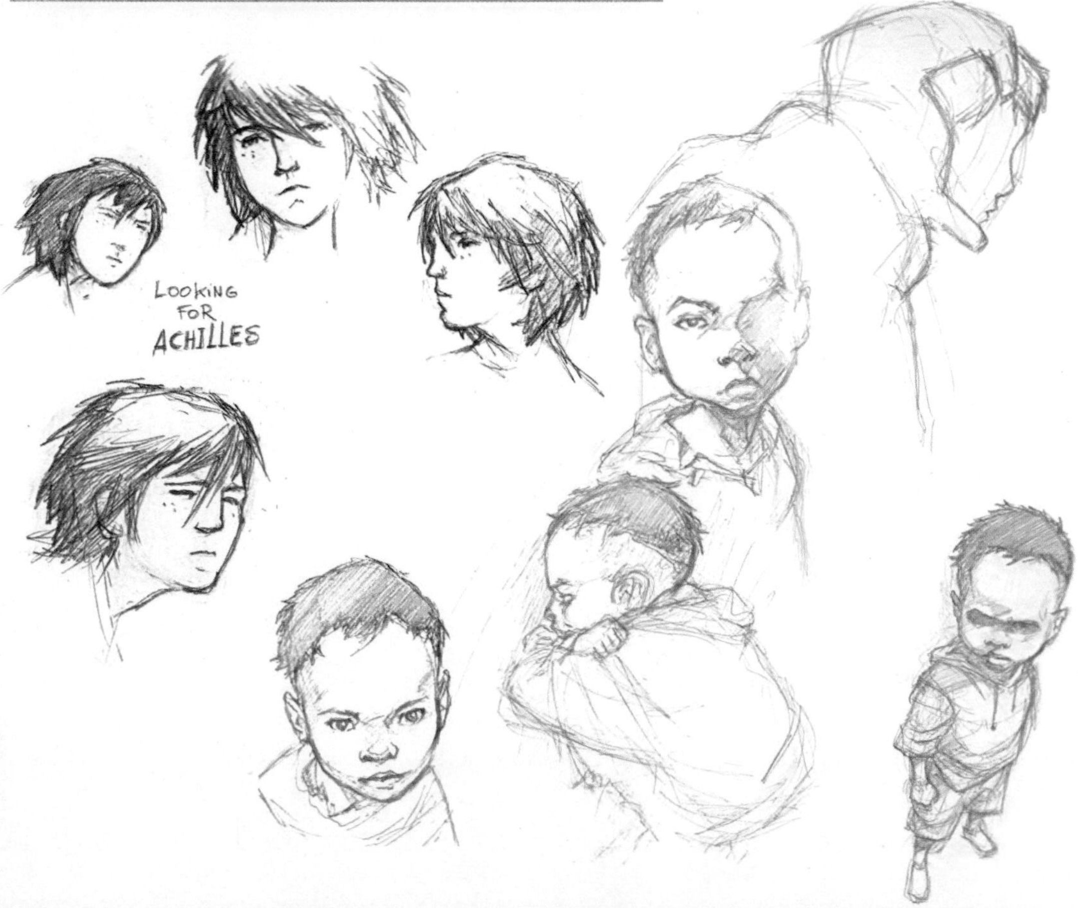
LOOKING FOR ACHILLES

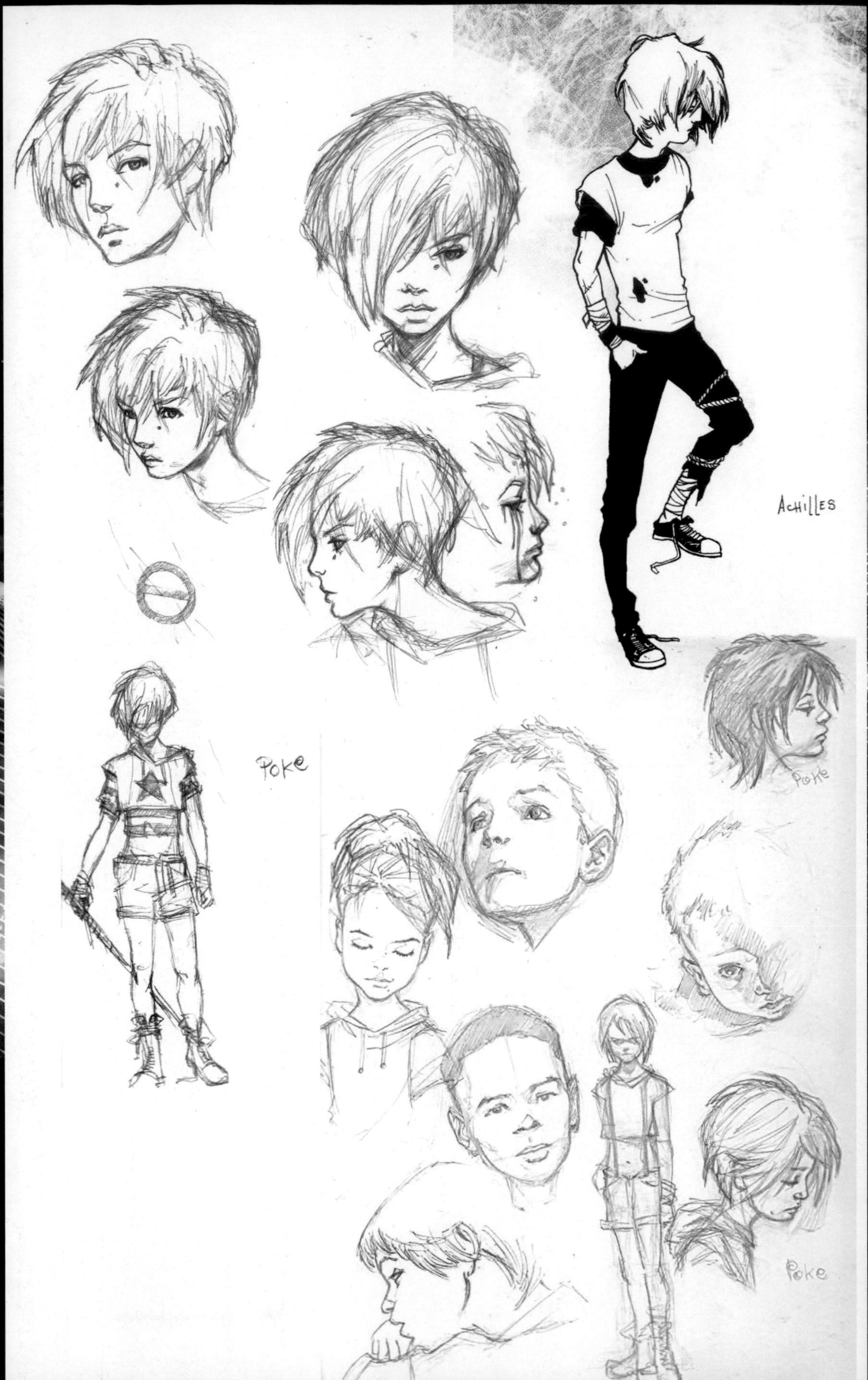
Achilles
Poke
Poke
Poke